FLYING UPSIDE DOWN

Flying Upside Down

TRUE TALES OF AN ANTARCTIC PILOT

MARK A. HINEBAUGH

NAVAL INSTITUTE PRESS
Annapolis, Maryland

Library of Congress Cataloging-in-Publication Data
Hinebaugh, Mark A., 1957–
     Flying upside down : true tales of an Antarctic pilot / Mark A . Hinebaugh.
       p. cm.
     Includes bibliographical references.
     ISBN 1-55750-389-3 (alk. paper)
     1. Airplanes—Piloting—Antarctica. 2. Antarctica—Discovery and exploration. 3. Airplanes—Cold weather operation—Antarctica.
     I. Title.
TL532.H55 1998
629. 13 ' 0998 ' 9—dc21   98-30923

Printed in the United States of America on acid-free paper ♾
05 04 03 02 01 00 99 98   9 8 7 6 5 4 3 2
First printing

To Charles and Lillian, who gave me
all the tools to succeed in life
and then allowed me the freedom
to find my own direction

CONTENTS

ACKNOWLEDGMENTS

I was attached as a transport pilot to Antarctic Development Squadron Six (VXE-6) from September 1989 to February 1992. During that period I completed three six-month tours of duty in Antarctica. Our mission was to fly the LC-130 and the UH-1N in direct support of the United States Antarctic Research Program as managed by the National Science Foundation's Office of Polar Programs.

This book is based on my daily journal, in which I recorded the experiences my crew and I shared during these three deployments. Everything in the book is true, although the sequence of events has been altered slightly. Additionally, since these events took place over a three-year period, I often combine material from two or more tours of service as descriptions of the events of a single day.

As for the individual members of my crew, I have chosen in this book to concentrate on those folks with whom I spent the most time. I regret that I haven't been able to include each and every individual I had the honor of flying with on the Ice.

In every adventure there are many people who have a significant impact on the events but whose efforts nevertheless go unacknowledged due to the short memory of the author who later chronicles that adventure. I want to recognize here, however, the following individuals, all of whom helped to make my personal journey a pleasure.

Lorilei Kornel, a top-shelf editor and patient friend who made sense of these ramblings. Capt. Keith Armstrong and Capt. Stacy Sebastian, two of the finest commanding officers I have ever had the privilege of serving with. Lisle and Meredith Rose, without whose support and encouragement this book would have never been possible. Kristi Squires, who attended to the minutia during subsequent editing, allowing me to retain some modicum of sanity. Sandy Russell, Cdr. Russ Jowers, Wendy Karppi, Morgan Wilbur, and the staff at *Naval Aviation News*, who not only gave me my shot at writing but also invited me to several grand Christmas parties. Myra Wilkinson, who, in addition to lending me her digs in San Francisco and her profound sense of humor to help me kick start this endeavor, also had to listen to my daily whine of "Bring me a treat." Sylvia Koskey, who gave me years of friendship, wrote me letters by the bushel, and never let me doubt myself. Louisa Agriesti, Sue and Steve Kullen, Carol Stafford, Mimi Morf, Janet Lee, Eleanor Fails, Susie Wright, Susan Johnsson, Linda Grale, Kay Kime, and Dave and Evie Church, whose letters and care packages kept me grounded and let me know there was light at the end of the tunnel during the grueling six-month-long deployments. Rich Francovitch and Laura Lambright, who have given me friendship, Mardi Gras memories (those that I can remember), inspiration, and support. My sister, Diana Ager, who served for years as my back-seat copilot. Dave Lovelace, who has given me years of understanding and who remains my best friend no matter what I do. Dr. Chris Smith, Esther Hendrickson, Fran Tyson, and Howie Levitt, who provided me with friendship and enlightenment on the Ice. Bill Sharp, Allison Yates, Bruce Witucki, the gangs at Southside and Union Streets, and everyone in Alexandria who never lost faith in my drive to publish this book, even when I seemed to be in doubt. My Washington, D.C., bubbas—George Haynes, Toby Pyle, Margret Starky, David Tull, and Charlie as well as all the good folks at Tunnicliffs, who have been ready to have my book publishing party for years. The Honorable Joe Taussig, Richard Healing, Fred Crowson, Lt. Sue Harvey, Annie White, Don Melick, and the staff at the navy's Safety and Survivability Office, who gave me not only good advice and encouragement but also a job. Dr. Murray Hamlet, the army's extreme cold weather guru, who lent me not only his years of cold-weather experience but sage advice and an awesome pair of socks. Kim Hubbs, Jack Elston, and the rest of my team at the VXE-6 Test and Evaluation Department, who by their hard work made me look good. Lt. Cdr. Ellen Roberts, who gave me space and a place to write this book.

Eric "Noodles" Mueller, who gave me a hand up and not a handout. Mike "Mr. Invisible" and Karen Nee, Roberto and Mary Guerrero, Sharon Nutter, John Adler, Patty Turney, John Serralles, Scott "FSA" and Nancy Allen, Dave Hegland, Ed Angel, Carol Bloemker (special thanks for that great internal into McMurdo), Sean Wise, Chip Cannan, John Dell, Jim Scott, John Higgins, Neil "Booger" Nostrant, Bob Fiacco, Greg Mclaughlin, Fred Spence, and Jim Palke (these latter three aka Larry, Darrell, and Darrell), Lou Evans, Glen Kyrk, and Gordo Linn (the infamous CAD brothers), Senior Chiefs Holloran and McCurry, Roy Williams, Chris Derby, Eddie Martens, Mike Frazier (thanks for hanging in there with me when everything went to hell on that approach into Western Samoa), and the rest of the men and women at VXE-6 who made my time in Antarctica not only enjoyable but safe. My patient editor, Gayle Swanson, who not only made me read well within these pages but graced me with her keen insight and an ample dose of southern hospitality. And lastly Tim, Mary, Jack, and Annie Lefebvre, who have provided me with years of friendship, support, car sitting, wok dinners, grilled oysters, a place in the islands, and a thousand laughs.

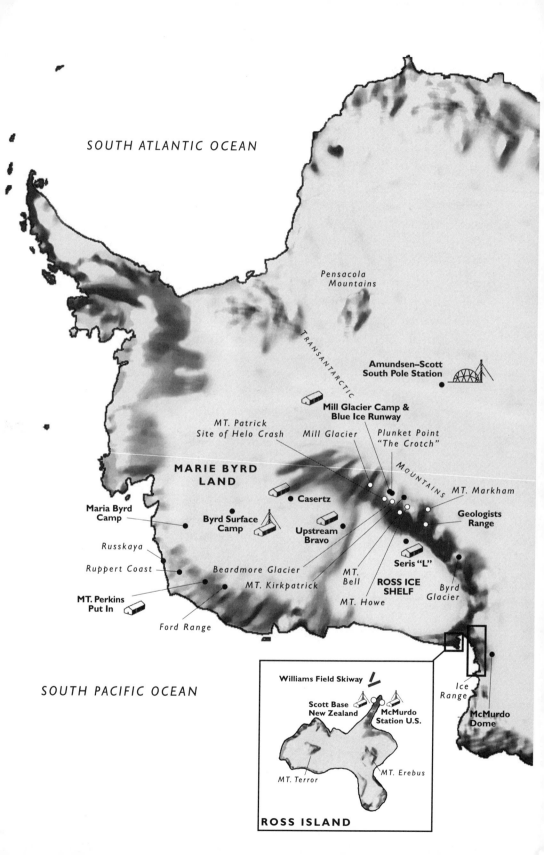

SOUTH ATLANTIC OCEAN

Pensacola Mountains

TRANSANTARCTIC

Amundsen–Scott South Pole Station

Mill Glacier Camp & Blue Ice Runway

MT. Patrick Site of Helo Crash

Mill Glacier

Plunket Point "The Crotch"

MARIE BYRD LAND

MOUNTAINS

MT. Markham

Maria Byrd Camp

● **Casertz**

Geologists Range

Byrd Surface Camp

Upstream Bravo

Russkaya

Ruppert Coast

Beardmore Glacier

MT. Kirkpatrick

MT. Bell

Seris "L"

MT. Perkins Put In

Ford Range

ROSS ICE SHELF

MT. Howe

Byrd Glacier

Ice Range

McMurdo Dome

SOUTH PACIFIC OCEAN

Williams Field Skiway

Scott Base New Zealand

McMurdo Station U.S.

MT. Terror

MT. Erebus

ROSS ISLAND

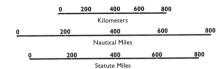

| 0 | 200 | 400 | 600 | 800 |

Kilometers

| 0 | 200 | 400 | 600 | 800 |

Nautical Miles

| 0 | 200 | 400 | 600 | 800 |

Statute Miles

QUEEN MAUD LAND

INDIAN OCEAN

● Vostok

● New Zealand
Science Group
Put In

WILKES LAND

VICTORIA LAND

Sturge I. **BALLENY**
Buckle I. **ISLANDS**
Young I.

Minna Bluff   Mt. Discovery
Black
Island
MT. Lister
Taylor Glacier
White
Island
Lake Vanda
Ferrar Glacier
Royal Society Range
Wright Valley
Olympus Range

**DETAIL OF
ICE RANGE**

DRY ICE

Antarctica. The white continent. The "Ice." It is the coldest, highest, driest, windiest, most isolated, and most desolate of places, by turns inspiring and daunting. The average temperature in the interior is 70 degrees below zero centigrade; readings of nearly 130 below have been recorded. Winds of two hundred miles an hour blast the coastline—the wind speeds actually go higher, but the impellers on the anemometers designed to measure them shatter and blow to pieces under the extreme force.

Despite millions of hours of research devoted solely to our understanding this vast frozen wilderness, it remains a mystery. Antarctica is the least known yet arguably the most studied continent. Picture a land of 5.4 million square miles, larger than the United States and Mexico combined, and all but 2.5 percent of it covered by a seven-thousand-foot depth of snow and ice—a depth that in some places reaches fifteen thousand feet. The snow has been accumulating here, undisturbed for millions of years, yet precipitation is virtually nil. The few inches of snow that do fall each year would amount to only one or two inches of rain. The humidity never rises above 2 percent, making this a drier place than the Sahara Desert. But despite its being the world's largest desert, Antarctica contains 70 percent of the world's fresh water, bound up in 90 percent of the world's ice. Should this ice melt, the oceans of the world would rise hundreds of feet, inundating the planet. Antarctica is an enigma: a desert of water, a continent of emptiness.

In this desert, however, is a savage beauty that I came to admire with all my soul. Flying over the continent or simply gazing across the McMurdo Sound at the snow-crowned peaks of the Royal Society Range, framed in an azure sky and glistening in the pale morning light, how could you not think of the magnificence and grandeur of the place, despite its hazards? Wherever I looked I saw the pristine Antarctic wilderness in its unspoiled splendor and felt pleased that this frozen paradise is inaccessible to all but a few. Selfishly I was glad there are no readily obtainable natural resources to exploit here, no industry, no easily available supply of fresh water (all fresh water here is made by melting snow or desalinating sea water), no areas suitable to farm or range livestock. Everything needed for human beings to exist must be shipped or flown in. And then everything brought in must be removed because in Antarctica's desert climate there is no decomposition. Whatever is left here stays here, forever intact, only covered by snow over the ages. Flying the continent I gained an appreciation for the fragile nature of the place and a profound respect for the natural order here. Antarctica changed me, as it changes all who spend time here. The day-in and day-out experiences of flying in this place—the exhilaration, frustration, boredom, and terror—are the fundamental subject of this book.

I first became aware of the navy's Antarctic Development Squadron, designated VXE-6, just prior to earning my naval aviator wings in 1983. I had no idea what the squadron did other than fly ski-equipped Lockheed C-130s "Hercules" transport aircraft in support of the National Science Foundation (NSF) in Antarctica. It wasn't until seven years later that I finally joined the squadron and experienced what Antarctica holds for those willing to pit themselves and their flying ability against the world's harshest environment.

Great God! this is an awful place.

—Robert Falcon Scott, *Wednesday, 17 January 1912*

On 25 August 1990 I sat in my Hercules with six pairs of eyes fixed on me. We were just off the skiway at Williams Field—also known as "Willy Field"—at McMurdo Station, the site of the skiway and home to the squadron's maintenance troops during the October-through-March flying season. It was now early spring in Antarctica, the start of the active season there. The temperature was 68 degrees below zero, and the wind was at 23 knots—conditions where exposed flesh freezes in seconds—and one of our engines was shut down. The propeller on the number-one engine had started fluctuating just over the Balleny Islands, forty-five minutes from the Antarctic coastline, and I had been forced to shut the engine down and land here at McMurdo. As polar transport aircraft commander (PTAC) it was up to me to decide our next move.

I was working single-plane operations (that is, working alone without the benefit of a rescue plane) during the annual midwinter fly-in, or "Win-Fly." Normal operating procedure in Antarctica is to keep two aircraft in flying status, each a backup for the other should trouble occur. But this requirement can be waived by the commanding officer (CO) in extreme circumstances. I guess WinFly qualified as extreme circumstances, because today I was on my own.

The annual season of Operation Deep Freeze—America's Antarctic exploration program—begins in August with WinFly. Engineers and other support personnel are flown in to Antarctica over a two-week period to build an ice runway and ready McMurdo Station for the main body of personnel that will be arriving in early October. WinFly coincides with the reappearance of the sun after four months of total darkness in the austral winter.

Freezing wind buffeted the plane. I closed my eyes and rubbed my temples and thought back to that first moment when, flying down from New Zealand in the skim-milk subdawn twilight, I saw the propeller rpm (revolutions per minute) gauge began to quiver, and I knew we had a problem. The fluctuation had been minor at first, but gradually it grew more erratic, the gauge needle sawing back and forth. Soon the plane began to yaw from side to side in an ever-widening arc.

At the first indication of a fluctuation I turned to the propeller-control panel to my right, placed the control switch for the prop from automatic (electrical control) to mechanical control and waited to see what would happen. Below us the Antarctic coast was eerie, bathed in the gritty silver light. Real sunshine was still weeks away. As I waited for the prop to come under control, I stared mesmerized out the window, listening to the droning engines, watching the endless gray of Antarctica's dawning summer.

The flight engineer grabbed my arm and snapped me out of my trance. "It's no good," Roy said. "We'll have to bag the number-one engine." He leaned forward as I seized the condition lever, nodding confirmation that I had the right one as I pulled the lever hard back to the stops. The prop wound down, then lurched to a stop. We headed for the skiway on three engines.

It could have been worse. The skiway, a runway plowed out of snow, was in OK shape—and considering that it was my first ski landing in six months and that we were descending through stiff crosswinds and that one engine was out, you could almost call the landing uneventful.

But now, here we sat. As PTAC, I was responsible for not only the crew and passengers but also the safe and orderly conduct of the flight. I considered the cockpit crew—my two copilots; two navigators; and Roy and Mike, the two flight engineers—who were all waiting for my decision. The thing is, Antarctica has a way of limiting your options. I could either let Roy get out and adjust the prop, possibly freezing himself to death in the process, or order the plane closed up and we could all trudge up to McMurdo Station and sit around waiting to be rescued. McMurdo offered the possibility of dinner and a room and a comfortable wait for the next plane to ferry us back to New Zealand. It might have been my choice except for the small detail that we happened to be sitting in the only plane available for twenty-two hundred miles. Of the three planes ferried from the United States to New Zealand for WinFly, mine was the only one in flying condition. Even when a second plane became available, conditions at McMurdo might be so bad that a prop repair on our plane would take several days—and that was assuming a prop could even be located. We had a spare, but it wasn't in working order, which meant the squadron would have to scavenge a new prop from somewhere in New Zealand or Australia.

Plan B was to send Roy out to adjust the prop in hopes we could get ourselves airborne again. Attempting a repair was risky. If I let Roy have a crack at it, I would have to shut down the other engine on that wing. If I shut it down, could we restart it? At 65 below, engine oil turns to the consistency of Jell-O and rotating parts stop rotating. The starters might freeze. I could make the whole situation worse. Was this an appropriate time to gamble?

Roy volunteered to go out and adjust the prop. I looked at him, trying to guess his thoughts. Roy was gutsy and no-nonsense when it came to flying, and he knew the LC-130 as well as anyone. But this was only our second flight together, and ordering him to repair the plane in these conditions was ordering him to risk his life—something I couldn't have done, even if we had flown a thousand missions together.

"What do you think, Roy? You really want to do this?" I stared hard, trying to judge his reaction.

He smiled. "Yes, sir. Won't be a problem. Should only take me a minute." Which was just as well, I thought, because any longer and he might freeze to death out there.

Like all good flight engineers, Roy cared for his planes as though they were temperamental children, respecting them but taking a firm hand when required. I knew he wanted to get the plane airborne, as we all did, but I had to decide if this was misguided machismo on his part or a realistic option. Locker-room bragging rights aside, we had to return this plane, and ourselves, safely to New Zealand.

I made my call. "OK, Roy. You can have your shot, but I want Mike with you all the time as your safety observer." Mike, I believed, would be at a lesser risk since he would be standing still, with his back to the wind, and could keep all his clothes on. Roy, on the other hand, would be twenty feet up on a ladder facing the wind and would have to take his outer gloves off to be able to reach the adjustment screw.

"Yes, sir!" He threw off his headset and started suiting up for the outside.

I rubbed my eyes and let out a long breath; in the freezing cockpit, it looked like a blast from a fire extinguisher. What the hell? If we were going to go for it, might as well go all the way.

"OK," I told the other crew members, "we're going to bag the number-two engine and let Roy have a stab at repairing the prop on number one." Animated conversation coursed through the plane as the crew energetically prepared to fix the problem. Together, as a crew, we would get this plane back to New Zealand.

I stationed Chris, the loadmaster, at the crew door to observe Roy and Mike for signs of hypothermia, such as dizziness or disorientation, as they worked. Roy, perched on a shaky twenty-foot ladder, unbolted the engine access panel and fiddled with the adjustment screw while Mike tried to balance the ladder from below. Even in good weather the adjustment was tricky, but in gray Antarctic twilight, in high winds and crippling cold, it seemed downright impossible.

Meanwhile a hardy band of onlookers had trooped down from McMurdo in a variety of vehicles to watch the show. Keeping one eye on Roy, I radioed our operations center in Christchurch, New Zealand, and informed them of our predicament. I asked the duty officer to relay my plan to the CO to get his approval for it, assuming Roy's repair worked and the prop held during takeoff. While we waited for the CO's decision, the crew reviewed my strategy, looking for holes, discussing potential problems, and planning emergency actions should further problems arise. I was following the advice of the Roman dramatist Publilius Syrus, who said, "It's a dangerous plan that won't allow for modification."

If Roy could adjust the propeller so that it was stable at 100 percent rpm when we started the engine, and it remained at 100 percent when I added takeoff power, and we could get off the ground, then we would continue to New Zealand. Even if we lost the engine again, we would continue north on three engines. If the propeller didn't work after Roy's adjustment and we couldn't get airborne, we would taxi back to the ramp at McMurdo and wait. Once airborne, however, we risked losing a second engine. The crew and I agreed that if this happened before we passed the coastal mountains, we would turn back to McMurdo. But if we could somehow manage to limp over the mountains, then we would continue the two thousand miles over open ocean to Christchruch. I figured if we lost a second engine over the mountains, I would drop down and fly the rest of the way to New Zealand at fifty feet over the ocean, or even just above the white caps if I had to. With two engines out, and carrying enough fuel to get us to New Zealand, we would have been way too heavy to climb high. The duty officer radioed back: the CO endorsed my plan and cleared us to operate as we saw fit. So now it was up to me.

It took Roy more than an hour to make the adjustment, with breaks every few minutes for him and Mike to come inside and warm up. But at last he climbed back into the cockpit and gave me a thumbs-up. I settled in my seat and initiated the checklist to restart my left-wing engines. To my relief, both engines started normally, and moments later the number-one propeller was holding steady as I advanced the throttles to takeoff power. We began tracking along the skiway, following the path made on our landing. The McMurdo group waved good-bye. I felt elated with our change in fortune.

We were barely airborne—and exchanging laughter and pats on the back—when Mike said, "Uh, sir, we've got a generator 'out' light on number one."

All banter stopped. We all felt something ominous, as if our self-congratulations had somehow caused the generator failure. By patting ourselves on the back too soon, we seemed to have jinxed ourselves.

Roy scrambled out of his snow gear and crawled under the flight deck to remedy the situation. He swapped cables and reset control boxes as the plane climbed slowly toward New Zealand. The crew was silent. Below us I could still see the line of vehicles from McMurdo making their way back to the shelter of the station. Roy frantically tried to get the generator back on line, but it was no go. The whole crew was tense. With an unpleasant sense of foreboding, I shut the engine down for the second time that day.

Still, we would stick to my plan. My crew supported it, my CO gave it his blessing, and the Hercules could fly nearly as well on three engines as on four. I tried not to think about the fact that we were leaving the only safe landing spot for two thousand miles. I rationalized my concerns. *It was perfectly normal to have some trepidation when taking such a risk. Don't think of it as being stranded out here alone,* I told myself. *Think of it as opening another page of Antarctic adventure.*

I thought of the early explorers who ventured through the Arctic snows with far less knowledge, equipment, and resources than we had. Our day could be woven into the tapestry of many other Antarctic days, fraught with unexpected hazards and concerns. *Wasn't it the challenge of this place that set it so apart from any other?* The willingness we had to proceed under any circumstances, the risk of failure as well as fame—these were experiences shared with many Antarctic adventurers who came before us.

Once outside, I raised my head to look round and found I could not move it back. My clothing had frozen hard as I stood—perhaps fifteen seconds. For four hours I had to pull [his sledge] with my head stuck up, and from that time we all took care to bend down into pulling position before being frozen in.

—Apsley Cherry-Garrard, *The Worst Journey in the World: Antarctic, 1910–13*

Adm. Richard E. Byrd began the modern age of Antarctic exploration, making five successful expeditions to Antarctica. During his first expedition (1928–30) he built the station Little America on the Ross Ice Shelf. From this base on 29 November 1929, he and his crew became the first men to fly over the South Pole. However it wasn't until twenty-seven years later, on 31 October 1956, that a Douglas C-47 "Skytrain," dubbed the *Que Sera Sera,* became the first plane to land at the South Pole. Today an average of ten flights a week make the six-hour round-trip from McMurdo Station to the South Pole during the flying season, October through February each year.

VXE-6 is a unique squadron in the U.S. Navy: its sole mission is to provide air logistics for the National Science Foundation's Antarctic Research Program. Flying the LC-130 ski-equipped "Herc" transport plane and the Bell UH-1N "Huey" helicopter, VXE-6 spends the austral summer (October through March in the southern latitudes) in direct support of Operation Deep Freeze, America's Antarctic exploration program. Based at McMurdo Station, these aircraft allow the United States to operate on the continent with a degree of flexibility, speed, and range unmatched by any other nation.

The success of Deep Freeze deployments depends to a major degree on VXE-6 aircrew performance. The work is arduous, unglamorous, and dangerous; but after forty years our aircrews have revolutionized air operations in Antarctica, a task unequaled in the history of aviation. With each successful flight VXE-6 lends further credence to Admiral Byrd's well-known assertion that aircraft alone could conquer Antarctica.

Our aircraft, the LC-130, is a mission-specific airplane. The Herc has, over the years, been the most modified and the most versatile plane in the armed forces' inventory. The air force has at various times refitted them for use as gun ships, hurricane hunters, special operations platforms, and a host of other specialized roles. The marines use them primarily as airborne fuel tankers, the Coast Guard for long-range search and rescue. And all the services use them to haul cargo and personnel. The C-130 is so widely used that you would be hard-pressed to find anyone in the military who hasn't spent some amount of time on one.

The navy uses Hercs in a limited capacity, however. A few of the planes, once stationed in Spain and the Philippines, were used as conventional cargo and personnel haulers before they were decommissioned, and others in Maryland and Hawaii were modified to send very low–frequency radio messages to deployed submarines. But unique in the navy's inventory is the ski-equipped LC-130, the Antarctic Herc. This is arguably the most specialized airplane in the world. Each landing gear is fitted with a ski that wraps U-shaped around the wheels, allowing either a wheeled landing on conventional runways or a ski landing on snow. The National Science Foundation owns these planes, but they are flown and maintained exclusively by naval aviators and mechanics, who spend six months a year supporting Operation Deep Freeze.

Hercs are perfect for polar work. The four-engine, eighty-four-thousand-pound (empty), ninety-seven-foot workhorse can take off at 155,000 pounds, nearly twice its own weight when operating on wheels, or up to 147,000 pounds when operating on its fifteen-foot-long, Teflon-coated skis. The four reliable turboprop engines make the LC-130 inherently safe. In Antarctica the excess power of the Herc's engines—coupled with the short takeoff and landing capability that is characteristic of all propeller-driven planes—makes work from skiways (runways plowed out of snow) relatively easy.

As anywhere else though, operating safely in Antarctica requires a complete dedication to, and knowledge of, proper procedure, and it doesn't take long on the Ice for you to realize that knowing such procedures is a life or death matter. When you have an emergency in Antarctica, you can't wait to look up proper procedure in the book. Even so, in Antarctica more often than not, normal procedures don't work anyway, so seat-of-the-pants-flying becomes an art form. As good as the Herc is, it's only as good as the pilots who fly it.

When I came to Antarctica for the first time, in October 1989, I looked forward to the adventure of a lifetime. In fact I volunteered for duty on the Ice. Of course some people thought I was crazy. When I look back on it all, I have days when I think they were right. From the very first moment we got here, we began to find ourselves in some pretty strange situations.

I trimmed the plane to fly on three engines. There was still no sun, nothing but a glimmering horizon of gray as we continued north toward the mountains. As we approached Christchurch, New Zealand, our staging base for heading south to Antarctica, I contacted Christchurch Tower and reported our position.

"Tower, this is X-ray Delta Zero Four. We are declaring an emergency. We have number-one engine shut down. Twelve thousand pounds of fuel and eleven souls aboard. Requesting the crash trucks."

"Roger, Zero Four, crash crew has been alerted. Winds 250 degrees at 12 knots. You are number one, cleared to land."

"Tower, Zero Four copies, cleared to land."

My copilot Sean rolled smoothly onto the proper glide path and course for the approach, then made the three-engine landing look like it was routine. He eased back the yoke (the pilot's steering wheel) and inched the throttles toward flight idle, touching down softly on centerline; he then put just two inboard engines into reverse, to maintain directional control while we slowed to taxi speed. When we were clear of the runway, I shut down the number-four engine to help more with directional control. As it wound down, I called the tower.

"Tower, Zero Four, safe on deck and clear of the active."

"Roger, Zero Four, taxi to your line. Nice job, sir. Will you require further assistance?"

This was controller talk for "Congratulations. You are not a huge fireball tumbling down the runway. But do you still want the crash crew to follow you to the ramp?"

"Thanks, tower. Zero Four, taxi to our line. No further assistance required."

Cheerful banter filled the cockpit again after nine-and-a-half hours of tense silence.

1

WELCOME TO

CLUB MUD

It was during the third week in October that my McMurdo roommate, Sean, and I were assigned our quarters for the season. We spent most of our first day back in Antarctica arranging the place to our mutual satisfaction—although because it wasn't much of a room, we didn't achieve much satisfaction. We placed our storage lockers together, dividing the area lengthwise, and then put our beds in opposite corners. We would share these quarters for six months. During that time, each of us having our own living space, even just a few feet of it, would be essential to the preservation of our mental health.

Our individual sleeping areas were cordoned off with curtains made of extra wool blankets. In addition to blocking the light, the curtains provided additional isolation, necessary because Sean and I worked different crews on different shifts and our sleeping schedules would be in conflict. The room's centerpiece was our uncomfortable and strikingly ugly couch. A shared bookshelf went in one corner, a two-drawer desk in the other. I lost the coin toss and became the owner of the bottom drawer. Through great foresight Sean had brought with him a small stereo with every imaginable accessory. I can endure almost anything if I've got music, and with his elaborate little setup, I felt almost decadent.

We had also been issued a small refrigerator apiece. The military recognized the premier requirement of Antarctic survival: beer. Our room was on an inner corridor, so we lacked a window from which to cool our precious supply—thus the refrigerators.

Once the room was in order, ugly but neat, I sallied forth to see my office. During the winter-over from March to October, when a minimal staff of about two hundred and fifty individuals maintain the station, someone had broken through the office roof and stolen ten thousand dollars' worth of extreme cold weather (ECW) clothing and gear. My ground job (my work when I wasn't flying) was test and evaluation officer of such gear, bringing the most up-to-date clothing and equipment to Antarctica to test with the goal of updating the Korean-era stuff that had been issued since Operation Deep Freeze began in the 1950s. My office—twenty-five feet long and fifteen feet wide, with an eight-foot drop ceiling and one small window, used to cool the overheated room—was crammed floor to ceiling with boxes, hundreds of boxes. There were boxes of boots, boxes of humidifiers, boxes of boot dryers, boxes packed with experimental gear and clothing. The place looked like a Wal-Mart storage depot. Carpenters had repaired the ceiling and created a secure storage area for our pilferables; however, with the usual military efficiency, no one had thought to provide a set of keys for the new storage lock. I had my petty officer go downstairs to the main squadron supply center to find a combination lock.

Once the office was secure and I had the combination memorized, I headed back to my room. The temperature wasn't much better than yesterday, 15 degrees below zero centigrade, and the stiff 23-knot wind (wind chill, minus-37 degrees) instantly reminded me that I was indeed in Antarctica. It was easy to forget that fact, sitting in an overheated building all day. As if to accentuate the miserable conditions, low clouds and gray skies prevailed.

On sunny days the sky in Antarctica is an indefinable shade of iridescent blue, so clear that you feel as though you could dive upward and start to swim. A "deep bluish-gray colour—a typical 'water-sky'" is how it was described in 1909 by one Lieutenant Bage, who was the astronomer and recorder of tides with E. N. Webb and J. F. Hurley at the South Magnetic Pole in Wilkes Land.[1] On water-sky days McMurdo Station is almost cheery. Almost. But grim, overcast skies like those today affected the mood of the town, pressing down on us with brooding malevolence reminding us that weather-wise, we were in a hostile environment.

McMurdo Station, Mac Town, the Hill. During the season you rarely hear it called McMurdo—a name reserved for tourists, distinguished visitors (DVs, VIPs), and fingies (FNGs, fucking new guys). McMurdo was constructed in 1955 as a staging base for inland research projects. It became a full-time base for scientific research in 1957–58 during the inaugural International Geophysical Year (IGY), the first year of a concerted international scientific and geographical effort. This endeavor was so successful that plans were made to continue the research program indefinitely, and it led to the signing of the Antarctic Treaty in 1959. After the IGY the station slowly metamorphosed into the headquarters of Antarctic research it is today.

Scientific utility aside, Mac Town is a dirty, frozen, overused, windblown mining town, built on lava rock and dust in a natural bowl, surrounded by snow and ice. It is built in tiers that rise like dirty brown waves from McMurdo Sound. Landlocked (or more appropriately "icelocked") on an island, the "station" is little more than a jumble of buildings as varied in appearance as their number, built on small graduated mounds surrounded by larger hills on the shores of a vast inland sea. There is a deepwater port with a pier made of ice, and on the opposite shore of the inlet, on Hut Point Peninsula, sits the historic first hut of British explorer Sir Robert F. Scott. It was here that Scott began his 1902 attempt to reach the South Pole, and the hut remains much the same today as it was when he left it nearly a hundred years ago.

McMurdo's most characteristic feature as a town is the extreme dissimilarity of its buildings. The place resembles some ramshackle Yukon settlement at the height of the gold rush. The atmosphere is like that of a mining town, too. This is the fringe of the Antarctic frontier; whatever people are when they arrive here, they soon become adventurers, their individual strength providing the only counterpoint to the overwhelming force of raw nature in this dreary outpost perched on the brink of a frozen Eden.

I certainly can't speak for all residents past and present, but most I have met were drawn here by curiosity about the unknown and the difficult. The place is like a test: are you afraid to stare into the vast nothingness of Antarctica? Some believed they could conquer a continent. We were all pioneers in spirit. Even as little as a few weeks of hardship under these intensely forbidding conditions is an adventure.

The town certainly has nothing noble about it. McMurdo is built mostly of prefabricated sheet metal, even buildings two or three stories high. The settlement centers around a large, beige structure with the romantic and adventurous name of "Building 155," which itself houses two mess halls with a common kitchen, a small store, a library, a liquor store, a laundry, a barber shop, administrative offices, the bank (a check-cashing window, no deposits), a twenty-four-hour radio and TV station, more than a hundred dormitory rooms, and a sauna.

From 155, the town's dirt roads radiate in all directions. Along the roads the remaining buildings loom like afterthoughts, thrown up as the population grew. No pattern, no forethought. Just jumble them together any old way: the LEGO school of civil engineering—if it fits, then snap it right in there.

Across the street from 155 is the cargo yard, dubbed "Hill Cargo." A Quonset hut houses army staff responsible for coordinating and preparing materials and personnel to be assigned around the continent and for the retrograde cargo to be sent back to New Zealand or the States. The twenty-five-thousand-square-foot cargo yard is walled off on two sides by large storage buildings and piled high with a seemingly inexhaustible assortment of vehicles, pallets, boxes of every size and shape, crates, wires, pipes, wood, cargo netting, and the strangest collection of fork lifts on the planet. The station's post office is sandwiched into one corner of the Quonset hut.

Dormitories come in three styles: tolerable, intolerable, and Jamesways. The tolerable, inhabited mostly by the scientists or their support personnel and some senior enlisted military, are large, newly constructed three-story affairs featuring a bathroom for every two rooms. The intolerable are the older dormitories, occupied mostly by junior enlisted military and Kiwi domestic help (that is, New Zealanders who clean the dorms, operate the kitchen, laundry, and so on). These two-story models have one bathroom per floor; each floor has twelve rooms. Then there are the Jamesways, ten-foot-wide, half-domed canvas huts with wooden floors and canvas curtains to cordon off living quarters from the central passage and warmed by a single heater running twenty-four hours a day to stave off the incessant draft. Sleeping in a Jamesway is like sleeping in your car at 60 below zero; we called them "ghetto huts."[2] The shuttle-bus drivers lived in Jamesways, poor souls. Thankfully the last of these huts was eliminated from McMurdo Station in 1991. I'm surprised the former occupants didn't get together and make a bonfire of them.

The entire dorm complex faces 155, with the newer buildings located closer to McMurdo Sound. Behind the dorms a road slopes down to the ice pier, where supply ships dock to off-load fuel and other supplies for the coming season. On the opposite side of 155 are specialized buildings like the fire house and the hospital (six beds!). There also stands the new Crary Science and Engineering Center (CSEC). A state-of-the-art facility for the support of international polar research, the center is built in three "phases," or tiers, like three steps going down toward the sound, with the tiers linked by enclosed, elevated walkways.

Adjacent to the CSEC is the Chalet, the station's A-framed nerve center and home to the National Science Foundation (NSF) representatives. Just below the Chalet on the shores of McMurdo Sound is the VXE-6 helicopter pad and its maintenance support building, called the "helo hangar." Next to the helo hangar is the station gym, with floor space so cramped that basketball teams are limited to four men per side. Across the dirt street are the VXE-6 administrative and operations offices, locally known as the Puzzle Palace or, more affectionately, Penguin Ops. Here the daily flight schedule is hammered out and managed by the operations duty officer (ODO).[3] The ODO mans the phones; juggles crews, maintenance, planes, priorities; and massages a few egos along the way. Pilots, scientists, and the NSF representatives rarely agree on priorities, and it's up to the duty officer to try to make everyone happy and ensure that missions are completed—an impossible job, so by the end of a week of duty everyone hates the ODO.

Fifty yards to the right of the Puzzle Palace is the cavernous supply building, where I had my office. The remainder of the station consists of a hodgepodge of specialized buildings, shacks, massive fuel-storage tanks, antiquated equipment, and dirt—the wonderful McMurdo volcanic dirt.

For getting around on the ground, there are snowmobiles, huge Delta vehicles with eight-foot-high tires, half-tracked trucks, World War II vintage jeeps and tractor trailers, pick-up trucks, four-wheel-drive passenger vans, and for the hardiest souls, mountain bikes.

And there are some hardy souls, believe me. People here, military included, have two main character traits in common: brutal candor and a pronounced devil-may-care recklessness. Back in the States they may be chefs, bikers, lawyers, doctors, students, or secretaries, but here the environment shapes them to its mold. They become adventurous and self-reliant—spurning civilization or maybe just running from the police—either description could apply to any number of the individuals I have encountered.

Something about the place encourages aggressive self-expression; yet I have also seen more tolerance here for the eccentricities of others. Biker types, who speak wistfully of barroom brawls and petty crimes back home, find themselves changed here. Overlooked by society back home, here they feel free, and they find sanctuary with kindred spirits. No one seems to mind the hardships of Antarctica once they have savored this bond. Adventurers require an adventurous place to meet, and Mac Town, where every day is an adventure, certainly fits the bill.

Thanks to the NSF, everyone in Mac Town is color-coded (or color-coated, actually). Military personnel wear green parkas, while science and support staff wear red. Kiwis working on the Hill in the dormitories or the galley wear military green, but those working at the New Zealand research station at Scott Base wear blue or yellow. In an instant, one may discern the role of an individual solely on the basis of the color of his or her coat.

There is also a slight transformation of character when the color-coating is applied. Red-parka people, for example, take on an air of superiority; they are grouped with the scientists—it's as if they instantly become chardonnay sippers and Democrats. Donning military green automatically places a person a notch lower—among the hired help, the beer drinkers. I've always thought this would make a good academic paper for social science research: "Color, Status, and Hierarchy in Antarctic Society." But, hey, some of my best friends wear yellow.

Most folks spruce up their parkas to stand out. Patches, ribbons, scarves, even duct tape adorns coats to break the monotony. These decorations also serve a secondary function at least three times a day: for identification when, at mealtimes, the walls are hung, floor to ceiling, with parkas. There always seem to be two or three bemused individuals wading through a sea of parkas, each trying to find the one with his or her own unique signature on it.

Despite the color coding, however, people do mingle over dinner or at the bar. The shared hardship of Antarctic life removes social barriers and brings together people who might not associate with one another anywhere else. Now, in retrospect, I see this fact as one of the most significant experiences of my Antarctic tours.

Back in the hall—the wing of 155 just above the galley where the VXE-6 officers were berthed—it's surprising to see how quickly folks establish their "homes" for the season. Each year an unspoken contest begins among the officers to see who can produce the most impressive living environment. With so few materials available, an inspired arrangement is widely admired and often imitated.

The main threat to Sean's and my comfort was the predilection of our cross-hall neighbor for listening to recordings of feline sex moans. Well, actually it was country music—Marty Robbins, to be specific. I have nothing against country music generally; it's just that hearing lonesome cowboy songs when I desperately need sleep is a severe test of my restraint. It took incredible focus for me to keep from walking across the hall and drop-kicking our neighbor's stereo into the Antarctic night.

For a while, we also had incessant telephone calls from someone convinced that my roommate was "Bill," and this individual would not be persuaded that "Bill" was not here. It went on for days and stopped only when I vowed to trace the call and place his phone where he would have real problems trying to dial it.

Entertainment of any variety was always at a premium in Antarctica; we didn't often have a chance to relieve the stress and monotony of our regular routine. One of the consequences of isolating a thousand-odd people in an Antarctic wilderness, in other words, is that they find some pretty unusual ways to entertain themselves.

There were the showers, for example. As part of our luxurious accommodations in Antarctica, we were permitted one two-minute shower (two minutes of actual running water) every other day. This plan was accepted by most as a suitable arrangement. Hell, under all those winter clothes and parkas, who could tell if you'd showered or not? But some of us looked forward to the showers as a civilizing event in an uncivilized environment. Unfortunately, no matter how carefully you adjusted the water, you got just one of two temperatures: freezing or, eventually, scalding hot. You could sometimes happen on just the right number of subtle adjustments that peaked the water to the perfect temperature, only to find yourself frozen or scalded instants later. It was on these occasions that I thought Satan might consider this for a new punishment in Hell. Imagine, condemned for all eternity to the military showers in Antarctica.

Nonetheless an imminent shower was approached with reverential regard, with the anticipation of a renewal of the spirit despite the fact that anyone stationed at McMurdo for more than a few days knew of the rapid and often unfavorable water temperature changes. This made it all the more puzzling why we continued to look forward to this torture, but we did. We continued to believe that perhaps this time the water would remain at the selected temperature for our two minutes—which, I might add, it never did in the entire three years I spent in Antarctica.

However, the showers did have their entertainment value. At times, when men were shaving in the bathrooms, the events were more interesting than TV. Standing a few feet away from these showers, shaving off the previous day's growth, you could count on being treated to one of the most unusual shows on earth. It generally started with an audible sigh, heard above the sound of running water, followed almost immediately by a shriek and the sound of flip-flopped feet frantically fleeing a frozen (or scalding) flow of water. An instant later a naked figure would scamper, gasping, out from behind the shower curtain. The newer the individual to the Ice, the better the facial expression. Overall I'd have to say that shaving while someone took a shower had to be our most consistent form of entertainment.

Even though I was constantly frozen or scalded, I felt I had no right to complain. I tried to rationalize my petty sufferings by remembering that just three generations ago and not more than a mile from where I stood freezing in my shower, men lived in small, drafty huts and slaughtered seals to burn the fat for heat and light. Those stalwart individuals were turned completely black by the soot the oily fat threw off. No showers, of course. After six months they must have reeked like dead skunks.

After a nice freezer burn, or a nice scald, depending on the day, I felt refreshed as I dressed for my next assignment. Dressing was no minor operation, either. Long underwear made of Nomex (a nylon-like fabric specially treated to be flame-resistant) was the first layer next to my skin, then a cotton turtleneck pullover and a Nomex flight suit. A pair of sock liners and thick insulated socks went under my heavy flight boots. Over all this were windproof Nomex overpants, a winter-weight flight jacket, a Nomex balaclava, a polypropylene "neckover" (an open-ended tube sock for the neck), two pairs of gloves, glasses, and a wool stocking hat. It was an ordeal to get into all those clothes every morning, but once I was outside in the minus-15 degrees centigrade weather, I felt comfortable. And at the end of a tough day, well, I could always look forward to the next hot shower.

During off-hours we traveled the main hallway of 155, dubbed "Route 1" because of all the foot traffic. It was the primary thoroughfare to mess halls, the barber shop, and the small, cramped store filled with Antarctic T-shirts, film, and books. I once purchased there a box of what promised to be fresh and chewy granola bars, only to break my molars as I bit into the first one. The Antarctic dryness desiccates everything; even chewy granola bars, hermetically sealed in foil, had the consistency of concrete. The remainder of the box went into the trash.

Life at the end of the earth has certain challenges. We learned to entertain ourselves exclusively with what we brought with us or what was provided by the NSF. Everything on the continent, beside the natural beauty, has to be shipped in. Mail deliveries provided our only additional form of diversion. And mail—all mail, any mail, junk mail—took on a kind of sacred importance. The first words out of every radio operator's mouth at McMurdo Center when news arrived of a flight coming south from Christchurch were, "How much mail do you have aboard?"

On mail days a thrill was in the air. Spirits soared, the condemned man got a last minute pardon. Everyone waited for confirmation that, yes, there was indeed an air force C-141 inbound with "freshies" (fresh fruits and vegetables) and thousands of pounds of mail, our umbilical cord to the outside. Mail was a bit of home, flown halfway around the world to put a smile on someone's face ten thousand miles away. Some people lived from letter to letter.

Yes, there were phones we could use, connected to the States via satellite and costing an astronomical amount, but calls were limited to ten minutes—including the dead time for "What did you say?" and the repeated statements. To me the phone was a negative tool, a poor means of communication that infused heartache in those who, once their call was over, found the isolation of the continent even lonelier.

But there was indeed the mail. Mail came from everywhere—from friends, family, acquaintances, businesses. And we got magazines and grossly outdated newspapers. Every cheesy advertisement was cherished. Antarctica creates the ultimate captive audience, and our mail was our freedom, a magical gift that allowed our spirits to soar over the frozen horizon to memories of home.

Before every season, I signed up for every catalog I could think of and subscribed to several magazines. I wrote to every friend, including people I hadn't heard from in years. I became pen pals with elementary school classes. "Wow, it must be cold there!" "How cold is it there?" "Do you ever get cold there?" And I corresponded with more than fifty other individuals. I wanted to increase my odds that with every delivery, there was something onboard for me. My motto: you've got to write them to get them. Besides, what's Antarctica without a Victoria's Secret catalog?

We mail-ordered hams, wine, smoked turkeys, cheese, beer-brewing supplies, books, clothes, stereo equipment, music, and photo supplies. We ordered anything and everything we wanted. The wait was the tough part. Mail was often bumped from a flight in favor of just about anything else, so it came slowly. The average time for a letter from home was about ten to fourteen days; a package (which had lower priority than letters) could take up to a month. One memorable day I received eight letters from friends, two boxes of goodies, and a videotaped Redskins game from my parents—I felt like I had just won the lottery.

Thank heavens for mail, because we needed something to do indoors when the Mac Town weather turned mild. Mild weather here is good and bad—good because it isn't a test of survival each time you venture outside, but bad because everything turns to mud as the snow and ice melt. During the endless night of winter here, a considerable amount of snow accumulates between the buildings, under pipes, and in cracks, nooks, and crannies—everywhere. This slush stays frozen and in place until the temperatures begin to climb above zero centigrade in mid-December.

The ice melt, when mixed with Mac Town's special brand of dirt, produces streets inches deep in volcanic-ash mud, a thick brown sludge so wonderfully foul and viscous that it pulls the boots right off your feet as you try to walk through it. Puddles abound. Mac Town is renamed Club

Mud. Hundreds of tons of accumulated snow melt; rivulets of mud flow unchecked to McMurdo Sound. Tramping around in this muck is a real chore. You sink up to your ankles, and the ooze swirls around and then sucks at your boots so that everywhere the streets are filled with obscene sucking, squelching noises.

The mud makes life here a new adventure. It coats everything and it's tracked everywhere, so there is no way to keep the floors clean. The folks responsible for cleaning the barracks spend nearly the entire day sweeping or mopping the decks, only to have them soiled minutes after they're done. It seems like the only thing that can extract the accumulated mud from your boots is a clean white floor. A squad of Kiwis sweeps up after us all—and sweeps and sweeps. For most people the mud is just an ugly inconvenience. For the Kiwi crew, however, it was a living hell. I often wondered if we would have any mud-related suicides among the clean-up crowd.

When the town is covered with snow, it's ugly but it seems serene. When the ice-mud comes, though, the place droops like an oil-covered bird. It looks dirty, used-up, soggy, and desolate. Junk and debris that have been hidden under snow now jut from melting ice cocoons. A mound of snow metamorphoses into a pile of rubble, old spare parts, or dry-rotted tires. Everywhere the unpleasant transformations take place.

Shuttle buses collect fat clumps of mud from the streets, which then jolt off as the busses hit ice at the transition between the land and the ice road to the ice runway. The mud clumps, in turn, attract heat and aid in the demise of the flimsy boundary between earth and ice. Civil engineers spend whole days building new and longer bridges from the land to the solid ice, trying to patch the area, but the whole place continues to melt back into the sea despite their efforts. The town is afloat in mud, ice, and trash. The mud does have one advantage, however: it isn't dust, which is what you get later, after the mud has dried. From bad to worse—at least mud doesn't make you sneeze.

When the streets are quiet, with only one bright orange shuttle bus idling at Derelict Junction, McMurdo has a certain mood.[4] Steam-jets crawl from pipes atop 155. A lone couple walks along the road toward Penguin Ops. At times, the whole place looks abandoned, a half-built nightmare, sinking in mud. Thank God for Sean and his music supply. Sometimes it was the only refuge from the place.

3

RUNWAYS ARE
FOR SISSIES

Operating on skis is much different from operating on wheels. As each season begins, all pilots in the squadron are required to fly two refamiliarization trainers, dubbed "A" and "B"—the first, where they practice landing on wheels and approaches to the ice runway; the second, where they refresh their skills for using the LC-130's most conspicuous feature, its massive skis.

The day I was scheduled to fly my "B" trainer, the temperature at preflight was 20 degrees below zero. With no wind and a perfect azure sky, though, the temperature felt almost warm. The flight schedule noted that there would be six pilots flying on this training evolution, which meant I would be sitting for quite some time waiting for the other pilots to qualify. Today the CO would qualify me on skis; then we would switch seats and I, as instructor, would qualify him. When the CO asked me to go first, I felt it was a matter of indifference since I would spend most of the flight watching others fly. However, waiting all that time wouldn't stop me from having some fun.

Since it was early in the season and we were operating exclusively from the ice runway, we would take off from there and transit the ten miles to the skiway, about three minutes flying time, to do our ski work. Given such a short transit time, a copilot/instructor is kept very busy preparing the plane to land on skis: he or she must read through three fairly lengthy checklists (thirty items), raise the wheels and lower the skis, adjust the flaps, as well as listen to and comprehend the pilot's landing brief. It's a heavy workload.

We hadn't been airborne for thirty seconds when I called for skis to be put down, just as the gear was coming up. The CO was still wading through the after-takeoff checklist, trying hard to catch up and get through the descent and before landing checklists before I actually touched down in about two minutes.

Roy and I had decided to rush the checklists during preflight just to rattle the CO's cage some. We'd planned on having to go around on the first pass because we were sure that he wouldn't be able to make it through the entire checklist in time for us to land. I called for flaps to be set for landing, two miles and less than a minute to landing, as the CO was starting the descent checklist. I then gave a quick "slide-and-go" briefing—reviewing with the cockpit crew the airspeeds for landing, the procedures that I as pilot would follow once we were on the ground, and what actions I expected the copilot, engineer, and navigator to do to back me up.[1] By the time we were half a mile out from the skiway and fifteen seconds from landing, the CO had just started the landing checklist, reading fast and furious, looking as though he might finish the landing checklist before I had to wave off.[2]

Fifty feet over the landing threshold, beads of sweat forming on the CO's brow, he ticked off the last two items on the landing checklist, and I landed. The skipper had rushed himself red. Roy and I were chuckling over the intercom as we slid along the skiway, and once we were airborne again, Roy gave me a nudge and said to the CO, "Didn't think you were going to make it to the end of that checklist there, sir."

The CO took the jibe and countered, "Yeah, I figured that since you have to fly with him this season, I didn't want you to have to witness one of Mr. Hinebaugh's pathetic go-arounds so early in the season. If you had, you might not want to fly with him anymore, so I figured I had better get him to land on that first pass."

Touché.

The skiway hadn't been graded yet and was in rough shape, but my practice landings were great, considering the fact that I'd done only two ski landings in the past six months. I completed five slide-and-goes and one full-stop landing before we moved on to the next phrase of the retraining.

Occasionally the weather here gets so bad that a pilot may not be able to see the runway, or skiway, in low visibility due to blowing snow, ice fog, and so on. In these situations the only alternative landing site is the white-out area: a flat, pie-shaped area adjacent to Williams Field that has been surveyed and is supposed to be free of crevasses. Pilots land in the white-out only when they are out of options. It is their last chance, and landing on instruments—in the blind, with nowhere else to go—isn't much for a last option. And on skis it's only worse because you never know what you might slide over in the open field.

These "B" trainers are pilots' only practice with these maneuvers prior to the season, when knowing what to do and how to fly the plane is what saves lives. I always took these training sessions seriously, since this was the only practice I would get before my ass was on the line and I had to do it for real.

A ski takeoff is a strange thing indeed. For a normal takeoff on wheels, it's a simple matter of adding power, keeping the airplane heading straight down the runway initially with nose wheel steering, then with the rudder once there is enough airflow over the tail to make the airfoil effective, and then accelerating to takeoff speed, pulling back on the yoke to raise the nose of the airplane, and taking off. The plane does all the work. A ski takeoff, however, is unnatural: the plane must be forcibly pulled into the air, a maneuver that requires a flawless mix of coordination, skill, and timing to perfect.

Ski takeoffs also pose the greatest potential for catastrophe that Antarctic pilots face routinely. As a matter of fact the only other group in the world that operates these with Hercs modified with wheel-ski gear, the New York Air National Guard, awards an air medal for every five takeoffs made on skis. If that system had been used for navy pilots during my time in Antarctica, I would have received more than eighty air medals. I'd be a regular hero.

When the aircraft is operating on skis, the large nose ski makes the nose wheel steering ineffective. And below 60 knots the rudder is also ineffective for nose control. Since it takes some time to reach that airspeed—which is fast enough to create sufficient airflow over the huge rudder airfoil—the challenge is to control the yaw, or the plane's heading, on the skiway with differential power, using the engines to control the plane's heading. As with a normal takeoff, the four power levers are advanced toward takeoff power. Beyond that, pilot technique on ski-takeoff varies: some pilots push all four up and control the nose with the two outboard engines, giving a little more gas to the right outboard engine to turn left and vice versa, while others use just the number-one engine to control the plane's heading (the four engines on a Herc are numbered from one to four, starting from the left so that, if you were sitting in the cockpit, number one would be the outboard engine on your left wing).

At 60 knots the rudder becomes effective and is used to steer the airplane. At this point the pilot places both hands on the yoke, and the copilot assumes control of the power levers. At 65 knots the pilot rotates the nose by pressing forward on the yoke, compressing the nose gear, and then yanking back smartly on the yoke to break the nose ski free from the snow. During a ski run, the surface friction of the snow against the nose ski is so high that the nose ski literally has to be "popped" off the deck.

Once the nose ski is in the air, the trick is to balance the plane. It is a real challenge to keep the nose high enough to prevent it from touching back down, causing an immediate deceleration, yet low enough to allow the plane to accelerate. With proper technique the pilot can balance the plane, accelerate, and slide down the center of the skiway on the two fifteen-foot-long main skis—145,000 pounds of plane in a 95-knot wheelie.

At approximately 95 knots the pilot yanks back on the yoke a second time and "jumps" the plane into the air. This is the point of true danger in the form of air minimum control speed (Vmca), which is the airspeed at which the airplane will be controllable and fly on three out of four engines. This speed is based on the weight of the plane, the outside temperature, and the pressure altitude.[3] In Antarctica the temperatures and pressure altitudes are so low that Vmca is always high, usually about 120 to 125 knots. During a normal takeoff, pilots always accelerate well beyond air minimum control speed on the runway before they get airborne so that if they were to lose an engine, they would already be at an airspeed where they could remain airborne and fly safely on three engines. Because of the surface friction associated with operating on skis, however, Antarctic pilots are not afforded that luxury. Consequently we routinely rotate and get airborne 25 to 30 knots below air minimum control speed. The best we can ever hope for is getting airborne at just above minimum flying speed.

For example, air minimum control speed was 120 knots the day of my ski refamiliarization trainer. If we had taken off on wheels, 120 knots would have been our takeoff speed, but since we were operating on skis, the surface friction allowed us only a maximum of 85 to 90 knots (minimum flying speed was 80), so we "jumped" to force the plane out of the snow and into the air and accelerated to air minimum control speed once we were airborne. Were we to lose an engine after takeoff, but before we had accelerated to air minimum control speed, we would be unable to control the plane's heading. It was risky stuff. If we lost an engine before hitting minimum control speed, the plane would be out of control. Our only recourse would be to reduce power on the symmetrical engine (on the other wing, the one causing the plane to yaw) and try to land straight ahead. Luckily, engine failures at takeoff are rare.

The second phase of the "B" trainer is held in the whiteout area, where we do some open-field work practicing ski drags and whiteout landings. Aside from a few major established camps or stations (South Pole, Byrd, CASERTZ—the latter name being an acronym for Corridor Aerogeophysics of the South East Ross Transect Zone), the entire continent of Antarctica is primitive and remote: that area, in its total, is called the "open field." Everything that scientists need to support their projects in the open field—as well, of course, as the scientists themselves—must be flown in to these locations, where there are no runways. In order to carry out these transports missions, Antarctic pilots must therefore make their own runways. We do this with the technique commonly referred to as a "ski drag"—that is, dragging the LC-130's skis through the snow by executing what is basically a minute-long slide-and-go.

Prior to a science party's being placed in the field, a crew is assigned to aid them in selecting a suitable site. Usually the PTAC and the navigator will meet with the science party's principal investigator (PI) to review the area of interest. The PI will relate what the party's primary goals are and where the scientists would like to establish their camp. The PTAC and the navigator will review the appropriate charts to see how close they can come to meeting the group's goals. The second step is a reconnaissance or "recce" (pronounced *wreck-ee*) flight. The crew flies over the area and looks for a suitable landing spot—one which is relatively smooth, as flat as possible, and appears to be free of crevasses. The PI will usually stand in the cockpit behind the pilots so that they can see the lay of the land from the air. Once the PI and PTAC agree on a site, a put-in is scheduled.

On the day of the put-in, the PTAC will overfly the area again, and once a suitable landing area is selected, the pilot will do two ski drags. A drag is a slide-and-go, except that the pilot doesn't let the nose ski touch the ground and keeps the power high enough to "ski" across the surface in a 90- to 95-knot wheelie (like a drag racer, front wheels in the air accelerating down a track). The drag is conducted for one minute—which, at 95 knots, approximates ten thousand feet. After one minute the pilot adds maximum power and takes off. The pilot then reverses his course and flies along the length of the drag to check for crevasses.

The theory is that, on the ground, the plane will be traveling fast enough to collapse, but not fall in, any snow bridges that may have formed over crevasses and may now be cloaking them. If the drag looks good from the air, the pilot then will conduct a second drag two wing-lengths away (about two hundred feet) from the first. On the third pass the pilot will pick the straightest of the two drags and land in the tracks. We then confine all further operations between these two sets of drags in our own crevasse-free area.

My first "B" trainer ski drag left much to be desired. I had no reference point on the horizon to track on—no mountain peak, no chunk of ice, no shadows, nothing. I ended up doing what Antarctic Herc pilots refer to as a "banana drag"—a long, arcing slide that from the air looks like a large banana sketched in the snow. Banana drags are common since the torque of the engines twists the plane's nose to the left, and without any visual reference point to steer on, the pilot is unaware that the plane is slicing through the snow in a long, slow arc. Ski drags must be straight, since in the open field these drags will be our runway.

Banana drags are bad in a training situation because you want to practice like you play, but worse is the ribbing you'll get from other pilots—that's hard to take. Sobriquets of "Chiquita" or "Cheeta" would follow me around for a week if I didn't nail the next drag. I lined up for my second drag facing White Island, so that one of its mountain peaks could be used as my reference steering point. Training on that peak allowed me to keep track of my progress and to continually correct my drift throughout the drag, thereby keeping the plane straight.

After my drags, I practiced my whiteout landing technique. We all practice this but hope we will never have to employ it. Caught in bad weather, out of gas, with no other options, we would have a whiteout landing as our last-ditch hope. It's a landing done solely on instruments. We might never see the ground until we've landed, and perhaps not even then. Once we're in the whiteout landing area, the technique calls for us to zero our drift, get as close as we can to a direct head wind, set power to establish a two-hundred-foot-per-minute rate of descent at 120 knots, and keep the wings level. Then it's just a matter of waiting until we blindly touch down.

This is the epitome of demanding flying. When it's for real, it's like flying in a milk bottle. The lack of any outside visual cues demands total concentration and an acute scan of the instruments. Pilots, whether seasoned or new, can easily get vertigo and stop trusting their flight instruments. This is an extremely bad situation. Any breakdown or lapse in concentration could end in an uncommanded bank or, worse, diving at the deck. The frozen ground doesn't care how you land. It accepts crashes as well as anything else.

I concentrated on my flight instruments alone and attended to the crew's essential calls of airspeed, altitude, rate of descent, and drift. I strenuously avoided looking outside. It seemed to take forever for us to touch down, but once we were finally on the deck, I recovered my normal breathing and heart rate again. If flown correctly, these simulated whiteouts take you to the edge of your concentration and test your self-control.

I completed my portion of "B" training with a ski takeoff in the open field. This is identical to a normal ski takeoff except we weren't on a smooth, packed skiway. Surface friction from soft snow in the open field is much higher, occasionally high enough that it's impossible to break the nose ski free. If the nose won't break free, the plane won't accelerate to takeoff speed.

At times you can literally plow through the snow for miles attempting to get the nose ski off. On this day I was lucky and broke the nose ski free in only two tries. We went bounding through the snow, pushing through small sastrugi until I yanked the nose free of the surface at 65 knots.[4] We shook and bounced along while we accelerated to 95 knots in a wheelie.

Thirty seconds later we broke free, extricating the plane from the clutching grip of the snow, immediately finding smooth, clean air to dance in.

As I went bouncing through the snow like a kid with an expensive sled, I could sense the power and intricate balance of nature, the tenuous balance between man and machine, earth and sky. As the aircraft gained the momentum to jump skyward, the snow, the sky, and the plane meshed together for a brief moment, and in that split second, the balance between flying and remaining glued to the undulating snow surface is either achieved or lost. It is the Antarctic pilot's ultimate challenge to control the aircraft during this transition. I was always happy when I won.

I swapped seats with the CO, who then went through the same program. He and I weren't grading each other overtly; together we were the most proficient ski pilots in the squadron. And since we two would be refreshing all the other pilots between us, it was incumbent, not to mention safer, for us to hone our skills together and establish standard instructions before we attempted to refresh the others.

Once he finished, I had to sit back as a passenger while four other pilots had their shot. All of them had varying degrees of success operating on skis. I admit to a little ego thrill as the CO had two other pilots use my ski drags, and not his, as references after these pilots had some difficulty keeping the plane straight during their open-field work. It was hard for me to sit on the bench seat behind the engineer and observe, but it did give me an excellent opportunity to observe mistakes so that I could be a more effective instructor when it was up to me to qualify other pilots on their "B" trainers.

We ended the flight four hours later by practicing instrument approaches at the skiway before heading back to the ice runway. As we prepared to land, our flight path passed over several groups of Weddell seals. "They look like giant ice slugs," Roy commented as they congregated in groups of twenty or thirty, slumbering on the seasonal ice, clustered around their access hole (their window to open water and three meals a day). It was always nice to see them again after being away for six months.

Following the last approach for the flight, we had a problem with the nose ski. The rigger strut failed. As the gear was raised, the nose ski, instead of coming up level, pitched upward and ripped apart the nose-gear fairing.[5] We made a full-stop landing on the next pass to check on the damage. It was substantial. Another few minutes airborne and I'm sure the whole fairing would have worked itself loose, departed the plane, and caused some real damage.

This was the same plane in which Rich (my PTAC during my first season) had run into a four-foot-high sastrugi at 60 knots out in the Geologist Range. The plane required massive rework and was never quite the same afterward. We were lucky this time; damage was limited to the fairing and a lost landing light.

The next morning I was met by a stiff, bone-chilling wind. The few minutes I had to wait for the shuttle bus to arrive were awful. Even totally covered from head to foot and with the drawstring on my hood pulled tight, closing the aperture around my face to a hole the size of a quarter, I experienced the wind as a knife that found its way to my core.

This morning I was to serve as the functional check flight (FCF) pilot. Once maintenance has repaired a plane, certain procedures (such as an engine or a prop change) require an FCF before that plane can rejoin the fleet.[6] An FCF pilot is generally a seasoned flyer who has demonstrated a high level of competence and understanding of the plane.

The day's flight profile called for us to climb to three thousand feet, shut down number-three engine, try to make the propeller spin backward (to see if the brake designed to keep the prop from spinning backward when the engine was shut down was working properly) by accelerating to 200 knots, and—if that worked—restart the engine and return. Simple.

We departed the ice runway and headed across the sound toward the Dry Valleys. The new propeller worked correctly; we had a textbook shutdown and restart. The engine worked so well that we finished the FCF in only twenty minutes, and since it was unlikely that we would fly again today, the crew and I decided to do a little low-level work down in the Taylor Valley.

The Dry Valleys are so named because of the lack of snow there. The Taylor Valley is broad and flat with rounded six- to seven-thousand-foot mountain peaks on either side that channel the Taylor Glacier from the polar plateau to McMurdo Sound. During October the sun is still low on the horizon, circling the Antarctic sky, gradually climbing higher as the season progresses and reaching its zenith in December. It never sets while we are there. When the sun is low in the sky, as it is early in the flying season, it makes for exciting and dramatic lighting. When the snow and rugged, windblown mountain peaks are tinged with subtle hues of orange and gold they lend an aura of softness to these stark vistas as they bask in the gentle glow of the slowly rising sun.

Although I had already taken several rolls of film of these same mountains, valleys, and glaciers during previous seasons, I continued to take more photographs. I sought out the minute, ethereal changes in the lighting here that were rendered all the more dramatic when I considered that everything I saw here was the same as it had been for millions of years. I think it was the constant subtle changes of light, when viewed against a backdrop of the utter indifference and frozen permanence of Antarctica, that most intrigued me. That light and the shadows it creates are the only real and visible changes that ever occur here.

The lighting, the clouds, the reflections off the snow—all made these mountains and glaciers appear to me as though I was seeing them for the first time. Viewing something in a slightly different light can give a totally new look to a familiar scene here or expose an unseen section of glacier, hillock, or mountain peak. The light sparked my imagination, and each new photograph I took seemed to exemplify the spirit of this frozen continent in yet another astounding way. At times when I was feeling spent, I would look again for the inconspicuous play between light and dark to rekindle my spirit through a passion for this unworldly place. In Antarctica, the most barren and desolate of places, only four colors prevail— white, black, brown, and blue. Yet with the aid of the sun I could see all the colors of the rainbow on the backdrop of snow and rock.

As we rounded the back side of the Royal Society Range, I was presented with a unique view of the two prominent peaks, Mt. Erebus and Mt. Terror, on Ross Island. The entire island was ringed by a low, dense fog so that their peaks appeared to float serenely on pillows of cumulus clouds. We spent over an hour drifting through those glacial valleys, like a massive gray bird held aloft by a steady breeze, moving slowly over a frozen landscape, basking in the gentle light of pale gold sun.

My primary copilot for the season, Tim, was at the controls. He started a long arcing turn from a point parallel with Mt. Discovery, a slow right turn that took us behind the rugged thirteen-thousand-foot Mt. Lister. Here he began a gentle descent down the Ferrar Glacier and kept heading down until we were at the confluence of the Ferrar and Taylor Glaciers. His next right turn brought us into the valley of the Taylor Glacier, where he leveled the plane at a thousand feet and accelerated toward the mouth of the glacier where it dumped into McMurdo Sound. Ross Island was now dead ahead of us, sixty miles away.

We wanted to get down to two hundred feet, but in the Taylor Valley we were rocked by down-drafts that poured down from the polar plateau, giving us quite a choppy ride at altitudes below four hundred feet. I had Tim check the altitude at five hundred feet and decelerate to 180 knots as he kept the plane squarely pointed toward the glacier's mouth. The fact that we could fly a huge airplane like this at an altitude of five hundred feet down a mile-wide glacier, dwarfed by six- to seven-thousand-foot mountain peaks, was a most impressive part of the job.

My sense of proportion deserted me as I stared up at the peaks looming over us. It's not uncommon, when at the controls of a large complex aircraft like the C-130, to feel that you are taking on the proportions of the plane itself: you become at once both massive and superior to the elements. Yet dwarfed in that valley, I knew we were mortal and insignificant, even in our large plane. The constant energy of the wind, like an invisible stream, could have slapped us down at any time. This vast, powerful, and unyielding continent demanded humility.

Once we exited the valley we were free from the severest winds so Tim accelerated to 250 knots, climbed to a thousand feet, and flew a beeline across McMurdo Sound to the ice runway. Ten miles from the field, I requested a ground-controlled approach (GCA) from the tower. Weather at the runway was cloudy and overcast, a sharp contrast from the exceedingly clear sky we had experienced in the valley just sixty miles away. Strangely enough, there were times when the runway would be covered with fog or low clouds and yet the valleys would be clear, mainly due to stiff winds that swept down from the polar plateau. But on the sound, over the airfield, the clouds thickened, became the color of snow, and tended to give the impression that we were flying blind, whizzing through a vat of sour cream.

The controller gave us headings to fly to align us with the runway and called our rate of descent until we were over the runway threshold. During any approach in Antarctica the pilot must pay such close attention to his attitude instruments that VXE-6 aircrews developed the "polar backup." This involves the entire crew in the approach and thus reduces the pilot's workload by delegating to the cockpit crew the responsibility for providing the pilot with time-critical information like airspeed, altitude, and rate of descent. In Antarctica the polar backup has proven so effective that aircrews practice it constantly in order to maintain proficiency while flying in the worst weather conditions in the world.

For a polar backup, the copilot is responsible for an outside scan and calls out the plane's airspeed and rate of descent. The engineer is responsible for actual altitude, and the navigator calls out the plane's drift due to wind. Once a crew has flown together awhile, the polar backup becomes a smooth and fluid process. In the cockpit it sounds like this:

COPILOT: "I have you one-twenty-five, down three" (125 knots, in a descent rate of, down three hundred feet per minute).

ENGINEER: "Two hundred" (that many feet above the ground, from the radar altimeter).

NAVIGATOR: "One right" (1 degree right drift due to a left-to-right crosswind).

From these bits of information the pilot can modify his or her approach and compensate or correct as necessary. This backup information is continuous from a thousand feet above the ground until touchdown.

"One-twenty-five, down four."

"One-fifty"

"One right."

Once we landed, I debriefed the maintenance chief, signed off the FCF paperwork, and gave the plane a thumbs-up. Then, after calling the duty office to see if there was anything else for us to do, I learned that the flight schedule had been canceled for the rest of the day.

One of our routine trips was to Byrd Surface Camp; occasionally, I flew as copilot to the skipper (our CO). Normally either the skipper or I would take our own crew and complete this mission, but as it turned out, he and I were the only two pilots who had completed both our "A" and "B" trainers and therefore were the only two qualified to fly on the continent thus far. While the skipper attended to some last minute details, I looked over the aircraft discrepancy book (ADB), received our weather brief, and did a final walkaround the plane before departure.

I noticed a small fuel leak six or eight inches from the number-three exhaust stack and reported it to maintenance. The leak had already been checked and signed off as WNL (within normal limits). I countered that the exhaust stacks heat to 900 degrees or better and could potentially ignite seeping fuel. A supervisor and several mechanics were dispatched at once. They gave the area a thorough going-over and reported that the leak was no big deal. They said that the seepage was from the auxiliary fuel cell and that all the fuel in that cell had been drained. "Well," I wondered aloud, "where the hell is the damn fuel coming from?"

The maintenance chief came to my rescue and ordered the bag drained again, this time from a low-point gravity drain, to ensure that all the cell was dry. An hour later, with the cell supposedly dry, there were still a few drops seeping through the aircraft skin. If we had had the time, the mechanics could have pulled the panels and dried things out, but as I learned, time was at a premium and we were already late. The skipper insisted we launch at once. I was still wary, but when I was briefed as to the urgency of our mission, I made the necessary preparations for an immediate takeoff.

The urgency lay with a Canadian "Twin Otter" crew who had flown down to Antarctica via South America and were traversing the continent from the Antarctic Peninsula. Their small twin-engine airplane had a limited range and wouldn't make it to McMurdo unless they got fuel at Byrd. Weather on the peninsula had forced the crew to linger longer than they had anticipated. So as soon as the weather broke, the Otter crew launched with just enough fuel to get to Byrd and, to save weight, less than two days' worth of food. On top of that, they were flying just ahead of a storm front that was bearing down on them from the rear.

Time was running short. It was up to us to get their fuel to Byrd so that they could land there, gas, and be on their way to McMurdo as quickly as possible. In Antarctica, fuel is life. It is heat, it powers planes and electrical generators, it melts the snow we drink, it is the juice that keeps us from freezing to death. In this case, it was the stuff that would enable the Otter crew to survive a major storm.

Any concerns I harbored about the fuel seep were relieved when the skipper said that I would fly the entire mission. This arrangement allowed me to make all takeoffs and landings and to fly as I saw fit to minimize the risk of any residual seepage. The skipper's theory was that if I was concerned about the leak, I'd fly the plane cautiously. He was right.

The three-hour flight to Byrd was uneventful. On the way the skipper challenged my knowledge of Antarctic landmarks. There are three, all major fissures, or active ice, on the Ross Ice Shelf and named (in order from McMurdo) the Big Ruth, Steer's Head, and Muffin's Delight. Dave, the navigator, whom we appointed as mediator, held our bets. I named all three of the fissures; the skipper, only one. By the time we were adjacent to Muffin's Delight, I was five dollars richer.

During the summer season the Byrd flight is one of the most tedious—an entire route of dull, flat white vistas. Only these three fissures, spaced about an hour apart, break the monotony. Generally when we flew to Byrd, the ice shelf was so cloudy that we rarely saw even one of these landmarks. Seeing all three in one day was a treat.

Descending into Byrd we flew through two distinct midlevel cloud layers at eight thousand and seven thousand feet, obscuring the sun so completely that surface conditions at the camp were nil and nil.[7] The skiway was nearly impossible to distinguish from the surrounding snow. It took us four passes, flying directly over the camp at five hundred feet, to locate it. The flags left at last season's end to mark the skiway were reduced to tattered red rags now, blown to pieces by fierce winter winds. They were of little help to demarcate the skiway.

I set up to drag the skiway, hoping it was still safe to land there. The Ross Ice Shelf is so unstable that crevasses can open up anywhere without warning. It pays to be cautious, even on an established skiway. Today the skiway was rough with the winter's accumulation of windblown snow but was free of crevasses, and we bounded to a stop on the second pass.

The weather and the poor condition of the skiway worried me. The skipper and I had dozens of such landings between us, yet this time we had had difficulty locating the skiway. I wondered how it would be for the Twin Otter crew, who had never been to Byrd before. I felt we should mark the skiway better, but we had too little fuel to be spending time on deck, and we had neglected to bring any extra skiway flags. We off-loaded our eight fifty-five-gallon drums of fuel and a pump. Our ski drags would have to be sufficient reference for the Otter crew to locate their precious fuel. I hoped that the wind wouldn't cover our tracks in the next few hours.

The landing and ski drags had been rough. The surface was a mess with the accumulated snow. The wind had pushed and carved the snow into uneven and distorted diamond-shaped drifts, five to twenty feet long and anywhere from six to thirty inches high. Most of the snow was soft, but the drifts were so high that the plane seemed to roll in angry seas more than slide across the ground.

As we taxied to the ramp area, the loadmaster lowered the ramp and raised the door for a running off-load. This is the most expedient way to get cargo out of the plane when pressed for time. With the ramp lowered, I added power, and the loadmaster released the locking pins, allowing the two large fuel-loaded pallets to slide backward down the ramp on rollers and right out of the plane. We drove out from under the load like magicians pulling a tablecloth off a table, leaving the dishes perfectly in place.

After the load was away, I didn't stop but continued to taxi back to the skiway. I aligned the plane back into our landing ski drags, advanced the throttles to takeoff power, and at once we began to leapfrog over the snow drifts, rolling and pitching toward takeoff speed. At 90 knots I pulled sharply on the yoke, and the jarring stopped as the wind lifted our wings and carried us skyward. We had saved enough fuel by completing an expeditious off-load that we decided to fly a recce over CASERTZ, an area less than a hundred miles away from Byrd where scientists were working to eventually produce a high-resolution aerial survey of a portion of West Antarctica. Using a Twin Otter and an occasional Herc flight, they will "look" through the ice with radar and other devices to map the bedrock layer that anchors the Ross Ice Shelf.

Before scientists are put into the field, a recce flight is standard procedure. The intended area of landing is located, and an initial pass is made at three to five thousand feet to scan the local terrain. A second pass is made at between five hundred and a thousand feet above the surface to locate any potential hazards such as sastrugi or depressions in the snow suggesting snow bridges, which indicate crevasses. The final pass is made at a hundred feet and below to determine the roughness of the surface and the sastrugi (they run parallel to the wind) and the predominant wind direction.

Once the recce PTAC believes the site safe to land, the proposed landing area is photographed by specially trained photographers for safety review by the operations officer, and a recommended landing site and direction are plotted on the applicable navigational chart by the navigator. This is done in case the recce crew isn't the same crew that does the actual put-in.

The weather at CASERTZ today was supposed to be marginal with a two-thousand-foot ceiling and one-mile visibility. On the first pass we flew three thousand feet directly over the camp and saw nothing. For the next pass I dropped down to fifteen hundred feet, and by ducking through a hole in the clouds, we located the camp. I then began a slow right-hand circle, allowing everyone but myself to get a good look at the site.

The CO said CASERTZ seemed to be in fair condition, no worse for the wear from the long winter. The skiway, however, had been roughed up by the high winds and drifting snow. It looked salvageable by a few passes with the snow plane, a motorless grader towed by tractors or snowmobiles to even the snow surface in preparation for a skiway. A smooth landing area saves the airplane from the excessive wear and tear of open-field operations.

The break in the clouds allowed just enough light for us to determine that the surface conditions were favorable, so we opted to stop and check the camp's condition. I completed a drag on the first pass and landed on the second. Despite its rough appearance from the air, the snow surface was fine, and although windblown, the snow itself was soft and powdery. I stopped the plane adjacent to the two Jamesways that served as the camp's galley and science center.

While an NSF representative and the scientists deplaned to inspect the condition of the camp's facilities, I wandered away from the camp in the opposite direction. I walked about a hundred yards from the plane and stood staring out across the frozen desert. Standing there, facing away from the plane in a light wind, I found I couldn't hear the engines anymore. It was an eerie silence, which I felt more than heard—like a breath frozen.

The weather worsened, and in a few minutes I could barely make out the plane. I felt as though my eyes had been wrapped in gauze. It occurred to me that the difference between a good and a bad day in Antarctica is cloud cover. When the weather is clear and fine, it is interesting to stand alone on the vast, white, frozen plateau and see the sharp contrast between the snow and sky. Gradients of blue range from pale, light, almost white blue near the surface to a brilliant royal blue, nearly black, as the sky meets space. The horizon on clear days like that is a vision of stunning clarity and proportion, an ocean of white meeting an ocean of blue.

However, on an overcast day like today, the clouds seem to stick to the ground and trap the light. The horizon disappears. White clouds combine with the white snow to form the illusion of swimming in milk. All white, all around. No surface definition, no horizon, nothing but a dirty gray-white of dead and dying light. On such days there is no drearier sight on earth than Antarctica. I hurried back to the plane before it was swallowed up by the milky white goo closing in around us.

Our takeoff from CASERTZ was as smooth as the landing; however, on climbing out, we had a minor problem with the autopilot. With an inoperative elevator channel (which holds the plane's altitude) we were forced to take turns piloting the plane, trading with one another every thirty minutes: the concentration required to control an aircraft in three dimensions over long distances is extremely fatiguing. Otherwise, the return trip to McMurdo was identical to the trip out to Byrd—except that we didn't see any of the predominant landmarks this time. Low clouds covered the entire ice shelf.

High winds spilled down from the polar plateau and out across the ice shelf. Hovering just above Mt. Discovery were two perfectly formed lenticular clouds that seemed to hang in the gale-force winds like kites. While these innocent-looking clouds appeared thin and fragile, they belied their true nature as harbingers of exceedingly dangerous turbulence. As I stared at the clouds, I thought of Professor Edgeworth David, leader of the first journey to the South Magnetic Pole, who wrote: "Towards evening, large clouds developed, much like the whaleback clouds which we had often observed forming over Erebus about the time of blizzards."[8] Occasionally we found ourselves being shaken roughly, feeling the effects of these clouds even when we were more than forty miles away from them and in seemingly clear air.

At McMurdo, I made a nice landing in a stiff crosswind and spent the next hour writing up the gripes on the auto pilot.[9] When we as a crew had finished our other postflight duties, the CO gave the crew a ride up the

"Hill" in his personal van.[10] I enjoyed riding in style (sitting in the front seat) and flying over the snow road to McMurdo thumbing our noses at the thirty-five-miles-an-hour speed limit.

After showering, I went to "midrats" (midnight rations, meals served from 0001 to 0130 for the late shift workers), where I ran into some helicopter pilots who filled me in on their group's latest activities. Out of fifty officers attached to the squadron, only ten flew helicopters, so they tended to band together. It seemed that one of the junior helo officers had had a run-in with the executive officer (XO) earlier in the day, an incident that had given all ten pilots a cause to bond—bonding for helo pilots consisting of a bout of heavy drinking. Being well-advanced in the present objective, they had then decided to see who could run and slide the farthest on his nylon flight jacket down the middle of dorm hall. Oh, the things one does for laughs on the Ice!

Mike Nee, a gentle giant who could bench press well over four hundred pounds, had slid the farthest and run headlong into the XO's door at midnight. Amid cheers and the adulation generally associated with such a feat, rumblings were heard from within the XO's room—a fact that had suggested the group should beat a hasty retreat. Quickly adjourning to the room next door to mine and thinking the coast was clear, they continued to drink. One of the younger pilots (the one purported to have had the original run-in with the XO) soon began to mock and mimic the XO as the others egged him on. His ribald imitation reached full swagger just as the figure of the XO filled the outline of the door.

Those in the room began to laugh nervously, wiggle their eyebrows and roll their eyes, anything to signal the helo pilot that the subject of his ridicule was standing behind him. The XO cleared his throat, and the whole room went silent. Mike—who had been standing off to one side, out of the XO's view—backed up behind a locker and kept quiet. The XO ticked off the names of those he saw in the room (everyone but Mike) and suggested they meet him in his office that morning at 0600. The crowd winced as the XO left. Mike immediately won the nickname Mr. Invisible.

Listening to this story as I ate midrats, I was glad that I had been flying—or I, more than likely, would have been involved and subsequently been invited to the XO's office also. That was something that so far I had managed to avoid, and I wanted to keep it that way.

On the last day of October, McMurdo was hit by a Herbie—the fast-moving Antarctic storm that lasts from a few hours to several days, with winds that can rage at over 100 knots. I awoke to find the town buried under a blanket of snow, a creamy white cocoon that was wrapped so tightly around the station that it created enough of a barrier to help fend off the biting winds. This Herbie—as all Herbies—was a monster, pushing before it high winds that slashed like knives through our protective layers and found its way in, around, and through the seams of our clothing to leave us numb and chilled to the bone. I had been truly cold before: once at the South Pole I spent about fifteen minutes outside when the temperature was 99 degrees below zero without wind. Today as I walked to Hut Point, however, the wind was blowing directly at my face, and although the temperature was only 40 below, it was cold enough to frostbite my face in about five minutes. I felt that I would never be any colder than I was just then, or at least I hoped I wouldn't. I was miserable.

As I walked back to the barracks, my fingers became stiff and then ached as I tried to flex them. My head felt stiff and tight. My eyes felt as if the fluid in them was freezing. My legs moved slowly as though I were walking in a thick, congealed, milky white gravy. I felt brittle. All motion was painful; it hurt being this cold. The wind-chill temperature was 75 below zero. At that moment I vowed to move to Florida.

4

WE BAND

OF BROTHERS

Our crew was fourth in a rotation of six crews, which was fine, except it meant we generally flew at night. "Night flying" in Antarctica is really a misnomer, since during the summer it never gets dark. This can be disorienting, but the worst part about night flying for me was getting used to having breakfast foods for dinner.

I hated wandering into the galley at 0700, hungry, red-eyed, dirty, and tired from an all-night flight, only to see all those fresh, well-rested faces staring back at me, chatting about the upcoming day. Then came the wonderful dinner choice: egg-substitute omelet or cold cereal with powdered milk? I never got used to that night schedule.

Our first flight of the season together was important because it was the first opportunity for us to see how the new crew would work together. The core of this season's crew had flown together last season, and we trusted and counted on each other. Last year, we enjoyed a safe and successful season, so we lobbied hard during the off-season to stay together for this year. To distinguish ourselves from other crews, we wore custom-designed patches on our flight suits, patches depicting Spaceman Spiff from the popular cartoon *Calvin and Hobbes.* Our motto described us as ten-feet-tall, bulletproof, and invisible—a reference to how one of us felt when he drank. The crew was made up of copilots Tim and Bob; Dave, the navigator (Ed replaced Dave in mid-December); Roy, our flight engineer; Chris, our loadmaster; and me, the aircraft/mission commander, or PTAC.

The PTAC's job is to ensure the safety and welfare of crew and passengers, the orderliness and smooth operation of the flight, and the successful completion of the mission. In an emergency, or in any questionable situation, the PTAC is the final authority. It is a heady responsibility. But with over three thousand hours in C-130s and two seasons flying in Antarctica, I reasoned I had a grasp of the dangers involved. I respected the place and the crew, and I flew the plane accordingly.

My copilot, Tim Lefebvre (pronounced *Le-fay*), was a second pilot (2P), which meant he was nearly ready to become a PTAC himself. Tim had a runner's build, not an ounce of fat on him. He kept his hair closely trimmed in a permanent flattop, but on deployment he grew a cheesy, tangled mustache that made him look like a teenage Zapata wanna-be. He was an excellent pilot. We had flown together most of last season, and Tim's flying skills bolstered my confidence and allowed me to be aggressive in tackling challenging missions, regardless of the weather. I trusted him. And when you trust someone on polar missions, you're trusting him or her with your life. Tim was vigorous and thorough in executing his duties, and for most of the season he completed all the paperwork that I was supposed to do before preflight. He anticipated well and was always aware of what was happening around him in the cockpit. For me, he was the quintessential copilot.

Dave Hegland, our navigator for the first half of the season, was the most competent and conscientious navigator I have ever flown with. At the navigator's station he was completely at ease, a master at his task. He could get us anywhere on the continent, using nothing but a sextant. He worked constantly, plotting and updating our courses, planning and computing his next "cel" (celestial) shot of the sun. He always knew our exact position. He was with me on WinFly when we flew from McMurdo to Christchurch on only three engines (the first time such a flight had been accomplished and, I hoped, the last time it would ever be attempted). Dave never lost his cool. He stayed focused and did his job.

Dave's real forte was the art of the internal approach. One of the unique features of Antarctic flying is that navigators must sometimes use outdated and temperamental weather radar to locate skiways for the pilots and then talk them down into the field. It is an extremely difficult technique, but Dave had perfected it. When I worried about landing in bad weather, I would glance over at Dave and he would cup his palms together—Dave-sign for "You're in good hands, bro."

I distinctly remember the first time I saw the Dave-sign. It was on our first WinFly together, and we were heading to Willy Field. Conditions were bad: an indefinite ceiling of less than one hundred feet and visibility of one-sixteenth of a mile, with no surface or horizon definition. As if the weather weren't sufficient trouble, all the ground navigational aids were out. I asked Dave to get me in with an internal approach, at least close enough so I had a shot at landing on the skiway instead of having to do a whiteout.

He nodded, then gave me that "good hands" gesture. He lined me up on centerline and called such a good internal that I made the field on the first pass. I never worried about his getting us in anywhere again. He was the finest navigator I've ever flown with—not to mention one hell of a guy, sharing my taste for good lager beer and reminiscences about the days when we were buff enough to lead climbs on Mt. Rainier.

Ed Angel joined the crew in mid-December when Dave left to be the officer in charge at Christchurch. Ed was also skillful in his own right. This was his second tour in the Antarctic, and I felt fortunate to get someone so familiar with the ice and internal approaches. As a crew we never missed a beat transitioning from Dave to Ed. He possessed an easy-going style that permitted the crew to warm to him immediately. He talked with a hint of a southern drawl, and he smiled constantly, which made him easy to like. And he was willing to do anything to help out. In the open field he generally followed Chris out the door, soliciting work and often tackling the jobs that no one else wanted. He was steady, helpful, and funny, and he did more than anyone else to keep our spirits on an even keel as the season dragged on into its final weeks.

Roy Williams, our flight engineer, was responsible for keeping the plane flying and for repairing the plane in the field. I have flown with many outstanding and dedicated engineers, and Roy was among the best. He knew every inch of the plane and could fix anything. If Roy told me the plane was ready to fly, I boarded it unhesitatingly. If something went wrong during a flight and he could get to it, it got fixed. The only time he couldn't get a piece of equipment on the plane to function properly was when it had been incinerated.

Roy's dedication was never in question after WinFly, when he climbed that ladder in 60-below temperatures to adjust the propeller to allow us to limp the plane back to Christchurch on three engines. He was a magician when it came to Hercs. He was invaluable in the cockpit, too. When I flew with an inexperienced copilot, he acted as an extra pilot and backed me up when the new copilot couldn't. He could think like a pilot, and if Roy told me to go around, or break off an approach, I did. He watched over "his" pilots and made sure we were safe.

Our loadmaster, Chris Derby, was our own Incredible Hulk. He worked out every day and was amazingly strong, a valuable asset when we had to load a plane in the open field. Chris's favorite joke was that we were only there to ferry him and his cargo from point A to point B. I had to admit this was more true than not. At McMurdo or the established camps, there might be forklifts to load or unload the eight-foot-square cargo pallets, and the loadmaster supervised the process. But in the field a good load-master was crucial. Limited fuel and weight considerations during take-offs and landings in the open field meant the loadmaster could make or break your trip.

Chris excelled in his role. Science parties were rarely packed and ready to go on departure days, despite twenty-four-hour notice that we were on the way. In these situations, for example, Chris seemed to be off the plane before we came to a stop. In an hour or two, a scattered field camp became an orderly and perfectly balanced stack of equipment in the back of our plane. Limited loading time meant everyone helped, but I have to admit there were times when I stared bug-eyed at Chris's frenzied activity and the amazing speed with which he could make a camp disappear, leaving behind nothing but clean white snow.

To ease the boredom on some of the more mundane flights, we listened to music on our headsets. Someone in the crew would always bring a portable tape player, and we'd scrounge up a patch cord that worked— Roy was scrounger-in-chief. The patch cord allowed us to plug the tape player into the intercommunications system (ICS) so we could listen to our own Radio Herc. It was a crude but effective copy of what the airlines use for their programming.

Unfortunately patch cords had a high failure rate. Once a working cord was found and the tape player set up, there was a hush throughout the cockpit. We had an unspoken rule: nobody touched the tape deck unless it was time to change the tape. Any other disturbance might put the whammy on the patch cord. Tape selection was strictly democratic, however. Majority ruled, unless the majority hogged the machine. The crew was fairly open-minded: if we listened to rock for a few days, we would switch to someone else's brand of music. Ed, for example, liked two kinds of music: country and western.

So with some woman wailing about a lost dog, or maybe it was a broken heart (all the songs sounded the same to me), we sailed through the freezing Antarctic nights. During these flights we established what I called our "C-W Tolerance Threshold": the level at which one ripped the headphones off and, uh, deselected Ed's music. Being PTAC has a few advantages.

We often flew with trainees on board. During one trip to the Pole, the plane ahead of us had produced a two-hundred-yard-long, fifty-foot-high contrail. It looked like a fog bank, and we had to wait for it to clear before we landed. Contrails aren't unusual at the Pole because the combined effects of low temperatures and low station pressures cause the water vapor in the exhaust of jet engines to immediately condense into thick, fast moving clouds. In the States contrails regularly string out behind airliners at high altitudes, where the temperatures can get extremely cold. What was interesting to me was that here at the Pole we were producing contrails while on the ground; we were on the ground at ninety-eight hundred feet above sea level with the temperature 68 below zero, so we were in similar conditions as the Stateside airliners.

We used the time for our student navigator to practice internal approaches, the last of which was very poor. We crossed the skiway 02 more than a thousand feet down from the approach end and 30 degrees off heading.[1] While Dave gave some additional instructional tips, I had to figure a way to land. The practice approaches had done more harm than good. Our contrails, the total effect from each of our three passes, combined with the contrail from the previous plane were such that we had in effect fogged ourselves out and couldn't see the end of the skiway. The day was windless so there was nothing to help dissipate the fog we had created.

I decided to take advantage of the dead calm and opted to land from the opposite direction on skiway 20 (180 degrees from and diametrically opposed to 02). I was pleasantly surprised to find that skiway 20 was so little used that it was probably the smoothest place to land on the continent. I would have landed in that direction every time if the prevailing winds at the Pole would have allowed.

We taxied to the pits (the area where cargo was loaded and unloaded) as the other crew taxied to the approach end of runway 02. They waited half an hour for the fog to clear before they could depart. The fog bank, hovering twenty feet over the skiway, was so thick that we saw only the Herc's tail when they made their takeoff run. The rudder knifed through the white strip of cloud like a gray shark fin.

We were on a tanker mission that day.[2] The rest of the crew relaxed as Roy pumped fuel to the South Pole's holding tanks. Roy finished defueling quickly, but we were delayed about thirty minutes attempting to locate our passenger. After six months in total isolation with the over-winter South Pole staff, he needed a surprising amount of time to say good-bye. Twenty minutes later, after I announced that we had to depart because we were short of fuel, he appeared. I told him if he wanted to stay awhile longer, he could always catch the next shuttle. He smiled and apologized for his tardiness, saying he did want to go with us. Evidently he knew the first rule of Antarctic aviation: never wait for the second shuttle. With him aboard we were on our way—or so I thought.

As we prepared to taxi, South Pole called on the UHF (ultra-high frequency) radio and asked us if we were ready to receive a pulmonary edema medevac (medical evacuation) patient. I asked if they could please repeat. They asked again, and I said I hadn't been briefed about any medevac. Had it just happened? I was informed that the patient had been diagnosed a few days ago by the South Pole doctor but had been unable to travel until that morning. As aircraft commander I hated to learn these kinds of details at the last minute. As the patient was loaded, our flight surgeon gave me a briefing on edema, which is altitude sickness, and its ramifications.

The Pole is at 9,301 feet above sea level, and the barometric pressure is always low, so the effective altitude that South Pole personnel normally experience is more like eleven to twelve thousand feet, sometimes higher. Most folks who travel to the Pole adjust to the altitude in a few days and deal with the headaches, nausea, and dizziness until their bodies adapt. Others can't adapt as quickly and have to be returned to McMurdo and sea-level pressure for treatment. To successfully transport an edema patient, one must bring them back to a sea-level altitude slowly, using the plane as a kind of reverse pressure chamber. This means we had to pay strict attention to the pressurization of the plane as we returned to McMurdo to make sure we didn't exacerbate his condition. I wanted to do a good job and not injure this poor fellow any more. As it turned out, however, the return flight to McMurdo nearly killed him.

We never needed more than five or six thousand feet to take off at the South Pole, so I was really surprised when we aborted our fourth attempt. The skiway had turned mushy, and each takeoff try in that soft snow was like a run in quicksand. We quickly concluded that if we were to get out of there we would need to try something more drastic. Fuel wasn't really a concern since the Pole station had plenty. They used the same fuel to heat their buildings as we burned in the plane, but there was always a hint of disgrace in taking on extra fuel, as if you had planned poorly. If for some reason the weather turned foul and you had to shoot a number of approaches, or you had experienced unusually high headwinds, sure the fuel was there. But on a normal mission, it was considered bad form not to complete the mission with the standard fuel load.

These ski takeoff attempts depleted the plane's fuel quickly, however. Roy made a quick assessment of our fuel and said we had enough for only a couple more tries. We discussed our options and decided to start our next slide with flaps up and to lower them full down as we accelerated. A full-flap takeoff was always our last-ditch effort to get airborne, and I hated to do it since it meant we had to take off even further below air minimum control speed than normally. The advantage was that a full-flap takeoff doubles the wing lift and thereby substantially reduces the weight of the plane on the skis. It generally works well, but then the downside is always the reduced safety factor: if you lose an engine with flaps full, no one is likely to survive the crash. It is a delicate balance.

I added maximum power. As we accelerated to 50 knots, we started to bog down. At 55 knots the copilot and I pushed forward and then pulled back on our respective yokes several times until we were able to bounce the nose ski loose from the sucking slush. The plane still wouldn't accelerate as we passed the "7" board, indicating that seven thousand feet of skiway remained. We lowered the nose slightly and accelerated to 60, then 63 knots as another thousand feet of skiway went by. I called for flaps to be lowered to 50 percent at 65 knots and 70 knots. Still 50 knots below air minimum control speed, I called, "Gimme flaps 100." Roy lowered the flaps full down.

At 80 knots, with the flaps 100 percent down, we finally broke free and clawed our way skyward, 40 knots below our air minimum control speed of 120 knots. The increase in airspeed from 80 to 120 knots happened quickly, once we were airborne. When I was sure we wouldn't inadvertently touch down, we incrementally positioned the flaps to 50 percent; at 120 knots we raised the gear. The nose ski came up bow high and hit the fuselage with a thud. We brought the flaps up the rest of the way to be able to fully concentrate on the nose ski problem. When the nose ski didn't retract properly, we extended the rigger strut (the device that levels the ski as it comes up) manually and raised the gear.

As we were coordinating to correct the nose ski problem, Roy, who had vacated the engineer seat to his trainee engineer on climb-out, tapped me on the shoulder and asked me if I felt funny. I hadn't noticed anything different, but I saw that our guest copilot had yawned more than usual and looked a little blue. As we passed through fourteen thousand feet, Roy checked the cabin altimeter and found that his trainee had neglected to pressurize the plane. I remembered that he had distinctly responded "checked" to the pressurization call on the after-takeoff checklist, but he had apparently failed to actually check.

Above fifteen thousand feet we would begin to pass out, so I flipped on the intercom and immediately instructed the crew and passengers: "Strap in and go on a 100-percent supplemental oxygen." Putting on my own mask before I started an emergency descent, I reduced power and pushed the nose of the plane sharply down and dove for the deck. Luckily it was a clear day above the polar plateau, and I leveled at three hundred feet above the ground.

Roy put on a portable oxygen bottle, went aft, and found that our safety valve (a backup valve to control the pressurization when the primary, or out-flow, valve didn't work) was stuck open. Once he got it closed, we were able to climb and repressurize. I feared the altitude might have harmed our patient, so I questioned Doc as to the man's condition. He told me that everything was all right, that the patient had been on oxygen since we departed the South Pole and was only shaken by the sudden drop in altitude. The man hadn't heard the announcement over the intercom loudspeaker and nobody had bothered to tell him what was going on, so he had believed this was the end.

Several days after this incident, I visited him in the infirmary and he related his experience to me in some detail. "I thought my luck had finally run out," he told me. "I felt we were headed down for sure. I remembered thinking as everyone around me started to put on oxygen masks and then the plane started to drop, *Well, if this don't beat all! I'm gonna die in a plane crash on my way to the hospital.*"

I laughed and asked, "Didn't anyone tell you we were having an emergency and what we were doing?"

"Nope," he sighed, "the Doc just looked at me kinda scared and then left." He smiled. "I felt a whole lot better when the plane finally leveled out." I could easily imagine his relief.

At the height of the crisis, I had announced that I wanted everybody on oxygen to check in over the intercom. Everyone had responded except my trainee loadmaster. After it was all over, I asked him to come talk to me. Why hadn't he donned his oxygen mask when I initiated the emergency procedure and instructed everyone to do so? He explained that even though he saw everybody else don theirs, and he had heard my order on his headset, he thought we were playing a joke on him.

His explanation made me cringe. Often new crew members are teased or have harmless practical jokes played on them as a rite of passage. And if I had instructed only him to put on the mask, then I might have been able overlook his error. But for him to choose not to follow a direct order, in a situation that might have incapacitated him, was setting a dangerous precedent. If he didn't follow orders when the emergency was minor, how would he react if we had had a major emergency, one that depended on his quick and correct actions? I told him that if he ever pulled a stunt like that again, I would personally strap him to the ramp and stick the oxygen bottle where it wouldn't do him any good at all.

As we approached McMurdo and were about to end this crazy flight, which I was very ready to be done with, I lowered the landing gear and knew we still had a way to go. The ski-equipped Herc has six landing-gear indicators, three for the gear (or wheels) and three for the skis. Antarctic pilots have a constant problem getting these six separate entities to work together and match up in the cold weather. It is in fact such a problem that someone had waggishly made drawings of quarter-sized slots on the instrument panels of several of the planes, likening the gear handle to a slot machine: you pull the handle down and hope for the best.

As we prepared to land, we played landing-gear slots. I lowered the gear handle, and the landing gear circuit breaker popped. We reset the circuit breaker twice, and on the third pull, all of the wheels came down and locked into place—and all the skis except the right ski had retracted. We have several backup systems to get the gear to the proper position, and we performed all the prescribed emergency procedures. But nothing worked. Roy cursed the gear system, threw his headset down, and went aft to look at the ski. When he came back to the flight deck, the ski was up and the wheels down. I never figured out how he did it, and I knew enough not to ask.

Since we had been having so much fun with the gear and skis, I hadn't paid close attention to the weather. Our forecast arrival weather for McMurdo had been three thousand feet broken ceiling, seven miles visibility, light snow, good and good (good surface and good horizon). An hour before we landed, we were updated to expect fifteen hundred and one mile. As we descended, I questioned the duty forecaster and learned that the previous forecaster had made a mistake and read the wrong page: we should expect a partially obscured five-hundred-foot ceiling and less than a mile forward visibility.

The crew landing before us radioed to say that the tower had called their landing weather three hundred feet with half a mile of visibility, which the forecaster confirmed for us. He added, "Oh, by the way, the winds have picked up and are 25 gusting to 30 knots. Have a nice day!"

I shut my eyes and sighed, as though that might help. Unpredictable weather was a constant headache. And to add insult to injury, weather briefs seemed to have become permission slips to fly rather than accurate descriptions of arrival weather. If, as the forecaster had said at preflight, we were to have at least a thousand-foot ceiling and three miles visibility for our arrival back at McMurdo, we were bound to try to fly the mission, no matter what the actual weather was at preflight. The frustrating part to me was that nearly all our weather forecasts called for at least a thousand and three for our return. Fortunately for us the weather that day wasn't too bad, and we broke out of the clouds to see the "rabbit lights" (sequentially flashing high-intensity approach lights) scurrying toward the runway as we approached two hundred feet above, less than half a mile from the runway.

We emerged from the fog to find a waiting ambulance to ferry Doc and his patient up to the Hill to begin the edema treatment. When they were on their way, I reflected that, all in all, things had worked in our favor: we were home, safe, and in one piece; I hadn't killed the medevac patient; and more importantly we had worked as a team through three separate emergencies.

5

THE WEATHER

SHAMANS

I have met with amused people who say, "Oh, we had minus fifty temperatures in Canada; they didn't worry *me*," or "I've been down to minus sixty something in Siberia." And then you find that they had nice dry clothing, a nice night's sleep in a nice aired bed, and had just walked out after lunch for a few minutes from a nice warm hut or overheated train. And they look back upon it as an experience to be remembered. Well! of course as an experience of cold this can only be compared to eating a vanilla ice with hot chocolate cream after an excellent dinner at Claridge's. But in our present state we began to look upon minus fifties as a luxury which we did not often get.

—Apsley Cherry-Garrard, *The Worst Journey in the World: Antarctic, 1910–13*

"How's the weather?" is no idle query from a pilot in Antarctica. Conditions change so rapidly there that timely and accurate forecasts are essential not only to safe operations but to our very survival. Getting those forecasts is not always as easy as you might expect, however. As pilots we often found ourselves at the mercy of the Weather Shamans, those wizards of subjective forecasting whose techniques ranged from solid scientific reasoning to wild-ass guesses.

On one flight from Christchurch to McMurdo, during the crew brief where we would discuss the particulars of that day's mission, we focused our attention on deteriorating weather conditions in Antarctica. Our weather information at preflight, as briefed by the Christchurch forecaster, was already four hours old, due to communication problems with forecasters on the Ice. We were not exactly getting the accurate, useful information one hopes for when flying in the planet's worst weather region.

However, our concerns didn't prevent the Christchurch forecasters—who, needless to say, weren't heading south with us—from making absurd assumptions about the Antarctic weather. Their original forecast that day was for a high ceiling at eight thousand feet, six miles visibility, winds of 15 to 20 knots with blowing snow—all in all not too bad. But the last observed weather condition at McMurdo, four hours ago, was only three hundred feet and less than half a mile of visibility. Naturally I questioned the forecast, but somehow the more I voiced my doubts, the more the Shamans rattled their magic shaman bones and insisted they were right. I was reluctant to launch, but since the forecast was good, I was obligated to try. All I could hope for was to get an accurate update before we passed PSR (point of safe return) and were forced to continue into whatever conditions prevailed on the continent.

Almost immediately after our 0700 takeoff, the bad news came in like an unwanted relative. Christchurch forecasters were finally able to relay the current 0700 observations from Antarctica: the winds had increased to 35 to 40 knots. Half an hour later, a news flash came from McMurdo Center: the station was in the throes of a Herbie. The weather was now a partially obscured two-hundred-foot ceiling and a one-mile visibility. Blowing snow, with a 16-below-zero temperature, and winds gusting to 50 knots blasted the base. The longer we flew south, the worse it got. The crew was far from devastated, however. In fact they began to perk up: just let it get a bit worse, and we could turn around and spend another night in Christchurch, drinking Kiwi beer. I shared their optimism; I knew the forecast we had received in Christchurch was no good.

By 0800 the visibility had dropped to one-sixteenth of a mile, due to winds at better than 50 knots; no surface or horizon definition was visible. The crew got rowdier as Dave plotted a course from our present position back to Christchurch International Airport. Eventually the Antarctica forecasters updated the weather for our arrival: an indefinite ceiling at four hundred feet. An indefinite ceiling has no base to it and often resembles a thick cotton blanket suspended in midair. Visibility for our arrival would be less than one-sixteenth of a mile, with heavy blowing snow and winds gusting to 45 to 50 knots, nil and nil.

I suggested that now would be an appropriate time to turn around. The crew considered this proposal and gave their professional opinions that this course of action represented the most appropriate response to the current weather conditions. At least I think that's what they said; it was hard to hear over the cheering. We turned around for another night of Kiwi beer and hospitality.

Just before the turn, I watched the Antarctic sunset, a thin tangerine line sandwiched between horizontal stripes of gray and black. The sun was an orange ball that moved from our right to our left along the horizon, bisecting the black Antarctic sky. Ahead of us the Southern Cross and the False Cross were plainly visible, pointing languidly toward the South Pole. Seeing the False Cross reminded me of our weather reports: you would be a fool to fly unquestioningly by either.

Back at Christchurch we headed to our hotel and, after a toast to the forecasters, played poker over a few friendly beers, talking of the sunset and discussing important intracrew issues, like what to get on our pizza. Later, safely in bed, I wondered if this forecast debacle was a harbinger of yet another season of quibbling with the Naval Support Force, Antarctica (NSFA) forecasters. As a body the NSFA serves two basic functions: it acts as the liaison between VXE-6 and NSF and, as such, prioritizes our missions; and it provides us our support services—tower controllers, long-distance radio communications, cargo and personnel prioritizing, transportation to the runway, loading, and fire, crash, and rescue services, as well as weather forecasting.

Since weather forecasts are mostly subjective interpretations, VXE-6 pilots, cautious by nature, are often at odds with NSFA forecasters as to the validity of their predictions. But the forecasters have the upper hand. If they say the weather is OK to fly in, then we are bound by our operations manual to fly in it. If the weather isn't quite what they forecast, we might find ourselves landing in poor conditions or worse, zero visibility. I often argued that the NSFA folks should forecast for the worst-case scenario rather than the best; but since NFSA also ran our flight schedules, that option never caught on. As long as we launched *on time*, NFSA's job was done. The rest was not its concern.

For example, one day in mid-November, a solid blanket of clouds enveloped the continent in a thick, white vaporous gel. The normally sharp contrast between the horizon and the land was dulled by reflected light in a dismal gray, empty sky. As we headed toward McMurdo, the weather was given as a three-thousand-foot ceiling, a forty-mile visibility, good and good. When planes are in the air, each Antarctic field station gives an hourly weather update for the air crews. An hour later, it was twenty-five hundred feet, forty miles, good and poor. Another hour, fifteen hundred feet and seven miles, poor and poor.

We landed forty-five minutes after that last forecast, breaking out of the clouds at a hundred feet with less than a quarter-mile forward visibility, nil and nil. I flew the approach to minimums.[1] Tim, in the right seat, caught sight of the runway as I was waving off and conned me in—that is, gave me steering directions as I continued to fly on instruments. The blustery 30-knot wind pitched snow from all directions and forced me to fight the plane all the way to the deck. I landed about halfway down the runway, losing the first five thousand feet of it as I tried to align the plane in the middle to gain advantage over the powerful crosswinds. With a sigh of relief, I felt us touch down. We taxied to a stop.

But when we deplaned, the maintenance-control building, a mere fifty yards away, was invisible, having been swallowed up by the swirling drifts. Apprehensive about becoming disoriented in the dizzying snow and getting lost between the airplane and the building (it has happened), I had Chris break out a rope from our survival equipment and tie it to the airplane. Then we staggered ourselves out in a line along the rope, keeping both the person in front and the person behind visible so that if we lost our way, we could at least grope our way back to the shelter of the plane.

The severity of the weather and the adverse circumstances in which we had just landed really sunk in when we reached Maintenance Control and were applauded by the maintenance crew and another flight crew for getting our plane back in one piece. No one had thought it possible. Looks of incredulity and remarks of "No way!" came from shuttle passengers on the ride back to the Hill as they learned we had landed at nil and nil, in a spinning white mass of confusion.

This wasn't the first time forecasters had given me bad information. Other pilots and I constantly argued against their subjective and overly optimistic predictions. We got no response. Forecasters didn't wish to give up their status as Shamans for any inferior group of people, especially not pilots.

In the lounge I ran into the forecaster just off duty, enjoying a drink. I told him facetiously that he had done a nice job calling the weather tonight. He smiled and said that the condition before we landed was just like he had called it: a nine-hundred-foot ceiling and a three-mile visibility, poor and poor (he had briefed us at preflight for our weather to be three thousand and three, good and good, for our return). When I said I had barely gotten in with a hundred-foot ceiling and a quarter-mile visibility, nil and nil, he said, "Yeah, right."

I thought of him sitting in a warm, sheltered building, drinking coffee and munching doughnuts, far from the maelstrom outside as he leisurely doled out inaccurate forecasts while my crew and I concentrated on just staying alive. The only word that came to me was *gall*. That's what it was: *sheer, in-your-face gall*. I was seriously pissed off, but what did I expect? They certainly couldn't control the weather; still, I don't suppose it was hard for them to grasp why we called maintenance chiefs, other pilots, anyone *but* the Shamans, when we wanted an accurate snapshot of the current weather at the runway.

I went to my quarters and wrote a few letters while the weather worsened outside. An hour later I could see no more than fifteen yards in any direction. The wind twisted through town, causing ten-foot-high twisters of snow to engulf buildings. I went outside to mail my letters at the post office, a short twenty-five yards away, and was planning to go on to my office to do some paperwork. My plans changed abruptly, though, when I left the post office and the wind whipped snow at me so violently I couldn't see.

I considered going back to the lounge to tell the forecaster what I had just encountered, but he would probably just smile a knowing smile and say, "Yeah, right."

The weather continued to dog us. The station was in the grip of a certified Herbie; 80-knot winds were buffeting the place, spitting horizontal snow through the streets. At Willy Field the visibility had gotten so bad that folks had had to run lines between the buildings to get around. Willy is in the open on the Ross Ice Shelf. It's completely isolated, connected to McMurdo only by a narrow seven-mile-long snow road from Ross Island. Everything at and around Willy is white, including the buildings, so when a Herbie blows in, the place becomes invisible. Residents batten down the hatches and wait out the storm alone.

There isn't much to Willy Field. Fewer than two dozen temporary buildings are distributed along a quarter-mile stretch of snow called, of course, Main Street. The residence buildings are mostly on the right as you approach from McMurdo.

The huts at Willy consist of two large, white refrigerated trailers joined together. They approximate double-wide trailers in size but look more like refrigerator boxcars. Quarters therein are small and windowless and are entered through insulated doors that give the places all the warmth and homeyness of a meat locker. There are ten twelve-by-fifteen rooms in each trailer, with two men to a room, but there are no bathrooms; those are fifty yards across the frost-bound street.

When you first get to Willy, you wonder why folks are always looking so anxiously for empty plastic containers. After the first Herbie, you understand. With the closest relief fifty yards away across Main Street, next to the mess hall, staying inside was a distinct benefit during stormy weather. The unlucky guy who didn't have a container and whose bladder wouldn't make it through the night got to grope his way along string ropes through the blinding white to find the johns or face wandering off in a storm, unable to locate a building that might be only a few feet away. What an ignominious death, frozen solid while in search of the loo.

On the Hill, circumstances were less dramatic. Our chow hall and bathrooms were located in the same building. The other buildings were closer together, too, and were of various colors and shapes so it was easier to tell one from another, even in a Herbie. Still, in all my years in Antarctica, I had never seen worse weather than we were having now. For three days malevolent 50- to 60-knot winds blasted through the town, roaring like ogres, until man and building alike moaned and strained under the barrage. In fact a remote weather station at Black Island, fifty miles away, clocked winds at 126 knots before the anemometer broke.

There was no snow on the tops of any of the buildings. It had all been pummeled off by high winds. Instead the snow collected on the leeward side of buildings the way an eddy current builds behind rocks in a river. There the snow gained a toehold and climbed high enough to cover the entire sides of some of the smaller buildings. Did I mention this was in the summer?

Late on the third day it appeared that the storm might finally break.

Earlier that day the wind had dropped occasionally so that I could see a hundred yards ahead for a few moments, although the raging tempest continued. We counted the lulls like labor pains, and they were definitely coming at closer intervals. Occasionally, when the wind died down for a few minutes, some of the more adventurous souls began to move around outside. The scene of those bundled-up figures struggling through the wind was a Chaplinesque comedy. They stumbled and strained, leaned forward to push headlong against the wind, which then inexplicably died, stranding the unfortunates on an icy surface in midstrain to hang cartoon-like in air for a split second before falling flat on their faces. When they struggled to get up, their feet spun like bald tires on an ice-covered hill. Finally they'd get up, only to be knocked over again by the fickle, mischievous wind. This comic dance might last upwards of twenty minutes before the poor souls gave up and turned around. In each instance I thought I could hear them sigh as they lay on their backs in the snow, completely worn out, contemplating the humiliation factor of crawling back inside on their bellies.

But cabin fever was setting in. I needed to get outside, so when the wind dropped to 40 knots, I walked to work. I felt as though the brunt of the storm was directed at me. The wind whipped the snow into a nightmarish frenzy of blowing white, blasting my face so that each time I lifted my head, I got a face full of wind-driven snow. I had to look at my shoes to make it to the office without going blind. My only thought as I walked to work was, *Thank God we made it home just before this hell was unleashed.* If we had been unfortunate enough to be only an hour or two later the other day when we landed, we'd have been forced down on the plateau somewhere to wait out this Herbie. If that had happened, I'd have been in a tent during all this, waiting for the weather to clear enough to permit another plane to come rescue us. As I walked, I imagined how terrible it would be, forced to wait on the flat, frozen wasteland, to pit our instincts and will to survive against such an overwhelming foe.

I recalled Robert Falcon Scott's diary entry when he and his two remaining companions, broken, exhausted, and out of fuel and food, waited ten days for weather identical to this to clear. Scott's 21 March 1912 diary entry reads: "Got within 11 miles of depôt Monday night; had to lay up all yesterday in severe blizzard. To-day forlorn hope, Wilson and Bowers going to depôt for fuel." On 22–23 March he wrote: "Blizzard as bad as ever—Wilson and Bowers unable to start—to-morrow last chance—no fuel and only one or two of food left—must be near the end. Have decided it shall be natural—we shall march for the depôt with or without our effects and die in our tracks."[2] The weather never cleared. As history records, the three men died in their tent.

In this wind, even with my bulk, six-feet-four-inches and 225 pounds, I found it extremely difficult to walk. As I rounded the corner of the supply building, a sudden gust blew my legs from under me, and my feet spun on the ice. I groped for the door handle just beyond my reach, lunged and grabbed it just before I fell, like a drowning man grasping for a life ring. I got the door unlatched, and the same wind blew me into the building. I was thrown in, along with about half a ton of snow, and immediately greeted by angry shouts of "Close the goddamn door!" Then, "Oops, sorry, sir" when they recognized me as I tried to muscle the door shut with my shoulder. Only with the assistance of two petty officers did I succeed. The wind was so strong that it filtered through every crack and cooled my normally hot upstairs office. I had worked for only a few hours when the cold permeated the office and forced me back to the warmth below. When the wind died some, I started off for home. This time the wind was at my back. I walked with colossal strides, assisted at each step by a 40-knot tailwind that propelled me four to five feet forward. I felt like Neil Armstrong walking on the moon.

The storm blew itself out after four days. The clouds parted, and blue skies prevailed. The upheaval left the town, that blotch in an otherwise pristine Antarctica, with a fresh blanket of snow, a mask to cover its ugliness. In reciprocity for all that is beautiful in Antarctica, McMurdo is proportionally repulsive. The mishmash of old and new, large and small, highrises and tin huts, all strewn haphazardly with bits of debris, gives you an overwhelming sense that you're in the middle of a dump. Telephone poles sprout like limbless trees at irregular intervals, their wires hanging in vinelike twists and tangles. Red warming huts, used by divers, have the appearance of mutant tomatoes left by the side of the road. Pipes coated with silver insulation snake along the ground, while antennas fantail from roofs like rotting palm leaves.

But after a major storm, all is white and peaceful. At such times McMurdo is an agreeable place, more like a ski resort than a working station. Concealed beneath a blanket of snow, as though wrapped in a white ermine stole, the town wears diamonds of ice. It's the finest this town can ever look, and it's a welcome sight after four long days of wind and snow.

The beauty of the town soon faded when we returned to work. The day the storm ended I was on the phone with the operations officer, who had called to relay a message from the forecasters that they were upset I had questioned their forecast over the radio as another crew listened. I explained that I had been perturbed as I searched for the runway in the low, dense clouds when only moments before, the forecaster had said weather at the runway was CAVU (clear and visibility unrestricted). This forecaster even contradicted the tower personnel, who were actually sitting in the midst of the fog. It came as no surprise when he told me that from now on I'd have to watch my radio communications with weather personnel and keep my comments to myself.

If the forecasters were able to actually predict what the weather would be, or if they at least listened to pilot reports, I might have given them some respect. But the forecasts for our past five flights had been dead wrong. I thought the forecasters deserved the criticism. Sure, they had a difficult time predicting the weather with their antiquated equipment. I'm confident they did the best they could with old information gathered from a handful of remote and less than reliable weather stations, plus a satellite system limited to two passes a day over Antarctica. But they would never admit their forecasts were "best guess," not gospel. They remained adamant in their predictions—this was how the weather would develop, period. Yet even though we knew the forecasts were unreliable, it was still very difficult for us to cancel a mission because of the weather. It boiled down to this: if the forecaster said fly, we were obligated to try to fly the mission. If the forecaster was wrong, we faced the weather alone.

This last Herbie also got one of our helo pilots in a little hot water. Had the storm stayed to the east or never developed, Barry would have been a local legend. But he ended up with egg on his face and a stiff talking-to by the CO. Two days prior, as helicopter duty officer of the day (HDO), he had given himself a little treat: he decided to take his longtime friend and roommate, Sledge, over to Lake Vanda to join the Lake Vanda Swim Club.[3] He also picked up one of our female pilots, Sharon, and another female, NSFA officer Tami, to go to Vanda for a swim.

Things had gone along splendidly, and it looked as though Barry was going to make it back to McMurdo without a hitch—when suddenly the weather closed in, forcing him to return to Lake Vanda and set the helo down. After waiting patiently for a few hours, they decided to spend the night. Barry thought a drink or two would lighten up the situation. As luck would have it, five minutes after his first drink Mac weather called and said it was clear enough now for him to return. Being a conscientious pilot, he admitted he had taken a drink (which meant that he had to stay out of the air until the morning). You could almost feel the chill that greeted him over the station common radio frequency as he explained his plight to the CO and the XO and then tried to explain how he was going to have to spend the night in the wilds of Antarctica with his buddy, two beautiful women, and a bottle of booze.

The weather was poor all week at Byrd Surface Camp. Several pilots had tried to get in, but all returned home unsuccessful. For each mission the forecast had been fair weather. When each mission failed, the air crew was held responsible for the wasted effort. We were scheduled for the next mission to Byrd. As I waited for our weather brief, I read the hourly observations, which said the weather hadn't improved there in the past three days. Needless to say, I was surprised when the forecaster told us the weather for our arrival would be fine.

It did look at first as if he might be right. The weather over the ice shelf was brilliant. A razor-fine line served as our horizon, while the sunny summer afternoon provided gentle shades of white, yellow, and orange to form subtle contrasts on a picture-perfect calm, flat, blazing white ocean of snow. We were afforded spectacular views of several of the major crevasse fields that broke up the endless white monotony of the Ross Ice Shelf. The crevasse fields Big Ruth and the Steers Head were dwarfed at our altitude. I had often flown over both without seeing them, but today the sun hit Steers Head in such a fashion that it did indeed resemble a steer's head, especially when I dropped my head onto my shoulder, closed one eye, and squinted.

The weather at Byrd was poor, significantly worse than our forecast of a thousand-foot ceiling and five miles visibility, good and good. We caught sight of the field at three miles, but as we descended to land, the surface and horizon blended so that both were nonexistent, lost in the white. The skiway flags appeared to float in the air, since there was no discernible contrasts to give us any depth perception.

We started to circle the field at a thousand feet, descended finally to three hundred feet trying to land, but the weather continued to deteriorate faster than we could descend and get lined up on the skiway below. The ceiling dropped to below two hundred feet and blended so well with the snow that we couldn't differentiate between ground and sky after three passes. I had read about how the weather could change from a cloudless sunny day to frenzied blowing white in a matter of minutes, but to actually watch it happen around me was something else entirely. I marveled at how rapidly the ceiling had dropped; fifteen minutes, and we were essentially flying blind.

It was disconcerting and confusing. My copilot for the day, who had a large ego but limited flying sense, was flying at that moment and became so disoriented that he banked slowly about 30 degrees to the left, caught himself, then overcompensated by rolling sharply into a 45-degree bank to the right. We were three hundred feet above the ground, immersed in a sea of white, so when he rolled back to the right he got vertigo—he didn't notice that we were falling fast. This took about three or four seconds. As he rocked back to the left, I grabbed the controls, leveled the wings, added maximum power, and pulled the nose up. Another couple of seconds and we would have been part of the whiteout.

I stayed on the controls with him, and together we climbed the plane back to altitude. We turned away from the field and set up for what would turn out to be a series of internal approaches to try to descend below the cloud deck, but we never saw a thing. After the sixth pass I called it quits. At that point all I could see, anywhere, was an ugly gray-white film. There was no surface, no horizon, no clouds; we were enveloped in moving gray soup. I radioed McMurdo to let them know what we had encountered and to tell them I was on my way home. A few minutes passed before the NSFA operations officer called back and rerouted our mission to CASERTZ. Since we were a tanker mission, carrying fuel as our cargo, he wanted us to give a shot at CASERTZ before we returned.

With all the maneuvering, one of our passengers became profusely airsick. She wasn't particularly heartened when I announced that we were proceeding to CASERTZ, forty minutes away, to see if we could land and drop our load of fuel there. Everyone else, however, was excited at the prospect of salvaging this so-far frustrating mission. Our crew considered it bad form to return to McMurdo without exhausting every possibility of making the most out of each flight, so we were happy to have a second chance.

We were only one hundred miles away from CASERTZ; the weather there was hazy, but it would be clear enough for us to locate the camp and skiway. I had the copilot set up for a visual landing. As we rolled into the groove (pilot jargon for being on the proper visual glide slope, aligned with the runway, and at the appropriate altitude), I noticed that, although he appeared to be aligned properly, he was lined up to the left and parallel with the skiway. My sight picture (what I expected to see when we were properly aligned) looked correct, but as we got closer to the ground, I watched as the skiway markers passed along the right side of the plane. We overflew the camp at five hundred feet and banked left and set up to try again.

On the next pass we again split the red and green flags that marked the left and right boundaries of the skiway, but again we found ourselves lined up to the left. The third time produced the same result. On the forth pass, feeling frustrated, I took the controls and flew right down the skiway and immediately recognized our problem. The crew that had landed there before us had off-loaded their pallets directly in the middle of the skiway rather than in the cargo area to the right of the skiway. On each pass we had split the skiway flags, but as we got closer and shifted our gaze down the skiway to fine-tune our line up, we had shifted slightly to the left each time to compensate for and avoid the four huge pallets we thought were in the cargo area. I was perturbed at the other crew's actions. By leaving their load in the middle of the skiway, they effectively blocked the entire access.

On the next pass I instructed the copilot to land to the left of the skiway, in the soft, unplowed snow. We taxied around the pallets into the pits adjacent to the fuel bladder. While Roy pumped the gas, off I walked to the station's main Jamesway to find out what had happened. The station manager was fuming. He told me the other crew had landed early that morning, dropped their cargo in the middle of the skiway, and departed— all without contacting camp personnel. He had awakened this morning to find the pallets where they sat. He apologized for leaving them on the skiway, but since the pallets contained several large, heavy items and his forklift wasn't working, he could do nothing to remedy the situation. I told him that I would look into the matter and talk to the other air crews when I returned to McMurdo. But aside from that, there wasn't much I could do except commiserate with him.

As I left the station's main building, I watched my plane being offloaded. Beyond the plane was nothing but an ocean of snow-covered ice. The horizon was an obscure line of milky gray over white, like a layer of ash on a plate of cream. There was nothing anywhere, just a flat, white sea of snow that stretched all the way to McMurdo and the Pacific Ocean.

Tim was in the left seat for takeoff. He initially had problems with the 30-knot crosswinds. On his first attempt we aborted after sliding sideways for several hundred feet. On his second attempt it was nearly impossible to keep the nose straight with the wind contradicting every input he made. On each attempt, as we added power, the wind caught our vertical stabilizer and pushed us in a giant arc so that we headed nowhere. Our only alternative was to get the wind at our backs and risk taxiing over uncharted ground, where crevasses were always an anxiety-inducing possibility.

A mile from the station we made a U-turn and added maximum power. We accelerated sluggishly to 50 knots and yanked the nose ski clear of the snow at 62 knots. Immediately we bogged down. We slogged along at 63 knots for five hundred or six hundred yards, until it was evident that we were slowing. I brought the flaps to 20 percent and we surged ahead to 65 knots, then 70, at which point I lowered the flaps to 100 percent, and we wallowed into the sky at 75 knots. I hated full-flap takeoffs. I considered them too risky, and I employed them judiciously only as a last-ditch effort. Yet we had done more of them in the past few days than I had done in all the past year.

When I caught sight of the ice runway at McMurdo in the shimmering blaze of the Antarctic midday, I wondered why the weather couldn't be like this everywhere on the continent every day. It was so clear I let the most junior pilot take the landing. He flared the plane at fifty feet (reduced the power to flight idle and raised the nose to land on the main mounts to cushion the shock of landing and at fifty feet he also flaired about forty feet too high). If we had been landing on an asphalt runway and not the ice runway (which gives considerably on impact), we would have bounced along for days.

Soon after we landed, Chris called from the cargo compartment: "Mr. Hinebaugh, that passenger that got airsick while we were maneuvering back at Byrd isn't looking too good, sir. She threw up everything else she had when we landed a minute ago, and now she's pale, dry heaving and gasping for air. I had her lie down back here, but I think she might be in shock."

I replied, "OK, Chris, I'll call medical. In the meantime, you're cleared to break into the survival equipment and get a sleeping bag." I immediately called medical and gave them a short description of her condition; then I called maintenance to see if any of the hospital corpsmen who occasionally fly with us were at the runway to help until the ambulance arrived.

We hadn't shut the engines down when one of the corpsmen hustled aboard. He and Chris helped the woman into a sleeping bag and raised her feet—the first steps in preventing shock. By the time I got to the back, she was delirious, asking for water. Our third pilot turned to get water from the flight deck, but the corpsman stopped him short: water, he said, would only exacerbate her problem.

The ambulance literally slid to a halt, backed up to the cargo ramp, and disgorged a doctor and two additional corpsmen; they were with their patient within ten minutes of my call. A flurry of activity surrounded her. An IV was started and a preliminary exam conducted even before she was transferred to a gurney. Gawkers and well-wishers joined the group so that for several minutes it looked like a huddle around her. Individuals would leave the circled group as their interest waned, only to replaced by someone else. Slowly the group gave way, and the stretcher was loaded into the back of the ambulance and rushed off to McMurdo.

That evening the doctor who had treated her approached me and told me that our crew's quick actions had really made a difference and that she was doing well. I promised I would pass on the good news before tomorrow's flight.

•

The annual Halloween party heralded the end of our first month back on the Ice. It was also the first major social event of the season, an extravaganza that got everyone buzzing with anticipation. The party, held in the gym, started at 2100. By 2130 the place was packed floor to ceiling. It appeared all of Mac Town had turned out to cram themselves into the tight space. With a dash of creativity, a few strands of crepe paper, and a smattering of well-placed paper bats, pumpkins, and witches, the dreary gym had been transformed for the evening into an even drearier spectral dance hall.

About three-fourths of the revelers were in costumes ranging from the sublime to the bizarre. Supplies were limited, yet I was amazed at how creative folks could be with the resources at hand. It was evident that hours had been spent on some of the more elaborate outfits. One woman had made a huge crescent-shaped headpiece from papier-mâché; another woman had boxed herself up like a huge birthday present with ribbon and a bow; someone else had found a rotating beacon light, wired it to a battery, and attended the party with a flashing-light hat. But my favorite (I felt he should have won the costume contest on inspiration alone) was a gent who had the chutzpah to attend wearing only bunny boots and red Fruit of the Looms.

We also had sea creatures, devils, toilet-paper people, box robots, fairies (both good and evil), garbage-bag wearers, the predictable bed-sheet togas, and a couple of cross-dressers. One fellow had done himself up so well that he decided to "come out" completely that night. This was well before the "don't ask, don't tell" era, so he was soon transferred off the Ice and discharged from the navy.

Music was provided by a band of support folks who made Antarctica their adopted home and brought instruments and played together year after year. They didn't play well, but what they lacked in talent, they made up for in volume. In the band's defense, they performed solely to provide entertainment for the rest of us. They practiced on their own time, spent a lot of time setting up and taking down, played to drunken crowds who constantly harangued them, and did it all without pay. Their reward was revenge; they had us, a captive audience, for their "music." Dancing was done in a crowd—with so few women, it was easier to dance as a group than try to pair up. A costume contest was held at midnight, allowing plenty of time for the contestants to wreck their outfits. Costumes were judged on crowd reaction alone, the golden rule for costumes being "the campier, the better."

Beer and sodas were sold at two makeshift bars for fifty cents each. Or you could bring your own, and most people did. Parties in Antarctica bordered on the edge of accepted behavior. No one really cared what anyone else did; there were no rules. Still, surprisingly, considering the mixture of alcohol and loud music, there were rarely any fights or trouble and only an occasional argument. Our "sanctioned" Halloween bash ended at 0100, but the party raged all over town in the dormitories until well into the early morning. Everyone drank too much, danced badly, and puked, and the degree of next-day hangover led to the rating of Best Party Ever.

Our stints in Antarctica ran for six months, from October to March. This meant that for three years we lost every Halloween, Thanksgiving, Christmas, New Year's, and Valentine's Day, plus any birthdays that fell within those months. We missed our families and our weekends. We missed important events like Super Bowls and national elections and large chunks of history like the Gulf War. We missed our regular lives for three years at the same time every year.

To combat these feelings of loneliness and deprivation, as well as the eventual boredom that comes from being in relative isolation for so long, we turned to ourselves and made our own entertainment. Drinking and large parties became a major outlet for us, a way for us to forget the people and the things that we missed and to live, at least for a few short moments, on another plane, where we could wipe out the fact that we were all desperately alone and in a very inhospitable place.

Today would have been a great day for being inside by a fire, in a hot tub, getting my shoulders massaged. I considered starting a small conflagration in the wastebasket and rubbing my back on the doorpost, but somehow the allure was missing. Instead, I went with the flight schedule. I later wished I had stayed with the fantasy.

Waiting for the shuttle bus at Derelict Junction, shivering and still tense, I tried to think of any excuse not to go flying. With luck, some problem with the plane would arise, something that required a prolonged fix. I asked Tim what he thought as we approached Willy Field, where there was no surface definition and a mere quarter-mile visibility.

"Total bullshit," he observed sourly.

Well, I could work with that.

At various times during the season one particular forecaster seemed to have it out for the crews. He was in the unique position not only of forecasting the weather but, as the NSFA Duty Officer, of being responsible for ensuring that all the missions scheduled on his watch went out on time. So it was always suspect when—on his duty days, no matter what the actual weather was—all our forecasts were always exactly the weather minimums that were required for us to legally take off and land back here at McMurdo.

Tonight, CASERTZ. I loathed that place with the special dread reserved for something both dull yet dangerous. CASERTZ represented a routine flight to a spot in the middle of nowhere, yet unusually horrid weather always seemed to prey on that area. I've often wondered if there was another place on the continent with such consistently awful weather. Perhaps gray weather produces gray spirits. Looking at the crew, I saw they were, to a man, a gloomy lot. Days like this, it's best to limit conversation to the mission at hand. Other subjects lead to answers like Tim's.

On such days, when Mother Nature was showing herself as the bitch-goddess with a big ice-chip on her shoulder, the ugly winds brought in with them the spirit of ill will, disguised as low, gray clouds. Even our normally affable Kiwi cargo handlers were irritable. They tried to load a ton of rotten food onto the plane, and it took nearly an hour to convince them that this wasn't a good idea. When the food was finally removed, our payload was nine shivering scientists, some frozen food, and a little fuel.

Airborne, I heard a definite "beat" in the props—a throbbing sound that you never get used to, no matter how long you fly these things, an unnatural sound like a chain saw trying to cut through too much wood. I let Roy, the engineer, and the 3P (third pilot, a copilot in training) deal with the problem as I concentrated on keeping us in the air. The number-one propeller had gone well out of limits to 104 percent (normal is 98 to 102 percent), an overspeed. The first step of emergency procedure is to switch from normal governing (the props' speed is controlled electrically) to mechanical governing, letting the spinning mechanics of the prop control themselves. I directed the 3P to "go mechanical on number one," but the prop stayed at 104 percent. I asked, "Are you sure you got number one?"

"Yes, sir."

I thought, *Well, this is just what we need—an overcast day, a squirrely number-one prop, a three-engine landing with no surface definition. Can things get any worse?*

Tim, who was sitting in the off-duty seat, stood up and calmly flipped the number-one switch to mechanical. The prop immediately stabilized out to 100 percent. The 3P had flipped the wrong switch—number-four instead of number-one. Both switches are positioned on a panel to the right of the copilot, so the pilot is blocked from seeing the switches and has to trust the copilot to hit the right one. A certain atmosphere of disgust came through the cabin, but at least we were not *in extremis*.

At altitude we tried the procedure to resynchronize the props, but this time the prop shot up to 106 percent, a severe overspeed, so we flipped the switch back to mechanical. Roy reached into his engineer's bag of tricks, but nothing worked. On top of our sour moods we were stuck with the droning beat of an unsynchronized prop for the next six hours, the kind of throbbing vibration that, after just five minutes, makes you want to inflict pain on someone. What the crew needed was something else to focus on.

We generally tried to determine early in the flight what we might be bringing back from a station or camp, our retrograde cargo—called "retro" for short. Chris, the loadmaster, liked to know early so he could plan ahead. Today's retro was three passengers and their gear. CASERTZ weather was forecast to be a thousand and three, so I didn't complain when I spotted the field at twenty-five miles. It was unusually good weather for this area—one of the rare times I could distinguish between the sky and the ground.

Once we were on deck, the off-load went smoothly. So, anticipating no delays, I called for our passengers right away. The trio came shuffling toward the plane. They looked like Sherpas, each dragging about three bags too many. Chris got them seated and stowed their gear as Roy finished pumping out the last little bit of fuel for the camp. I called Mac Center to update our return forecast and was pleased to hear that it was to be two thousand and seven miles visibility. I hadn't finished getting the answer "Great!" out of my mouth when one of the passengers wandered up to complain that he was missing a box.

Of course he was. He had only known we were coming for twenty-four hours. He had probably spent the last three days packing. Of course he couldn't find his box. Another flight was scheduled for tonight. Couldn't they pick it up? I didn't want to miss our weather window. But no, no, no, that wouldn't do. The contents of this box were apparently of the same significance as the Magna Carta.

So we sat on deck, burning gas at the rate of four hundred dollars a minute, and searched for the special box. We scoured the plane for thirty minutes and finally found the box—where else?—in his boss's luggage. The boss sat stone-faced throughout our search, shrugging his shoulders. It's great what a little Antarctic isolation does for labor-management relations. We took off immediately.

We were no more than fifteen minutes out of CASERTZ when we got a strong left jab in the form of a special weather observation for McMurdo: our two-thousand-foot ceiling and seven miles visibility had suddenly become "sky partially obscured at eight hundred feet and less than three-quarters of a mile visibility, dropping fast." Surface and horizon definitions were nil and nil. Time for another blind landing.

I was pissed at the forecasters again. When we had entered the clouds at seven hundred feet, I had passed that information back to the weather office. Unfortunately the forecasters do not use pilot reports ("pireps") because pilots, as any forecaster can tell you, are idiots; ergo, no matter what conditions they claim to be flying through, well, they're wrong.

I discussed my options with Mac Center. How about landing at the Willy skiway, which was relatively clear? But, as I was informed by an astute controller, landing at the skiway would have to be cleared through the ODO and, "There ain't no gas there."

Well, naturally it would be better to try a whiteout landing with four engines in mechanical governing. I looked at my crew. They were shaking their heads in disbelief. Time to give up on this Bozo and work things out for ourselves. We all felt the fear that comes from going into a clouded-over field when your plane is low on fuel. It means you don't get a second chance. If we hadn't wasted all that time at CASERTZ, we would have had a greater margin for error. Dave did some quick calculating and figured we could get to the Pole with gas to spare, so that's the way we pointed the plane. I called Mac Center and informed them of our decision to divert to the Pole for gas. They rogered the call and contacted the Pole to find out if they had anything that needed to be flown back to McMurdo.

The Pole weather was clear, so we landed, gassed, and took on a few passengers in less than twenty minutes. I talked to the Pole radio operator on VHF (very high frequency) as we fueled. He couldn't believe what we had been going through that day with the delays, diverts, and bad weather calls, and he laughed when I told him that the real reason for the divert was a little employee-manager lack of communication. Did I mention that after all the worry over that precious box, the contents turned out to be paint?

Our flight home was uneventful until we hit "papa 2," one of our mandatory reporting points en route to the Pole.[4] A crew who had just landed at McMurdo came up on HF (high frequency) and told us they had broken out at three hundred feet and less than a mile visibility, with no surface or horizon definition. About ten minutes later Mac Center radioed and said the forecasters were calling the weather for our arrival as three thousand and three, good and good. I asked if they had just heard the last crew's pirep of three hundred and one, nil and nil? They said they had but they were calling for three thousand and three, good and good anyway. Whom was I supposed to believe? My money was on the crew who had just landed.

When it was our turn in the barrel, we broke out at three hundred feet and maybe one-mile visibility. We were lined up for a landing on the main skiway, but there was a lively 40-knot crosswind blowing from the northwest, so I opted to land into the wind on skiway 33. During our circle the tower controller asked, "How high are you right now?"

I responded: "Three hundred feet. Why?" They needed a reference mark, and since we were circling just at the base of the clouds, they used us as a measuring stick. We circled to the left and headed down the boulevard of Willy Field. Halfway down the block, still at three hundred feet, we made a shallow right-hand turn to line up with the off-duty skiway and then set the plane down in a cloud of snow and ice. Often if we reversed our engines when the snow was loose and grainy, the props' reverse thrust would kick up the snow, blowing it in front of the plane as we slowed down, creating our own personal whiteout. To escape this we accelerated through it: today, as we pulled the throttles into maximum reverse, the blowing snow was kept in check by the stiff breeze we created.

On deck I called the field conditions into the weather office, but I got some sarcastic asshole on the phone who adamantly informed me that the weather was indeed just as they said: fifteen hundred and three, poor and poor (which didn't even match the last observation they had given me ten minutes ago, three thousand and three, as we descended to land). I told him that I had just flown through this crap and that the tower used our altitude for confirmation of the cloud deck's base.

He said, "Yeah, right"—and then hung up.

Crew 4. *Left to right:* Tim Lefebrve, Dave Hegland, Neil Nostrant, Ed Angel, Chris Derby, Roy Williams, and the author. Kevin O'Conner

The author striking a pose at the entrance to the South Pole station. Ed Angel

Mt. Patrick and the Beardmore Glacier as viewed from Mt. Bell. Atop the Mt. Patrick plateau are the remains of the abandoned crashed helicopter that the crew often flew over.

The author's bird during a put-in as the crew established a field camp in the Pensacola Mountains.

The broken rigger strut damaged at Mill Glacier.

Near whiteout condition in town during a herbie. Winds at the time were about 40 to 50 knots.

The author at the Vostok station ceremonial pole, pointing toward his boyhood home in Washington, D.C. Ed Angel

Emperor penguins. Mike Nee

The author at the ceremonial igloo built at the Soviet's Vostok station. Ed Angel

The Soviet scientists who hosted the author's crew at Vostok.
Left to right: Vladimir, the author, Alexev, and Camille. Bob Fiacco

Two plane pull-out of SERIS L camp.

McMurdo Station and the yearly resupply ship. Polar explorer Robert F. Scott's first hut is the structure in the foreground.

The author with an Adélie penguin. Gordon Linn

The twin peaks of Mt. Markham.

6

HAPPY CAMPER

SCHOOL

Working as the test and evaluation officer was an unusual job. I loved doing it, for there are few opportunities like it in the navy. Since the squadron deploys to Antarctica every year, we've taken the lead in improving the navy's extreme cold weather (ECW) clothing and equipment. When I started the job, the navy was still using 1950s-vintage clothing for polar work. Bulky, awkward, and uncomfortable (though warm when you were standing still, it became ineffective when it got damp with body moisture) to work in, these outdated clothes were in plentiful supply. Our marching orders, however, were to procure the very best ECW clothing and gear available from any source, public or private, to determine what worked and what didn't, and then to disseminate, as widely as possible, all the information we'd gathered.

Since its inception in 1988, our small T&E (testing and evaluation) effort had become recognized worldwide. We field-tested everything from food to tents and sleeping bags to boots for the army, air force, and marines. For the navy, we were the primary field-testing source for all new ECW gear. We procured a few items from the British, and even tried some French-designed long underwear. We traveled extensively, looking for new gear or lecturing on lessons learned in Antarctica, and during my three years as T&E officer I gave dozens of talks on the subject of cold-weather personal protection, speaking to all types of audiences ranging in size from four to four hundred.

The T&E group consisted of six dedicated people, who did most of the data collection while we were on deployment. We weren't supposed to sift through the data and publish our results until we were back in California, where we were afforded additional time, manpower, and computers to digest the data to determine what gear was useful and what was not. Our efforts introduced a number of new items into the navy stock system.

For example the army had developed several pieces of clothing for its troops made from high-tech fabrics called the Extended Cold Weather Clothing System (ECWCS). This was basically a camouflaged Gore-Tex parka, pants, and synthetic-pile underwear. And even though we were a T&E group, it was difficult for us to convince the army quartermasters that sailors in Antarctica needed army supplies. But for me the best part of the job was its constant evolution. There was always someone with a better idea or an improved article of clothing. Individuals with new, revolutionary, or radical ideas sought us out, and on occasion we tested some pretty strange items. One year a gentleman sent us a peculiar set of gloves, handmade of wolf fur with calf-leather palms. I tried a pair. My hands looked like they were being eaten by a rabid muppet. His idea was simple: if your hands were cold, you simply balled them into fists, thereby turning the gloves into giant mittens or, more appropriately, giant paws. It turned out that although the muppet gloves weren't very practical for working around airplanes, they were so good for general purposes; they became the most sought-after gloves on the continent.

Even minor pieces of gear could mean survival in Antarctica. Before heading south each season, we began our Antarctic life with a mandatory lecture series on the safety and survival equipment we carried on our planes. The parachute riggers (PRs), who are responsible for inspecting and maintaining all our survival equipment, went over every piece of gear and explained where in the plane it is stowed. Overland survival gear is carried aboard in the "box and sled." The box is a two-by-two-by-twelve-foot wooden structure that holds enough freeze-dried emergency food and supplies to last twelve people seven days. On an eight-foot-long banana-shaped sled are strapped tents, sleeping bags (rated to 60 degrees below), extra food, fuel, stoves, pots and pans, and various other items to make an emergency a bit less hopeless. During lectures the PRs would break down one box and sled to show where the items were arranged in each.

Once we had sorted through all the survival gear, we practiced pitching the survival tent. The tent went up smoothly enough in the warmth of a gorgeous spring day, but I was never sure how easily it would pitch in a real survival situation, with crew members probably in shock and being whipped by freezing winds. My hope was that I would never see inside that box or sled except during these annual demonstrations.

My issued ECW flight gear consisted of "Chips" (heavy-duty, thickly insulated flight boots made by Chippewa Boots); four pairs of wool socks; two sets of waffle-weave long underwear; a thick, heavily insulated Korean War–era parka; a pair of multipocket overpants with liners (again, of Korean War vintage); a pair of insulated wind pants; a winter-weight flight jacket; my bunny boots (white, heavily insulated boots that despite their comical appearance were often the only thing between me and losing my toes to frostbite); more wool socks; leather gloves with liners; a balaclava; an ear warmer; a pair of green canvas, rubber-soled mukluks with thick wool liners; a pair of heavy, fur-backed mittens; a "Russian" polar hat with ear flaps; a scarf; a hood; some sock liners; sunglasses; and one large yellow bag to stow it all in.

From now on, we would each carry such a survival bag on every flight. Your "yellow bag" was your best friend if you got forced down on the continent. It also contained a packet of survival information and certain basic survival items including matches, candles, and glacier glasses. These personal items augmented the survival gear in the box and sled and gave us a fighting chance if we underwent a forced landing.

One evening I was slated to brief five new crew members on some ECW gear they would be taking into the field with them to test during their Antarctic survival class—or, as we liked to call it, Happy Camper School. They would leave the next morning for two fun-filled days on the Ross Ice Shelf a few miles from town, just off Ross Island in an area with the cozy name of Windless Bight, where they would receive practical instruction in how to survive if forced down in the open field.

There are many reasons that you could find yourself in the wilds, reasons ranging from the frightening to the frustrating to the merely embarrassing. You could crash, for example. Or you could experience a malfunction serious enough to force a landing. Or you could just plain get stuck in soft snow while trying to take off and run out of gas. Learning to survive in the harsh environment was serious business.

Survival school was taught by professional mountain guides, mostly from New Zealand. As a prelude to survival exercises the next day, this evening our group of five joined twenty science support personnel at a windowless two-story building on the outskirts of town. The Berg Field Center (BFC) housed mountaineering supplies and served as a staging area for several science groups. Scheduled was a slide show on the rigors of Antarctic survival. The show highlighted Antarctic dangers and explained crevasse detection and avoidance, as well as basic mountaineering skills. The listeners grew very quiet watching the slides.

Next we got a lecture on techniques and equipment to maximize chances of staying alive until a rescue was possible. It was good for me to refamiliarize myself with basic survival techniques and to see if any new techniques were discussed. The audience then broke into small groups to practice tying a few basic knots.

I waited while the instructors covered the schedule of events for the next two days. Then I helped teach our new crewmen how to tie and use prussic knots. The prussic, an aid in climbing vertical surfaces, is a basic mountaineering knot that is easily tied by wrapping a smaller loop of rope around the main climbing rope. The situation in which you would obviously need it, but one that no one liked to think about, was if you fall into a crevasse and survive: you would use the prussic knot to get out. The small loop of rope is wrapped around the climbing rope three times, with each succeeding loop inside the last. This leaves a loop that, when cinched down, can be used as a foothold. The prussic can also be played up the climbing rope as a movable handhold or foothold. The technique is simple to master when the knot is tied correctly. Later I watched as my group practiced the knot and the technique by hauling themselves up a rope suspended through a trapdoor in the upstairs floor.

With the conclusion of the instructional portion of the evening, the participants were issued crampons, ice axes, web belts, two three-foot pieces of 6-mm line for prussic-knot loops, and one hundred fifty feet of 9-mm line for climbing, plus sleeping bags, ground pads, and a list of personal items they would be required to bring. The crew seemed pretty excited about their new acquisitions.

After class I herded them to my office to issue a new type of three-man tent we wanted to field test, a new sleeping bag, two different types of glacier glasses (very dark sunglasses), new leather gloves with what was described as a "breakthrough" in thin, effective insulation, and two pairs of high-tech socks—plus, this being the military, a pile of evaluation forms for each item. The crew could use these items alternatively with those they were issued in survival school so they could make comparisons on which ones were most effective.

As I handed out the T&E gear, most of the questions were not about how to test the equipment but about what to expect from the upcoming two-day class. It was evident that the group was apprehensive about spending a night sleeping in the snow. Tomorrow's weather forecast predicted a cold, gray, miserable day, so I advised the students that, as further preparation for their coming ordeal, they should seek out as much hard alcohol as possible. My gouge to them was to keep as busy as possible until about 2200, then drink heavily, go to sleep, and try to forget about the cold.[1] Somehow, though, this didn't assuage their fears, so I invited them back to my room to relate my experiences in Happy Camper School. In detail.

In my room, spread out on the couch and floor, and under the calming effect of a couple of beers each, they listened while I told them how I had, two years earlier, arrived at Happy Camper School just before 0800, prepared for the worst. The weather for my first Happy Camper experience had been miserable, 20 degrees below zero, with gray overcast skies and a whipping wind. Walking to the Berg Field Center, where we were to muster, a first-year copilot named Frank Scott Allen—nicknamed "FSA"—commented on the spits of snow that swirled around in eddy currents between the buildings. He said they looked like icy versions of the dust devils he used to see back home in Texas. Milling around outside the BFC were forty shivering, glassy-eyed, and dread-struck survival-school classmates. We stood in color-coated groups of five or six, grumbling about the dismal weather, hopeful that school would be postponed. Not likely. Everyone wore something different; the military members wore their olive Korean War parkas and overpants, the science support staff wore their bright red down jackets and black overpants, and the group of Kiwis were dressed in yellow parkas and bib overalls. The only similarity among us was our shoes: we all wore bunny boots. The huge, white, ultra-insulated boots made us look like life-size versions of Mickey Mouse instead of the tough-ass polar explorers we thought ourselves to be.

Our hopes of a last minute cancellation were dashed when at 0810, six vans pulled alongside the BFC and our mountaineer instructors dropped out with cheery grins and shouts of "Good morning!" Our faces dropped as we were told school was a "go" and we could begin piling our baggage (we were encouraged to bring everything we were issued to find out what combinations of clothes worked best for us in different situations) into the vans. No one moved. For several minutes a murmur hinting of anarchy ran through the crowd. Perhaps the instructors were joking. Perhaps we should defy their orders, pick up our satchels, and head home. A second, then a third call came for us to "load up" before we stiffly hefted our bags of clothing and boarded the vans to set off for Scott Base, about a mile away. The crowd of students in my room now, having heard this story, groaned. No hope for cancellation for them, either.

At Scott Base, as I went on to tell the new group, we had transferred all our baggage onto a large sled towed by a Nodwell, a huge tank-like tracked brute of a machine that for an hour clawed through the snow on a line parallel to the sloping arm of Mt. Erebus that forms Hut Point Peninsula. Eventually we were ferried out onto the Ross Ice Shelf and our camp. Riding in the Nodwell was nauseating. It moved in the jerky, twisting motion common to all tracked vehicles, and my stomach was turning somersaults.

Halfway to the camping area, we had stopped and were broken up into groups of ten for instruction in basic climbing techniques. We practiced using an ice ax and cutting steps in the snow, and we learned about crampons as we climbed three hundred feet up the steeply pitched leeward slope of the peninsula. For the next two hours we climbed up the hill and then slid down the hill, practicing various methods of self-arrest, with and without the aid of an ice ax. I was amazed at the abrupt change in attitude by the group: just a few minutes of sliding down the hill replaced loathing with the high-spirited enthusiasm of kids.

We launched ourselves with vigor down the hill, going head-first, bottom-first, backward, forward, on our stomachs, on our backs, every which way, then trying to right ourselves and stop our downward momentum. With everyone hurling themselves down the side of a mountain, a contest quickly developed to see who could launch the most bizarre out-of-control free slide and still be able to stop.

I told the new students that I personally preferred to self-arrest without the aid of the ice ax, and I explained how. Launching myself down the side of the mountain (simulating having fallen and now sliding out of control), I would then maneuver my body so as to end up on my stomach, with my feet downhill. Next, using my fingers and toes as brakes, I would push myself up into a modified crouch, which resembled a bent-knee push up, and hold that position until I stopped. I was always amazed that such a simple technique worked so well.

Next my Happy Camper School group went to practice stopping with the ice ax. The idea was to place the haft of the ax beneath your body with the claw facing down, using your body weight to force the pick end of the ax into the snow. This claw was very effective and stopped you quickly. We had ended the session with our version of the grand finale. Our instructor, a wonderful Kiwi named Mary Anne, formed our group of ten into a large chain—bums downhill, legs uphill, linked arms and legs with me at the bottom of the chain pointed downhill (the disadvantage of being the largest person there). We launched, sliding and screaming to raise the dead, and arrived at the bottom in a chaotic fashion, a massive, flailing pile of arms and legs, heads and bums. The only drawback to this stunt was that we had to climb back up and retrieve our gear. I've always believed that some things in life are worth the extra effort, and this was, without a doubt, one of those times.

There was a relieved laugh from around my room as the beers took hold and the apprehension of tomorrow's activities began to ebb. I opened another beer and took a long pull for effect before continuing. The morning's exertions worked up an appetite in all of us, I explained, so it was a letdown to eat a lunch of cold pizza, nuts, cranberry juice, and a tasteless cake while sitting cramped in the Nodwell. After our lunch we rode farther out onto the ice shelf to build our shelters for the evening.

Building a shelter out of snow is an art. And the type of shelter that a group of three or four decides to build speaks volumes about that group. Some groups build simple shelters, a pit in the snow with cut blocks of snow pressed together for a roof. Others build modified igloos. My group— FSA, Lance (a squadron navigator), the Doc (the squadron flight surgeon), and I—decided to build the granddaddy of snow shelters: the snow mound. The instructors estimated it would take us four hours to construct, but since there wasn't anything else to do, we accepted the challenge. Our shelter eventually took on epic proportions. It turned out to be a feat on a par with building a condo out of Popsicle sticks—only slower.

We began by piling our bags together in a heap and then burying them under about eight feet of snow. We then packed the snow down well on top of the bags and then tunneled in to dig them out. This left us with a natural cave to expand, and we had to do some expanding indeed before it was large enough to accommodate us. We had a difficult time digging, piling, and packing that much snow, but we had the bags covered in a little less than three hours. Tunneling in to the bags was laborious and at times claustrophobic, as snow from the low, narrow tunnel constantly shifted and fell in our faces, hinting that the thing could collapse at any time.

After another two solid hours of tunneling, we located and dragged out our bags. With the bags removed, the work went much more quickly. What had been a one-man operation now became a team effort—shift work. FSA and I hollowed out the room using shovels, axes, and a snow saw, which turned out to be the most valuable tool because it allowed us to cut huge blocks of snow from the interior. We worked an hour and then were spelled by Lance. He worked like an ox, elated at the heavy work, as Doc stood close by the entrance offering encouragement and plenty of hot chocolate laced with peppermint schnapps. After six and a half hours of arduous, back-breaking work on what was supposed to be a four-hour job, we were ensconced in a shelter of massive proportions. The snow floor was seven feet square, and the ceiling was over four feet high. The roof was an eight-foot layer of well-packed snow that would stay in place even in high winds but was still thin enough to allow in enough pale blue light for us to read by.

However, before we agreed to sleep in our cave, we felt we should test the roof, just to prove to ourselves that it wouldn't cave in. Mary Anne told us that the heat from our bodies had melted the layer of snow that constituted our ceiling and created a layer of ice strong enough to support the roof. Just to be sure, one by one, we climbed atop our snow pile. It held. We celebrated by cooking dinner on our Coleman stove and drinking more cocoa and schnapps.

Then, after our dinner, FSA and I wandered around the camp to look over the other shelters and to invite our neighbors to our snow mansion for cocktails. I had a hard time calling our area a camp, since a camp, in my mind, suggested some kind of uniformity. Here, more than a dozen shelters were thrown up, dug out, and piled together in an area the size of a football field. None faced the same way. Somewhat in the center, a nylon tent served as the privy. Fifty yards away stood the Nodwell, idling with the heater on for those who just couldn't take the cold.

We returned to our shelter and opened a bottle of Jack Daniel's. Magically we became the best little bar on the ice shelf. Eventually we were joined by others from the camp and had eight very Happy Campers crammed into our shelter, sipping whiskey and feeling wonderfully warm. What a great bunch of guys. What a wonderful igloo-full of pals. More whiskey, anyone?

The group in my room smiled at the thought of a comfortable ice shelf. I continued telling them my story: at 2300 we had bid our fellow Happy Campers adieu and popped into our sleeping bags, where I was exceedingly comfortable until I had to go to the bathroom at 0300. This would be a major ordeal, and time was against me and my bladder. In my state it would be next to impossible to force myself out of the whiskey-tinged warmth of my sleeping bag, put on my bunny boots, and stagger naked out into a blast of Antarctic air. This could be my most challenging survival moment of the trip. As I lay there, I remembered a particular bit of cold weather medical advice given by one Dr. Murray Hamlet, who recommended avoiding metal poles when urinating in Antarctica. I shuddered. Thinking of myself floundering around outside half-awake, I considered the consequences of ignoring Hamlet's advice as I answered nature's call. I lay in my sleeping bag, debating whether to go out. To pee or not to pee. That was the question.

Thirty minutes passed before I summoned enough courage (my bladder had a lot of input into that decision) to edge out of my sleeping bag, find my bunny boots, and crawl naked out into the sunny night. I didn't go far, and I was out just long enough to know that I would never *ever* walk naked in Antarctica again.

I slept soundly until 0630, when I awoke with a terrific hangover. An Antarctic hangover is the worst. With no humidity in the atmosphere there, you lose your fluids quickly and dehydrate, and alcohol only exacerbates the dehydration. It took me nearly an hour to muster the energy and courage to back out of the cave and face the raw, cold, new day.

Continuing my description of the Happy Camper School experience for the newcomers, I explained that after breakfasting on coffee, water, rock-hard freeze-dried raisins, and aspirin, we had packed our gear and were picked up by the Nodwell at 0800. Heading back toward Scott Base, we stopped after about twenty minutes and divided into teams of ten to twelve students per instructor. We strapped on our crampons, roped three or four together to a hundred-and-fifty-foot-length of climbing rope, and headed up a steeply pitched hill. At the first rise, we found ourselves amid a crevasse-filled field. We proceeded slowly, picking our way through the field as Mary Anne explained how to detect and avoid crevasses. We had just gotten through the first field and crested another small hill when a call came in over the radio that severe weather was moving in from the ice shelf. The head of the survival school insisted that all groups leave the mountain immediately before the weather got any worse.

The winds began to pick up. What had been a relatively nice day of minus-10 degrees and 10 knots of winds rapidly deteriorated into a life-threatening situation. The winds increased to 30 to 40 knots in less than twenty minutes as the storm developed rapidly, perhaps churning into a Herbie, which would mean real trouble. High winds began to propel the snow in sheets thick enough to blind us. It ripped and grabbed at our coats and pushed and pulled at us as we wound our way back through the crevasse field, desperately trying to retrace our steps. The billowing white sheets of snow melded the dull white sky with the ground to make each step tenuous. At times I couldn't see the ground or my feet below my knees.

All was white. There were no contrasts, no shadows. It was like being wrapped head to toe in gauze. I shuddered as I recalled that it must have been conditions identical to these that killed Robert F. Scott and his companions in 1912. I certainly wasn't any more cheered by stomping blindly through a crevasse field in the middle of such a storm. At one point the wind became so fierce we were forced to stop, form a circle, and hunker down as a group in the snow and wait for the wind to abate. After a few minutes the wind did die down a bit, but we could no longer see our tracks back to the Nodwell. Under these conditions it would have been suicidal to continue. We waited for nearly an hour before it cleared enough to find our way back to the shelter of the Nodwell.

Other groups began to stagger in. Within an hour all the groups save one had arrived. The instructors tried to raise the missing group via radio, but their efforts were useless since nothing could be heard over the constant howl of the wind. We waited two more hours, everyone crammed in the Nodwell. The wind abated somewhat. As soon as we could see fifty yards ahead, we struck out in small parties to locate the missing group. Our party of five wound its way back through the crevasse field and, after an hour, found the errant group huddled in a shallow snow cave. They cheered as we came into view. The poor guys looked as if they had just received a last-minute pardon from a death sentence.

The instructor said the wind had come up so fast that they lost track of where they were and decided to hollow out a shelter rather than risk the crevasse field blind. The instructor tried to raise somebody on the radio, only to find the batteries dead. So they waited. As each hour had passed, their paranoia increased. Without food, water, or a radio they had planned for the worst to happen, quickly. I made a mental note of their psychological state. Should I ever be forced into a survival situation, I told myself, it would be crucial to be able to maintain a positive outlook.

We helped them back to the Nodwell; then Mary Anne decided that the weather was good enough for us to practice rappelling and prussicking. We threw a line off a cliff and started down. I was in mid-rappel when the wind mounted another assault. Halfway down the rope I was blown sideways, nearly parallel to the cliff edge above. The wind was so strong that I hung on with both hands, clawing at the ice face with my crampons, trying to stop the swaying. The gusts blew my hood and hat off, leaving my head exposed to the full force of the wind. My face began to ache and burn, my eyes felt as if they were freezing, and each breath filled my mouth and nose with snow. I couldn't see the ground below me, but I knew it must be less than fifty feet, so I clawed myself upright, pushed off, and rappelled, sliding and swinging down the rope as fast as I could.

Luckily I had done a fair amount of mountaineering on my own, so I got to the bottom quickly. I unshouldered my backpack, yanked out my balaclava, my neckover, and my goggles, quickly covering my face and head. When I had begun to warm up some, I searched for a way to get back up to the rest of my group. I found myself in a narrow couloir, maybe fifty feet long. The snow was blowing so thick that I couldn't see the top. I tied one end of the rope to my climbing harness and started along the gully.

Near the far end, I located a three-foot-wide chimney and wedged myself in. By pressing with my legs and feet on one side and my back on the other, I worked my way, inch by inch, up the fissure. With one leg stretched to the wall and the other planted under my butt, I lifted myself with the leg beneath me, until I could go no higher. Then, holding myself in place with my outstretched leg and my back, I changed legs and repeated the process. Near the top, the crack opened up so that I had to keep my legs nearly fully extended to remain wedged in. I planted my right leg behind me, my left leg in front, and shifted all my weight to my legs. Then I used my ice ax as a pick and clawed at the snow just beyond the lip of the crack until I felt that I had a solid hold. I held onto the ice ax as I kicked both feet into solid footholds in the face of the crack; then I took a deep breath, kicked, and pulled myself free.

After lying there for a moment, collecting my breath and my thoughts, I followed my rope back to the group. They were all staring over the edge of the ravine. I strolled up from behind and rejoined the group, who were peering over the edge. "What are you looking for?" I asked.

They all jumped a foot. It had been nearly forty-five minutes since they had heard from me. They were about to give me up for dead. Mary Anne, not amused, decided it was time to knock it off and head back. We took our time picking our way down an adjacent hill to the shelter of a small heated trailer. There, stripped to our underwear to dry our sweat-soaked clothes, we ate lunch and waited for the other groups to trickle in. While we waited, there was no talk. We all just sat chewing and staring straight ahead. The last group came into the trailer an hour later, just as the survival coordinators at Scott Base decided it was too dangerous for us to stay out any longer and called us back.

When the last group was fed and checked for frostbite, we climbed in the Nodwell and began the long trek back to Mac Town. After a harrowing day in the weather, the group looked haggard. I watched as the others staggered away toward their rooms, dragging their gear behind them. The weather had worn us out completely. It wasn't until I had a warm shower and was back in my room, tucked into bed with a beer and a book, that I started to feel like myself again. I was a Happy Camper, all right. Happy to be alive.

As I finished my story, the new students laughed nervously. I assured them that I had been having a great time up until the weather hit on the second day and that I would do it all again if I could. I lied.

1

CHICKEN COOKIES

When you're stuck on the Ice two thousand miles from the normal amenities of daily life, details become important, and those details include food and drink. One day I was summoned to the wardroom for an all-officers meeting (AOM) at 1400. Generally I loathed these informal meetings, held weekly, since they were little more than a Bully Pulpit for the CO, XO, and department heads. Usually the junior officers tried to look interested as the squadron leadership talked shop.

This particular AOM was mostly administrative BS, but one announcement caused my ears to perk up: the entire wardroom (all the officers) had been invited to New Zealand's Scott Base for an informal "chin wagging." During the flying season, we—that is, the United States Antarctic Research Program (USARP)—worked closely with the Kiwis; in return, they'd invite us for a cocktail party a few times a season. Although it was less than two miles away, we rarely went to Scott Base unless invited, so I always considered an invitation an honor and jumped at the chance to share in some hearty fellowship—not to mention that the Kiwis stocked the best beer on the continent.

The supply of U.S. beer is brought down a year before it's used. With all the cooling and heating it goes through, American beer ends up tasting like formaldehyde. Kiwi beer, on the other hand, is flown in fresh every week or so. The worst Kiwi beer I ever tasted was still better than most American-brewed beer.

On Saturdays, station routine and flight operations generally stopped at 1900. Since Sunday was our only day off, Saturday night was the sanctioned night for parties, a night to let down your hair and blow off steam. In McMurdo it was affectionately dubbed "Saturday Night Live," and it often took on the atmosphere of a fraternity initiation. The entire station drank, caroused, and howled for a good time. To borrow the wisdom of Robert E. Lee, who said, "It is well that war was so terrible—we should grow too fond of it,"[1] it was good that Saturday happened but once a week, or we would have grown far too fond of it.

Sean and I caught the 1930 shuttle bus to Scott Base. The bar was at one end of the main building, separated from the dining room by a folding wall that limited the bar to about twenty-five by forty feet. Sudden occupation by fifty or so people certainly made it cozy. The bar itself was big enough for only half a dozen barstools. This meant ordering a beer became a shouting match at times. And of course the more you shouted, the more everyone else did, too. On the walls hung artifacts and souvenirs from various expeditions that had started or ended in the bar at Scott Base. Entertainment was conversation or, for the more adventurous, a pint-sized pool table with one-inch balls. The floor was covered with an ugly but, as I was to learn, cherished carpet.

My first evening at the Scott Base bar began inauspiciously enough with a major faux pas on my part. I entered the bar, and as I stood waiting for a beer, someone grabbed me. My captor, Graham, held up his hand and yelled that court was in session. A hush fell over the room. Under his breath he asked me my name and then said, "Ladies and gentlemen, I give you Mark, who has found it necessary to violate our laws and enter herein with his shoes on!"

The crowd gasped "No!" as I stared involuntarily at my feet, which were trying desperately to kick off two tightly laced hiking boots.

Graham continued: "I submit to you, the upstanding, law-abiding, shoeless people herein, to decide what fine we shall impose. Shall we lop off his feet?"

"Yes!" the crowd screamed as I tried to back through the door.

Graham, seeing my bewilderment, asked, "Didn't you read the sign on your way in?"

"Sort of," I stammered.

"Ladies and gentlemen," he proceeded, "Mark here seems like a good lad. I think we should let him off with a lighter sentence."

"Boil him in oil!" someone shouted.

Graham said, "No, we've done that already this week. I know! Let us fine him all that he has in his pockets and allow him to buy everyone drinks as his penance."

Four large fellows grabbed me and turned me upside down—not an easy feat with someone my size—and shook me until every last penny I had fell out. It was a swift trial: within two minutes I had been tried, found guilty, and summarily fined twenty-two dollars and change for my transgression.

Graham led me to the bar and bought me a beer (with my money) to ensure there were no hard feelings. I told him that I could live with the fine but that I could swear there was no sign on the door. He led me outside and pointed at the door. Those cunning Kiwis had a sign all right. It was written in Japanese. Graham handed me a beer and patted me on the back. So much for my trial by Shoe Court.

Of the fifty or so people in the bar, about half were Kiwis and half were VXE-6 officers. Only about a dozen were women, who found no lack of dance partners once the music started from the stereo. We drank, played pool, sang great bar songs, including "Going up Sunshine Mountain," wherein the chorus is repeated and those not off the floor are pointed at and shamed into compliance until every last person in the bar is off the floor in some manner. Tables, chairs, the bar, anything that could be stood upon was, until we were all up. We let up a boisterous cheer when the last person standing on the floor found refuge on the bar.

The Scott Base portion of the evening ended when the remaining McMurdo folks piled into a tracked vehicle and were driven back over the hill by the lone sober (or so he professed) Kiwi. I went straight to bed, but judging by the noise up and down the hall, the party continued until the liquor dried up. From time to time I would hear drinkers yelling outside my door, but I stayed in bed—and I was thankful for it when I watched those party animals crawl, moaning and hung over, to the bathroom the very next afternoon.

Sunday I slept in and then caught up on neglected correspondence and watched a weeks-old football game on video. That evening I went to dinner late. It was the ever-popular pizza night, and if you went any time before 1830 (dinner ends at 1900), the line was around the block. I finished late and then stopped in on the Sunday science lecture already in progress. On most Sundays different scientists would lecture for anyone interested in what they were studying in Antarctica. The topic for that evening was the benthic ecology of the McMurdo Sound. I was just seated when the fellow next to me said, "I don't know about this guy. He just said he's been looking at the same population of sponges for fifteen years. He says he's not actually sure if some of the sponges he observes are still alive or not."

I listened to the scientist describe sponges found in the sound. People began to get up and filter out, including the gent next to me. He rolled his eyes and said he was going to the bar. I asked if I could join him, since all this talk about sponges had made me want to soak up a little something myself. He introduced himself as Bob and said the distinguished scientist giving the lecture had collected data that were vast but unimpressive. We walked to the Officers' Club (called the "O" Club for short), and after we had settled into our beers, Bob continued. "That guy has way too many unanswered questions for working on a project for so long," he complained. "His research sounds more like a high-school senior project than pure scientific research." Bob swigged down some beer. "This guy isn't a stellar example of the typical polar researcher, but there are a few scientists here that have me stumped how they continue to be funded year after year."

As Bob and I talked, I noticed that the bar was filling up. Everyone seemed to be talking about the disappointing lecture. Bob continued: "There is another guy who has been doing research here for twenty years on a biological antifreeze produced by fish that inhabit Antarctic waters [saltwater doesn't freeze at 32 degrees because the salt and pressure lower its freezing point; sea water in Antarctica ranges from 28 to 29.5 degrees]. He identified the antifreeze molecule years ago that allows the fish to lower their freezing point just enough to survive but he hasn't done anything with it."

Bob drained his glass and ordered another beer before he started again: "Other scientists who have studied the molecule speculate," he spat the word out, "that the research may lead to development of inexpensive, nontoxic, biodegradable alternatives to road salt, aircraft deicing solutions, what have you." Bob was on a roll now. "But even the guy that found this stuff in the first place is skeptical about wide-ranging applications—but he does think his research could lead to food additives that could prevent ice crystals that give ice cream that gritty consistency." He pulled at his beer and shook his head pensively. "Imagine that! Twenty years of Antarctic research to make better ice cream."

Apparently Bob now felt the need to defend the rest of his fellow scientists, because he spent the remainder of the evening talking about the relevant and important, leading-edge research that would give mankind a glimpse at how the universe was born or would unlock the secrets of our world by revealing the records of past eons that are buried beneath the Antarctic snows. It wouldn't be until much later that I would learn how prophetic Bob had been about some of the disappointing science conducted there.

Monday we were back on duty as usual and did a mission to Byrd. Low, dull clouds had moved in and covered the entire Ross Ice Shelf. When I had completed my flying duties at Byrd, I felt hungry, so I slid the plane's seat back and went to the cargo compartment to take a look at what was in our in-flight box lunch. VXE-6 air crews operate around the clock, so they routinely miss at least two meals at the McMurdo galley. This being the case, all flights are provided with box lunches. During my three seasons in Antarctica the contents of the box lunches never changed. The only variety was in the desserts, which were either last night's leftovers or the coming night's selection, depending on when the box lunch was packed at McMurdo.

The box lunch always contained enough for a crew of nine: three loaves of bread, a pound of American cheese, a pound of mystery meat (usually something that resembled salami), one jar of smooth peanut butter, one jar of grape jelly, two dozen small bags of airline peanuts (or, occasionally, rock-hard raisins), a dozen boxes of cranberry juice (or cranapple, crangrape, or the like), condiments, and dessert. It also usually included round, boneless fried chicken patties, which we called "chicken cookies."

We lived for dessert. Whoever on our crew got to the box lunch first would check the dessert and report back to us. If the dessert was considered noteworthy, it could be the saving grace of an otherwise dull flight. Once you've eaten the same bland food for two meals a day for three years, you start getting peculiar cravings. Veteran air crewmen ate strange combinations of foods just to keep things interesting—concoctions running to the bizarre. One favorite: chicken cookie with jelly. Mostly, we all lost weight.

It was still early in the season so I opted for that old standby, the peanut butter and jelly sandwich, otherwise known as the PBJ. I never missed home so much in my life as when I took that first familiar bite. PBJs notwithstanding, a diet of chicken cookies and American cheese can make one quickly turn to the liquor selection for relief. Off-duty, we weren't shy about drinking, but after a few months on the Ice, you learned the limits there, too.

Waking up with an Antarctic hangover has to be one of the most unpleasant experiences imaginable. It combines severe dehydration, dry throat and mouth, headache, and nausea—but all double what you experience with a normal hangover. It feels, basically, as though you ran headlong into a brick wall during the night and then fell asleep in the desert with your mouth open. You feel thick-headed and bruised on the inside. But even that wasn't much of a deterrent for most people.

Our Antarctic work week ran from Monday morning until 1900 Saturday night. Working ten or twelve hours a day, six days a week, lent itself to blowing off a little steam on Saturday night. The key was moderation, but that advice was rarely heeded. What we required was the release of energy. We needed the chance to howl at the remoteness to try to prove we were unafraid of this beautiful but god-awful continent. We celebrated our freedom from the daily grind—a lot.

8

A COZY LITTLE

ICE SHELF

We began what was to be an eventful day with a run-in with the squadron's ODO. The Transport Aircraft Commanders Briefing Package (TAC-PAC)—a portfolio prepared by the ODO to brief the PTAC and crew on the day's mission—read that we were bound for Upstream Bravo (Up B), but it lacked any load or passenger information (so we didn't know what we were carrying) and leg-loads (so we didn't know what the last two crews' experiences had been) and even a put-in sheet (so we didn't know the condition of the camp skiway). In other words, it lacked all the pertinent data necessary for the flight.[1] We wasted nearly two hours in an attempt to locate the information we needed; in short, we wasted our time doing the ODO's job.

There were always frustrations associated with flying in Antarctica. The nearly always poor weather, the numbing cold, the occasional deplorable state of the aircraft, the lackadaisical attitudes of some of the support staff, the seemingly endless waiting for paperwork—all of these things were out of our own control, and they always added up to headaches for the air crews. It was bad enough that those of us in the military who were counted on to be punctual were ourselves subjected to delays because of less-than-punctual scientists or VIPs. But when we had to take matters into our own hands because of ill planning on the part of one of our own, we experienced the ultimate frustration.

•

To get to Up B we fly a heading between South Pole Station and Byrd. It's an interesting, albeit short, flight. We cross the dull white Ross Ice Shelf for half the flight, but the other half we fly over two massive ice streams as we pass from the ice shelf into Marie Byrd Land. These fast-moving ice streams resemble huge glaciers except that glaciers are bound by mountains, while these ice streams thunder through slower-moving ice.

Up B is at the apex of Ice Stream B and is one of five major ice streams connecting Marie Byrd Land to the Ross Ice Shelf. The term *ice stream* is really a misnomer: these "streams" rival some of the largest rivers in the world. Ice Stream B, for example, is thirty miles wide, over three hundred miles long, and half a mile deep. As for speed, these streams flow at about ten feet a day, while the ice surrounding them flows only ten feet a year. The ice that forms the Ross Ice Shelf originates here, flowing to the sea and replenishing the ice shelf, which continually calves icebergs as it moves imperceptibly out to sea. When I considered the fact that we were more than five hundred frozen miles from open water, it was impossible for me to imagine that this ice over which we were now flying would one day wind its way to the sea. Yet it will.

In the midst of all this active ice a camp had been established on a small patch of snow. We located the site and circled once to get a feel for the lay of the land and to check the surface conditions. The area was surrounded by major crevasse fields. I thought that whoever selected this spot for a skiway did an outstanding job, because the skiway was located on the only stable snow for miles. Tolerances were so tight there wasn't more than a quarter-mile clearance in any direction where I couldn't see large, shallow depressions in the snow—the primary indication of major crevasses.

We found the old skiway, with its flags and mesh panels all in fair shape, which surprised me since the station had been inactive for the past two seasons. We also spotted the week-old ski drags of the recce crew. Their leg-load report read they had difficulty finding the skiway through the haze, so they decided to do a ski drag and land in it instead of wasting gas searching for the skiway. The decision to drag prior to landing was a fortuitous one for them. Their drag, about less than a hundred yards from the skiway, was inadvertently made in a crevasse-filled field. Their tracks exposed a crevasse that was ten or fifteen feet across.

They had been extremely lucky. From three hundred feet in the air, the crevasse looked like the open mouth of a hideous frozen ice creature waiting to devour a Herc appetizer. Having seen the tracks of the recce crew drop off into the oblivion of that gaping maw, I renewed my profound respect for the value of the ski drag.

During a ski drag, the plane should be traveling fast enough to collapse any snow bridge that may have formed over the mouth of the crevasse, fast enough to skip over the crevasse itself (unless of course the crevasse is so huge it could swallow a plane). Our drags today worked out well, but it was still unnerving to think about the consequences of crossing a plane-eating crevasse. My mental picture of this was Wile E. Coyote of *Road Runner* cartoons, running across a burning bridge just as it drops away in ashes into a chasm. The coyote falls just as he reaches the other side, landing far below in a tiny puff of smoke, then walking away, bobbing up and down, like a deflated accordion. Had we fallen through a crevasse, we might have looked like an accordion, too, but somehow I didn't think we'd walk away.

We landed on the old skiway on the second pass in a stiff 30-knot crosswind. Despite the high wind, the snow was reassuringly smooth. We had a limited amount of space in which to taxi and drop off our pallets. The first crew had dropped their pallets in the center of the cargo area, forcing us to squeeze between the snow mounds that were the buried buildings and pallets.

The group of nine whom we brought in, coming here to open up the camp, were obviously old hands. I was awed by the practiced efficiency that marked their movements. Even before we were able to off-load the first of our pallets, they had deplaned and were involved with the task at hand. The camp manager got to work on the radio and established communications with Mac Center, while the remaining personnel dug for the tunnel leading to the snow-covered Jameswazs. The only indication of buildings underground was a wooden box sticking a foot or so above the surface to mark the entrance.

We dug away the snow and found the hatch. Once it was chiseled open, we crawled down a ten-foot ladder to a second entrance below, gaining access to the main room in minutes. The entire three-building Jamesway complex was buried by ten to twelve feet of snow. Inside, the main building felt dark and eerie. In the dim light I saw chairs in place around a table, half-opened boxes of food on the shelves, and the heater that look as though it had just been shut off and would fire up immediately. You could swear the station had been abandoned only yesterday and not two years ago. Only the accumulated snow in the corners and the two-year-old calendar gave the truth away.

Finding myself alone momentarily, I pulled out a chair and sat in the gray silence to visualize folks having a communal dinner or whiling away the hours around this table while the winds howled above. Despite all the lore about unlivable conditions in the center of the continent, I found that alone in the dark there, I felt calm—as though I was once again protected in the womb. I found that when I imagined the table bathed in soft light, the heater chugging away to keep the cold at bay, with several close companions about, this placed seemed exceedingly agreeable.

In that moment I sensed that I was more than just a bit player in the history of Antarctica: I was a part of the continent. In an instant I stood at the Pole with Roald Amundsen and Robert Scott, I froze in a make-shift hut with Apsley Cherry-Garrard, I endured the austral winter alone with Richard Byrd, and I understood why they all wanted to come here. It was their need to know, to understand not only what lay ahead on the trail but also what lay dormant inside each of them, what they would find within themselves as they faced the far horizon and trudged out into the unknown.

My stillness was dashed by a box of supplies landing with a thud in the entrance. It was my cue to leave—or find myself pressed into station duty. Back above ground I was reminded of how different Up B was from the other outlying stations around the continent. Most of the other stations were on flat, white plains, but here a natural bluff rose from the homogeneous sheet of white. It was the only rise I had ever seen this close to the ice shelf. The mound, the result of up-welling ice at the stream's source, was over two hundred feet high and dominated the landscape for miles. I traced the escarpment line from surface to crest, where it reached up into the clear blue sky and pressed against it like an ice cube in a curaçao cocktail.

The camp manager sidled up to me and remarked on the beauty of the view. He had a faraway look in his eyes, as if he were staring through, rather than at, the bluff. He told me he had yearned for two years to get back out here, and he couldn't believe he had actually made it. He had been Up B camp manager for several years before it was temporarily closed, and he spoke of it as his camp. He suddenly snapped out of his reverential mood, made an indiscriminate gesture toward the camp, and abruptly excused himself, explaining he had much to accomplish before the next plane arrived. He seemed eager to be rid of us, so we obliged him. The camp crew stopped working long enough to assemble in the cargo area and wave good-bye, but I still felt like we were house guests who had overstayed our welcome.

After liftoff I turned 90 degrees to the right, immediately following that with a 270-degree reversal turn to the left. Our world toppled to the right as the horizon line bisected our windscreen. We rolled back to the right, and I pulled hard on the yoke to bring the plane's nose around. This maneuver placed me in a perfect position to overfly the camp. I rolled out of my turn, descended to a hundred feet, accelerated to 250 knots, and as we crossed the buildings, I rocked the wings as a crude farewell. Nine stalwart souls waved back.

On our way home we were instructed to lend assistance to a plane that had incurred major nose-ski damage in the open field. Normally the crew could have assessed the damage themselves via a small inspection window aft of the nose-wheel well. Unfortunately when the ski came undone, it smashed the inspection window, and the crew could no longer see through it. They had no idea of what they were up against. A low flyby at a hundred feet off the deck in front of maintenance personnel was no good; the plane would be traveling too fast for us to make anything other than a snap judgment. Instead we were to join on them (fly in close formation) not only to describe the problem but also, with the Lockheed technical representative aboard our plane, to offer technical expertise. (Tech reps, employees of the Lockheed Corporation, were permanently assigned to the squadron as expert engineering advisors.)

We returned to McMurdo, refueled, picked up the tech rep, and dropped off all nonessential crew members. We were airborne again in less than thirty minutes. The plan was to rendezvous with the stricken plane about a hundred miles out of McMurdo. We switched our tactical air navigation system (TACAN) to "air to air," which gave us distance and relative bearing to the other plane; we caught sight of each other when we were eight miles apart. I called the other PTAC, Scott, and told him to switch to an obscure ultra-high frequency (UHF) so we could talk without interruption.

I called, "X-ray Delta Zero Four, X-ray Delta Zero Two. You up?"

"Zero Two, Zero Four. Hey, Mark, how you doing?"

"Zero Four, Zero Two. Not bad, Scott, but we're too heavy to get any higher right now. Can you descend about two thousand feet?"

"Zero Two, Zero Four. No problem. You want to stay in loose trail [behind us] and join on us in trail. I don't want to change power settings until I know what the plane looks like."

"Zero Four, Zero Two. OK, Scott, agreed. Go ahead and leave the power up. I'll catch up with you when you're level again at twenty-three [thousand feet]."

Once they had descended, I joined on them, flying twenty feet off their right wing and slightly below them at 160 knots. It was readily apparent that the nose ski was severely damaged. It was drooping badly and looked as though it might fall off any second. The major problem appeared to be the nose-ski rigger strut, the piston that keeps the ski level as it comes up. It had detached from the aft bulkhead and lay atop the ski like a wounded duck.

"Zero Two, Zero Four. So what's it look like?"

"I've got my FE [flight engineer] looking at it right now, Scott; hold on a second. OK, he says that the rigger strut has been pulled clean off the aft bulkhead and is dangling—the good news is you're already bow high." (The nose ski was already pointing up in front, which meant if they had to land with the ski in its present state, at least the ski wouldn't auger into the ground on landing, and second, if they could raise the ski, then the rigger strut wouldn't be necessary since the ski was already nose up.)

"My nav [navigator] said on her last cel shot [a celestial shot of the sun to confirm the plane's position] that she could see one of our HF antennas had come loose but wasn't sure if it was still on the plane or not. How about taking a look for that while you're here?"

"OK, we're going to swap sides now and fly underneath you and check the other side." I drifted back and crossed under their plane, assuming a mirror position on their left. Roy, using binoculars, spotted the antenna draped across their left wing, caught in the slot between the inboard and outboard flaps. The remainder of the wire trailed behind the wing, beating against the fuselage. The sixty-foot-long antenna posed a real threat; if it unwound when they slowed or reversed engines on landing, it could be sucked into one or both engines, causing them to fail and possibly causing the plane to crash.

"Scott, the wire is still there, but it's not in a very advantageous position. My FE says the antenna has broken free of the aft attachment point but is still attached to the front. From here it appears to run across the top part of your left wing just aft of number two [engine]; it's wedged in between your inner and outer flaps on the left wing and the trailing end is probably causing your loadmaster to tell you he's hearing something beating on the side of the plane."

From the other plane I heard, "Great."

"Scott," I said, "let's worry about the ski first. We're seventy miles out of McMurdo; let's go ahead and descend and take care of this on the way in."

We began the long, slow descent toward home. The tech rep went through every option he could think of, and together we all decided that the best course of action would be for them to try to raise their skis. I felt they were in a no-lose situation as far as the ski was concerned. If it came up, great; if not, it would probably fall off and land harmlessly in the middle of nowhere.

"Scott, my FE and the tech rep agree you should raise the skis using emergency ski up [the backup system to raise the skis if the normal system failed], so let us know when you're ready to give it a shot."

A few moments later: "We're ready on this end."

"Give me a second and I'll call when we're in position." I reduced power, drifted back, and eased off to the right to watch without being in harm's way, in case the nose ski departed the plane. When we were in position, we gave the signal and they raised their skis.

The main skis came up immediately, but the nose ski wavered, tentatively rose a little, then stuck. It was up enough that some tire showed beneath the ski, at least enough tire to land on. "It looks good, Scott. You've got three, maybe five inches of tire showing, and the ski looks steady, so I think you're OK there. Let's discuss the antenna. We've talked about it on this end and believe that if you lower the flaps, chances are the wires will dislodge; then, it's anybody's guess. We think your best bet is to land no-flap, then reverse only the outboard engines. Landing no-flap will also let you keep your speed up so the wire stays back and out of the way."

"That's what we thought, too. I guess we're as ready as we're ever going to be. You go ahead and land first; we'll be right behind you."

"Let's run through your landing sequence," I told him, "so you can go think it through before you do it for real." We walked through each step, so they could play out in their minds what to expect. This was an unusual combination of emergencies, so we thought it prudent to rehearse the scenario. It seemed trivial, but it was the most valuable type of drill because it forced them to concentrate on the problem at hand without being lulled into the routine of a normal landing, which this one certainly wouldn't be.

"I guess we've done all the damage we can," I said to Scott. "Good luck! We'll see you on the ground." I hoped I sounded convincing, since they faced a bad situation. If they were able to use their flaps, they could land slowly and not worry about reversing their propellers to stop. But with the wire so close to an inboard engine, they couldn't risk reversing without having the wire caught in a propeller and risk pulling the plane or prop apart. They were now forced to land fast (landing with flaps, they'd descend at a slower airspeed) and use minimum reverse (so as not to catch the wire); and since they were landing on the ice runway, their brakes were useless. About all they could hope for was that they could slow down enough using the little reverse thrust to be able to stop before they ran off the end of the runway and plowed into the snow berm. All in all I was glad I was in our plane.

We broke off from our formation to commence our approach. There was a morbid but practical reason for us to land first. If something did happen to them on landing, at least we would be safe on deck and not circling waiting for a clear runway. We descended quickly and flew straight to the field to land expeditiously and get out of the way. We taxied to our parking spot on the ramp and finished our postflight checklists; then we joined the maintenance troops to wait. Crash vehicles stood ready at either end of the runway, their lights flashing. An ambulance waited next to the midfield tower. The atmosphere was tense, everyone waiting to see the plane as it approached the field.

We spotted the aircraft about eight miles from the runway. They flew a long, flat, straight-in approach with flaps up. In this configuration they approached the field fast and, nearly level, began descending slowly. They passed the approach end of the runway low, at about twenty feet, and everyone around me sucked in their breath. Even as the stricken airplane passed, it didn't seem to make a sound. A moment later, we heard the sound of engines easing into reverse to try to slow the plane. It broke the silence, and a cheer welled up from the crowd and enveloped the station.

I watched and waited until they had parked next to us. I was amazed the nose ski hadn't fallen off. Up close, I could see that it was dangling precariously at the end of a few thin hydraulic lines. When the engines had stopped and the hydraulic pressure fell to zero, the nose ski came completely undone and hit the ice with a thud that kicked up a shower of snow. I caught Scott's eye and gave him a thumbs-up as he sat in the cockpit unbuckling his seat belt. He smiled and returned my gesture, a tacit acknowledgment that was worth more to me than a pot of gold.

I thought about the significance of the flight as I walked back to Maintenance Control to fill out my paperwork. Scott and I had never been close or overly friendly, but an Antarctic misfortune had pushed us to overcome our differences and work together to conquer our own small corner of the world. We brought two crews and two planes home safely—we couldn't have asked for or expected any more from each other, and in the process we gained a mutual respect and trust.

Even on our regular routes, nothing was ever routine. A hundred miles out from the South Pole Station, I radioed the Pole HF radio operator for a weather update. It didn't look good. They were calling conditions partially obscured with an indefinite ceiling and a horizontal visibility at less than a mile. I reminded myself of the promise I made after last season: that I wasn't going to be a cowboy again this year. If the weather was as bad as the Pole radio operator was calling it, and I didn't have a shot at getting in, I'd turn around and head home, no glory-boy stunts.

But as we descended to search for the skiway, I quickly realized that I enjoyed going into poor weather—that I thrived on the challenge and had made a mistake by making myself a promise that I couldn't keep. I had to face the fact that I was an excitement junkie; at least, the fear wasn't ever boring. As long as we adhered to strict safety procedures, poor weather was just another obstacle that required a great deal of concentration to overcome.

As soon as we reduced power to descend, we were in the klag (pilot jargon for ugly weather, or overall cloud cover). The Pole's GCA and TACAN (a navigation aid that gives the pilot not only the azimuth but also the distance to the tramsmitter, TACAN was developed to aid pilots in locating their aircraft carriers in the 1950s) systems were both temporarily down, and there were no UHF or VHF communications established yet. So it was just us against the weather. Our only good news was that the Pole folks had dragged a chain across the length of the skiway that morning, so at least the skiway should be smooth.

Dave gave an excellent internal approach that lined us up with the approach end of the skiway. We descended to three hundred feet and continued inbound. At about half a mile out, I picked up the skiway panels, so I conned Tim in. Conning—another procedure that is a staple of Antarctic aviation—is used in conjunction with the polar backup. During an approach, while the pilot concentrates on flying the airplane on an exact course, as given by the navigator or the ground GCA controller, he or she listens for the crew's vital polar-backup input (airspeed, rate of descent, and so forth). This allows the pilot keep the plane on course by concentrating on the plane's flight director (a combination of attitude gyro and compass) while adjusting power to correct for airspeed deviations or the degree of descent, without having to keep cross-referencing his or her other flight instruments. By allowing the pilot to concentrate only on the plane's heading, conning allows the craft to fly a much more precise course over the ground. It is the copilot's job to stay "outside" the plane, looking for the field. As the plane gets closer to the ground, the copilot keeps looking for the skiway, staying "outside" while the pilot concentrates on flying a precise course "inside." Once a copilot acquires the field, he conns the pilot in to landing, by stating "easy left," "easy right," "come to a heading of," "begin decent," or "descend at" a particular rate—in this manner he guides the pilot through the landing procedure. Conning is integral to flying in Antarctica because of the lack of contrasts. If pilots were to look outside the plane during their approaches, they might become disoriented, so allowing copilots to conn them until the skiway is in full view assures that the pilots are always positively controlling their planes.

Tim's landing wasn't too rough, but we dipped when we touched down, as though one of the main landing struts had collapsed, and it was all Tim and I could do to keep the wings level as we stopped. Our problem became what to do now since we were listing badly to the right, with the outboard propeller spinning just inches off the ground. I felt it was safe to taxi clear of the skiway, so we did, slowly. Roy thought the intense cold here at the Pole must have affected O-rings in the strut, causing them to fail from the surge of hydraulic fluid when we touched down. Once we stopped, Roy went out to look at the starboard struts and confirmed that the forward strut had failed completely. He said it appeared that the hydraulic fluid had completely pissed out on impact so that the entire weight of the right side of the plane rested on the rear strut. He said the only thing he could do to remedy the situation out here was to try to balance the plane by shifting fuel between wing tanks after we unloaded.

Off-loading in the field is hell. It is loud; the noise coming from four turboprop engines whining at ground idle (minimal power on the engine) is deafening. The engines also produce contrails that blanket the area in a thick layer of fog. Because of these, visibility behind the aircraft today was limited to only two or three feet. So we sat in the pits, listing badly to the right and producing a thick, fast-moving fog only inches behind the exhaust pipes, as we tried to decide how best to off-load our cargo in such formidable conditions.

To add to our dilemma, Chris called up from the cargo deck to tell me that the plane's cargo door, which was normally held open by an up-lock, wouldn't stay in the up position because the lock was frozen open. Someone would have to stand in the doorway and hold the door open by using a switch located in the mouth of the ramp. This further complicated the off-load. The Caterpillar Tractor forklift was so large it afforded only a few inches clearance when the forks were inserted into the plane's cargo compartment. With someone standing in the doorway when the forks were in place in the cargo bay, with nearly zero visibility, the slightest false movement either way could be disastrous for the plane, the cargo, the forklift operator, or anyone standing in the cargo bay. Running an nine-ton Caterpiller into as large an object as a C-130 would not be pretty. Dave volunteered to man the cargo door "up" switch.

For every off-load at least one person had to stay in the cockpit to monitor the engines and be prepared to shut them down if there was an emergency. We also positioned a safety observer (usually the navigator) away from the unloading but still in a position to monitor the off-load. The safety observer stayed on the headset, in constant communication with the cockpit, and watched and coordinated between the loadmaster (who was off the headset) and the pilots. Since we couldn't see behind us, we counted on Dave to be our eyes in the rear of the plane and let us know what was going on.

Chris talked with the South Pole cargo director, and together they decided the best way to proceed was to turn on the high intensity loading lights and to position them so that they pointed out the back of the plane to act as fog lamps. This would give the forklift operator a visual guide. I didn't know the cargo director personally, but he appeared to me to be the perfect man for such a dangerous job. He possessed unbounded energy and seemed to be everywhere at once. He was covered head to toe: he was dressed in a one-piece, thickly insulated set of red coveralls and wore thick work gloves, and his face was always hidden behind two balaclavas, a pair of tinted ski goggles, and a floppy-eared hat that he tied under his chin. I could distinguish him only by his glowing red nose and ice-encrusted blond mustache.

Chris, Dave, and the Pole cargo director, all screaming to be heard over the noise of the engines, coordinated the efforts of two forklift operators. Visibility behind the plane was nil, perhaps two or three feet. To get in close enough to see the loading lights, the forklift operators had to maneuver their nine-ton tractors to within inches of the plane, without really being able to see anything. The three yelled, gesticulated wildly, and stopped often to reevaluate. Chris used a length of line tied to the back of the cargo compartment to walk the forklifts in inch by inch.

When Dave, positioned in the door, could see the forklift's loading lights through the fog, he would tug on the rope to signal Chris that the Caterpillar was in sight. Then everything stopped, and Chris repositioned himself between the forklift and the plane. From there he brought the Cat in to the cargo bay through a series of shouts and hand signals to the Pole's cargo director, who relayed the information to the forklift operators.

Just before the forks entered the plane, Chris moved up onto the cargo ramp, where he directed the final placement of the forks under the pallet. Once the forks were spotted (that is, in the correct position), the pallets were eased onto the waiting forks—the maneuver was like pushing a package into a friend's outstretched arms. After the load was adjusted, the huge machine lifted the load slightly, rumbled backward a few feet, lowered the load, and backed straight out. The whole operation had been a strange improvised dance.

The forklift operator had done an excellent job getting the forklift centered into the leaning mouth of the cargo compartment and then extracting the pallets without hitting the plane or Dave—all while moving cautiously through the dense, fast-moving fog and a bone-numbing 78-degrees-below-zero cold. In fine, clear weather, off-loads are challenging enough, but today, with the rear visibility just inches, it required intense concentration and extraordinary teamwork. To off-load three pallets generally takes twenty to thirty minutes; today it took us more than an hour to off-load two pallets.

After the successful off-load, while Roy leveled the plane as best he could by transferring fuel in the wing tanks, Tim and I walked thirty yards to the Ceremonial South Pole so Tim could take a photo of me. We were out of the plane for less than five minutes, but in the minus-78 temperature we were stiff and nearly frozen by the time we made it back to the warmth of the cockpit. It would have served me well to remember that our manuals classify anything below minus-40 centigrade, with only 6 to 10 knots of wind, as a class 5 wind chill—meaning that exposed flesh freezes in less than a minute. I concluded that those figures were absolutely correct.

We were outside maybe two or three minutes, and in that short time my camera case became so rigid I couldn't work the snaps. Our fingers stiffened and were nearly useless; even our pace was labored. In addition to subzero temperatures, there was an extremely low station pressure of 28.07 inches of mercury (standard sea-level pressure is 29.92 inches), which meant that we were at an effective altitude of over thirteen thousand feet. At altitudes above ten thousand feet the air becomes so thin that many people to have difficulty breathing. I'm lucky; altitude doesn't affect me. Roy, Chris, and Tim, however, had to go on supplemental oxygen to stave off the effects of altitude sickness before we taxied for takeoff.

The South Pole has been the ultimate conquest of hundreds of explorers and the goal of thousands of others over the past two centuries. As I waited for the crew to ready the plane to taxi, I thought of Capt. Robert Scott and his ill-fated expedition. Had he known the outcome, would he and his companions still have come? I was inclined to believe so, but I could only wonder about their mind-set when, on Tuesday, 16 January 1912, Scott wrote:

> The worst has happened, or nearly the worst. We marched well into the morning covered 7 ½ miles. Noon sight showed us in Lat. 89° 42' S. [within about fifteen miles from the Pole], and we started off in high spirits in the afternoon, feeling to-morrow would see us at our destination [the Pole]. About the second hour of the march Bowers' sharp eyes detected what he thought was a cairn; he was uneasy about it, but argued that it must be a sastrugus. Half an hour later he detected a black speck ahead. Soon we knew that this could not be a natural snow feature. We marched on, found that it was a black flag tied to a sledge bearer; near by the remains of a camp; sledge tracks and ski tracks going and coming and the clear trace of dogs' paws—many dogs. This told us the whole story. The Norwegians have forestalled us and are the first at the Pole. It is a terrible disappointment.[2]

What courage it took to make that trip under such arduous conditions, with such unending obstacles, only to experience the ultimate frustration of knowing that their dream of reaching the South Pole first would go unfulfilled. At least we could return to McMurdo in about three hours. Scott and his companions never did see their base at Cape Evans, seven miles from McMurdo, again.

Roy had done an outstanding job of balancing the fuel in the wings to offset the canter caused by the blown strut, and we taxied back to the end of the skiway. But we were forced to wait while the contrail that had formed over the skiway during our taxi cleared. After five minutes the visibility was good enough for us to see two thousand feet, so we started our takeoff slide. As soon as we had left the ground, we were swallowed by low clouds, so we climbed straight ahead for two miles to avoid becoming disoriented by the overcast.

While one day at South Pole Station the weather could offer absolutely horrid conditions to operate in, conditions the next day could be totally unpredictable. Our first two hours out of McMurdo, en route to the Pole, the entire Ross Ice Shelf and Transantarctic Range from the Beardmore to Byrd Glaciers was covered with a creamy pall. We saw nothing below us.

Once we were beyond Plunkett Point—that black, V-shaped mound of earth that is the last point we see prior to the vast, flat, white plain that is the polar plateau—the clouds simply stopped.[3] It was as if we had transcended our own physical world; we sat perched at the edge of the spiritual world, each minute a step closer to that ultimate reality.

The Pole weather was fantastic—clear with a sharply defined horizon and light winds, the temperature a balmy 15 below. It was warm enough for the station personnel to download the plane while wearing only light jackets, jeans, and tennis shoes. We worked without our jackets. We then taxied out and started our takeoff slide at midfield, becoming airborne after only twenty-five hundred feet. *Why,* I asked myself, *was yesterday nearly 80 below and today only 15?* I didn't know, but I liked the warming trend.

Good weather had a way of warming our spirits. The crew always seemed a little more cheerful on calm, clear, warm days. I was happy and felt that nothing at all could ruin a day like that. As we climbed, at about fifteen hundred feet, I had the 3P engage the autopilot. On the older model aircraft, like the one we were now flying, the autopilot has four switches—one each for controlling the rudder, ailerons, and elevator and a separate switch for altitude hold. Today, as the 3P engaged the altitude-hold function, the machine immediately pitched the plane down violently into a steep six-thousand-feet-per-minute dive toward the snow below. I grabbed for the yoke and thumbed the autopilot emergency disconnect.

So much for positive thoughts. The emergency disconnect button on the yoke immediately shuts off the autopilot. I hit that, and the plane was again under my control. I trimmed the plane as best I could, and after discussions with the copilot and engineer, we decided—in the interest of science—to fly a constant-power cruise climb profile all the way home, just to see how high we could get. For this particular profile we would let the plane climb as we burned fuel and became lighter.

With the low-pressure altitude in Antarctica we can climb much higher than we can in the States, so we thought we might try for a world record for Hercs, which is now somewhere around forty thousand feet. As we climbed through thirty-six thousand, I sensed how tough it was going to be to break the record. We had been climbing for two hours now at a hundred feet per minute and were still well off the mark. As we were up there in the rarefied atmosphere, it was as if we were floating on clouds. The normally noisy plane was nearly silent; with the nose pitched up we were hanging silently in space on the props. All around us was a ghostly white shroud of diaphanous stratus clouds. It was as if we were in a dream, floating serenely along the edge of sleep. We were left with the curving white Earth softly spreading out toward the horizon, an endless eternity of dreams.

We hit 37,750 before we ran out of steam—any higher and I would have had to jettison some of the crew. They seemed as interested in breaking the altitude record as I was, and they suggested that I be the one who was thrown out. That being an impossibility—I was the person who'd signed for the plane, and I'd be in serious trouble if I were not with it when it returned—we pointed the nose at the ground and sped up.

I pasted the airspeed counter on 270 knots, and the wind tore at the wings. We dropped like a rock. I leveled the wings to check our descent at four thousand feet. We were between Black and White Islands when the bottom dropped out. One second we were at four thousand feet, then in an instant two thousand feet and falling—we had been caught in a wind shear. We lost two thousand feet in less time than it takes to read this sentence. It felt like we were on an out-of-control elevator going down. I added maximum power and pitched the nose up to a takeoff attitude. At eight hundred feet we began to climb out from the shadows of the peaks of the two islands. It had happened so quickly I hadn't had the time to think or to be scared. At fifteen hundred feet I reduced power to cruise the remaining ten miles at 150 knots.

In the States pilots are taught the warning signs of an impending wind shear, but in Antarctica those warning signals are never evident. Today we had a visual on Willy Field at fifty miles, and there wasn't a cloud in the sky between us and them—no rolling plumes, no rotor clouds, no lenticular clouds spilling off the ice shelf, no preceding turbulence. Just *ba-boom*, and down we went. I was just glad we hadn't been at five hundred feet.

Winds at Willy were calm, so I lined up for a straight-in approach to skiway 15 and landed without further incident. After postflight I needed a cigarette and a beer. It just goes to show that even when the coast seems clear, the weather monster can still sneak up and kick your ass. All the clubs had already closed, so there was just one thing to do now: hit the chiefs' barracks. It was a den of debauchery. Chief petty officers are the backbone of the navy. They are the all-important middle managers who run the day-to-day business of getting things done. But when the chiefs are off-duty, they know how to have fun.

There is a special bond here in Antarctica between the officers and the enlisted personnel that is unique in the services. Together for six months, in close quarters in an extremely isolated location, sharing a difficult experience, we develop a special brand of trust, and we count on each other for our common survival. Tonight the chiefs' hut was rocking. There were twenty-five or thirty people stuffed into an eight-by-ten-foot room, swilling beer, sweating profusely while dancing to 1960s rock and roll and singing our lungs out, screaming at the silence that surrounded us outside.

My two favorite senior chiefs were there directing the party. They were in their element, so they decided to hold a kangaroo court. One started: "Senior McCurry, do my eyes deceive me, or does it look to you that Lieutenant Hinebaugh here could use a shave?" *I can't imagine why, since I've been up and at work for only eighteen hours now.*

Senior McCurry responded: "Senior Holleran [his troops loved him, but they also had a field day with his nickname, Hollern' Holleran], I was just about to mention that fact, but I couldn't believe that a refined gentleman like Lieutenant Hinebaugh would attend a fine affair like this without shaving first."

I stood bemused in the middle of the room, still in my flight suit. Senior Holleran said, as he inspected my face, "Well, I hate to do this to you, sir, but we'll have to find you guilty of not shaving before entering the chiefs' quarters. Fine is two [slight pause], no, three shots of Jack Daniel's. Step up to the bar, sir."

Chiefs are, as a whole, avuncular by nature, but Seniors McCurry and Holleran took it upon themselves to take excellent care of their maintenance troops. Additionally they took exceptionally good care of the junior officers assigned to lead them. It is a time-honored relationship between a junior officer and his or her chief; they either make it or fail together. During business hours we maintained a cordial yet respectful relationship. I was respected, called "sir," and treated like a prodigal son by the chiefs, even at 0430 in their darkened Hooch, drunk on Kiwi beers, singing "Louie Louie, I gotta go now."

•

We made as much of the holidays as we could. Just prior to Thanksgiving my crew and I had the privilege of spending three days in Christchurch and then bringing home the bacon, literally. We were flying in a supercargo of ten frozen hog carcasses—Mac Town's Thanksgiving pork. During the eight-hour flight home I thought a lot about the three days we had just passed in New Zealand. I had reveled in excess, overindulging in a spate of unadulterated debauchery. It felt good to let all the tension go, to stuff myself on whatever I wanted, to sleep in a comfortable bed, to have a hot shower that stayed hot for more than ten seconds, to find some solace in the darkness. Far from the Ice, I felt calm knowing that at least for these few days, Antarctica could do me no harm. I was safe from merciless weather, ignorant forecasters, and the danger that typified this season. I was rested and ready to return, even though a voice in my mind screamed, *Stay!*

As we approached the ice runway, I was surprised to actually have pleasant feelings about it—the weather was smooth and clear, the place seemed fresh and new to me again, like I was seeing it for the first time. Fifty miles from the runway an air force C-141 reported it was ten minutes behind us. Since these planes have no other option than to land on the ice runway, they get landing priority. If we landed first and crashed, they would have no place to go. If they crashed, we could just crank down the skis and land at Williams Field.

The tower called and asked us to circle the field for twenty minutes. Instead we circled the an active volcano Mt. Erebus. There was no plume rising from it today, so we were able to peer into its blackened bowels. The sides fell away quickly from the rim and dropped perhaps a thousand feet to what appeared to be a small blue-green lava lake. But we were impatient to deliver our cargo. We circled until the C-141 was on deck, and then, when the pilot was unable to stop the plane, we circled some more. Finally we were able to land on our next pass, just in time to save Thanksgiving. *Bon appétit, McMurdo.*

We postflighted quickly to catch the shuttle up to the Hill because today an important Antarctic event would take place—the Penguin Bowl Holiday Classic. I showered, dressed, met up with Sean; my helo buddy Berto Guerrero; and his roommate, John Adler. Together we commandeered a shuttle bus to Willy Field for the annual game. We brought champagne and became a tad unruly. Cindy, the shuttle driver, was unimpressed with our antics until I produced a bottle of bourbon she had requested from Christchurch. Nothing like a bribe to calm the natives—judging by her look and the hug she gave me as I handed her the bag, I'm sure she would have driven us to the Pole at that point.

We arrived about five minutes into the second quarter of the game. The Penguin Bowl is one of those long-standing and slightly suicidal traditions that seem to develop wherever military types are stationed. It's a full-contact, no-pads football game played entirely on ice, pitting our beefiest VXE-6 members against any and all comers. It seemed that this year, the all comers had practiced a little. At the close of the first quarter, the score was six to zero, against us.

Midway through the second quarter, they scored again. It wasn't looking good for us. Small fights started to break out on the field. Accusations about the use of ringers started to fly. But somehow the two sides played on. VXE-6 saw a thin ray of hope just before the half. A long bomb placed us on the one-inch line—an interesting line concept on a sheet of solid ice, where you're as likely to slide a touchdown as to run it. One inch later, a score. And the extra point was good. We retired to the officers' quarters at halftime, trailing by less than a touchdown. Now came the traditional beer and Knute Rockne speech.

Jubilant, we screamed our readiness for blood, glory, and victory! VXE-6 must ride the wave of past brilliance! In the twenty-odd years of Penguin Bowl history, VXE-6 had won all but one game. The present game had all the intensity of a classic Redskins-Cowboys rivalry.

We drank some more beer. Winning was our ichor, our tradition; we were invincible, we were winners, we were Penguins, damn it, and we would win again today. Our boys bravely staggered back onto the ice field for the second half, which commenced with a fumble recovery. One of our guys scooped the ball up midfield, then slid, slipped, and slogged his way toward our goal. He appeared to be running in slo-mo, muscling his way through the gelid, hail-like snow. Twenty-five feet from the goal, he slowed, raised his hands in a celebratory pose, and promptly dropped the frozen ball. We drank some more beer.

The pigskin stayed there for what seemed like an hour while everyone slogged upfield toward it, pumping steam from their noses like a stampede of moose on a frozen Maine pond. Finally a mass of groaning, swearing bodies piled on. VXE-6 lost the ball. We also lost the game. Final score: all-comers, eighteen; VXE-6, seven. We retired again to the officers' hut for medicinal beer, excuses, and chants of "Next year, next year!" Penguins may slip down, but they always get up again.

Thanksgiving, the meal, was something to behold. The fine china and silverware were brought out and dusted off, polished chafing dishes held steaming concoctions, and mess cooks, who usually looked like Cookie of *Beetle Bailey* fame, dressed up to look like haughty New York chefs. They were proud of the food they served this day, having prepared the meal so carefully that it made the many bad meals they produced all year fade like a bad dream. The cook who carved the steamship round and the turkey wore a fine, stiff-collared, white linen coat, a high chef's hat, and a charming smile. He nodded graciously as he cut and served our portions.

With the turkey and roast beef came all the trimmings: steamed shrimp with cocktail sauce, relish platters, cranberry sauce, stuffing, freshly baked rolls, assorted vegetables, mashed potatoes—the works. For dessert, there was pie: mincemeat pie, apple pie, cherry pie, key lime pie, and of course pumpkin pie, all with real whipped cream. The food even made palatable the hour's wait we spent trying to get at it.

Sean, two other friends, and I sat down to dinner with ravenous appetites and a few bottles of wine I had brought back from Christchurch. Our plates were piled high. Forty-five minutes later, we pushed away from the table and loosened our belts, stuffed but supremely satisfied. A short walk around town somewhat reduced the bloated condition that mysteriously comes upon me every Thanksgiving.

Before bed I met up with Sharon, one of our pilots, who gave me a detailed description of last night's annual king and queen ceremony. On Thanksgiving eve, this strange ceremony traditionally takes place at Willy Tavern, the drinking establishment for Willy residents who don't wish to come to the Hill for drink or entertainment. "Ice couples" cross-dress, parade their wares, expose their alter egos, flirt with the audience, and do whatever they deem necessary to win the title "King and Queen of the Ice."

The squadron members had thought that Sharon and her partner were a shoo-in. Sharon was statuesque and well-proportioned—a fine example of womanhood, with clean, smooth lines and extremely short hair. Her partner was also tall, with long, flowing tresses braided into two Heidi-like pigtails. Sharon had worn pants, a thick coat, boots, and sunglasses. Her partner had worn a grass skirt and sported coconut shells for a brassiere. From her report, they had been in the running until the end, when a second couple outperformed them with an on-stage display too lurid to mention here.

Tonight's brief was pushed back three times because of leaks, seeps, cracks, chips, and malfunctioning or missing parts. Then, just when it seemed we would never see the plane ready, I received a call saying that we could indeed give it a go. By the time I arrived the plane was fueled, loaded, and ready. I had the copilots call for a weather forecast (it was reported to be fine) and then file a flight plan as I looked over the aircraft discrepancy book. I often wondered if people would drive their cars if there were as many things wrong with the vehicles as we did with these planes.

All the planes were air-worthy, and the majority of gripes were minor, but I will always remember the look on the face of one of the scientists one day as he watched me paging through the ADB and asked me what all the pink slips were. I explained that they represented problems with the plane that had yet to be fixed. With a look of incredulity he asked, "Do you really think we should go flying with so many?"

I don't think I assuaged his fear any by responding, "Sure, we all gotta go some time."

Our flight to CASERTZ today was more boring than usual. Just beyond Minna Bluff, the ice shelf was covered with a layer of clouds at five thousand feet—nothing to see today. At sixty miles out of CASERTZ, Dave reported the field on radar as we let down into the clouds. At twenty-five miles he had picked out the skiway and begun to give us headings to align us. At two thousand feet above the ground we still were socked in. We let down to one thousand feet and began to pick up some surface definition. The weather briefing had the surface and horizon definitions (gained directly from the camp personnel in this case) as being fair and fair, which may have been the case six hours ago, but now it was tough to see any definition at all. At seven miles, aligned with the runway I could begin to make out the blurry outline of the camp on the horizon. We lowered the flaps and then the gear and ran through the landing checklist. At three miles and three hundred feet I was just able to make out the red and green flags that defined the skiway, but it wasn't until we were over the threshold at fifty feet that I could finally make out the windblown surface of the skiway. Just another day at the office.

Our cargo for the day consisted of three pallets and some loose-loaded items on the ramp.[4] My training loadmaster asked if she could lower the ramp as we taxied in; since this was generally considered standard operating procedure (SOP), I gave her the go-ahead. As we taxied, she asked what I planned to do with the loose load. I explained that I wanted it to go off with the other stuff: when we drifted the other cargo, we would place the loose load with it.[5] I thought I heard a barely audible "Uh-oh." But I wasn't sure, so I kept quiet.

Once we were in the pit area, I had her drift the cargo, which is SOP— we stop, unshackle the pallets, and lower the ramp so that as we add power, the pallets slide gently backward, down off the ramp and into the snow. After we had completed the drift, my regular loadmaster, Chris, came back on the headset (he had been off ICS, setting up for the off-load and trusting his trainee to pass on communiqués from the cockpit) and asked if I wanted to leave the loose load where it was. I told him I had instructed that it was to be put out with the three pallets. He responded that the trainee had told him that I wanted it thrown out as we opened up the back end— which meant that the loose load was probably scattered on the skiway. I had to laugh. It was an "Uh-oh" I had heard, after all. I kept wondering when she was going to tell me, or maybe she was going to let me find out for myself because I was just about to taxi over it.

I stopped the plane, and we all went over to move the stuff. I was seriously nonplused with the support staff here. While we were transferring dozens of boxes, hoses, and frozen food across the snow, this Bozo from the camp drove by on a skidoo with a sled. He didn't even attempt to help; he just stopped and watched us. I motioned him over and told him to load his sled with as much as he could, ferry it to the main building, and then return to get what remained. I explained we were in a hurry because we were short on fuel and needed to get going. He shouted that he'd need to get permission to help. I nearly throttled him. I promised I would speak to the camp manager on the radio as we taxied out and explain to him that

I had enlisted his service, and I promised I would make sure the manager was onboard with my plan. I kept thinking of what I'd heard last year about the CASERTZ people: they were indeed "the first to complain, the last to help."

While we burned time transferring the loose load, the weather continued to drop, compelling us to make quick preparations to depart before we were forced to stay overnight. By the time we were ready to take off, the winds were so strong that we had a slight problem staying on centerline, and once we rotated, we were fighting for our lives staring at the cold-faced instruments and trying not to develop vertigo. We raised the gear and flaps as we passed fifteen hundred feet above the ground. No use taking chances changing the flight characteristics of the plane when another pilot was fighting just to keep the thing flying. At three thousand feet the clouds began to thin again to the point where I could see patches of blue. By five thousand feet we were breathing a collective sigh of relief, staring into the sapphire emptiness of space.

The return trip was uneventful until we hit Black Island, where we ran into every pilot's nightmare, wind shear. We had descended to five thousand feet when suddenly we were hit by the violent downdraft and stopped our descent after a three-thousand-foot drop. As we approached the field, tower changed runways on us, forcing us to fly down Main Street Willy at three hundred feet. It was a special wake-up call for all those late risers. I was personally glad we had the extra flight time; it gave my flight suit an extra few minutes to dry.

At the Hooch the crew made a beeline to my room for nightcap shots of Rebel Yell, before breakfast. The last few days had been extremely challenging to us as a crew, so I thought a small celebration of our being alive and intact would do us good. A few shots later and feeling no pain, and considering that this was our "nighttime," I shouldn't have been bothered by the fact that it was 0730 to the rest of the station. I usually hated to be in the bathroom with all those freshly awakened and shaved faces, especially when I was so bleary-eyed and reeking of whiskey. However, this morning it was sinfully delightful. I felt we deserved to experience that intangible sense of absolute freedom and total self-indulgence by drinking in the morning. It was a wonderful, euphoric feeling of release. What the hell. We had earned it. Our morning drinking could become ugly, I thought briefly as I drained a vodka-grapefruit with my omelet. But after surviving a wind shear of that magnitude, I felt that we had earned the right to drink whenever we wanted.

As I look back, aside from exercise in the small gym, drinking was basically our only outlet. There were a number of workshops, classes, and projects that folks here could participate in, but all these activities were conducted during regular hours, usually in the evening. An air crew's schedule was so erratic that we could never have attended any of these classes on any kind of routine basis. That left us with the gym, drinking, and the occasional video for our recreation. And after a hard day at the office, too few to us took to the gym instead of a pop-top can. I should know.

9

ICE FOLLIES

In early December there is always an abrupt change in the weather in Antarctica. The incessant, bone-chilling winds ebb to near-calm, and the temperature starts to climb above zero. Initially everyone around the station felt it was an eerie and uneasy time, and we trod softly to prevent any unrest among the weather gods. No one wanted those winds unleashed again. By mid-December, however, the low clouds had begun to burn off, giving way to a constant bright blue sky. As long as the weather remained good, the station folk were cheery, and McMurdo took on a whole new look—scrubbed, trimmed, and starched, ready for a first date. I, on the other hand, never trusted the weather and felt that these patches of mildness were too good to be true. As a cautious optimist I enjoyed the balmy weather; as a pessimist I waited for the clouds and winds to return.

With the warmth, getting to the runway became yet another peculiar entertainment for us. The trip, which normally took fifteen minutes, now took more than thirty. The ice road to the runway was melting. The jacked-up four-wheel-drive vans that ferried us to and fro were up to their doors in water, and those doors are two and a half feet off the ground. Wide cracks developed in the ice, making the drive nerve-wracking as well as treacherous. The rough landings we sometimes experienced seemed mild compared to the bus rides. They were scary, frustrating, and inconvenient—perfect Antarctic amusement.

When the vans couldn't make the trip because of the water, we were ferried out to the runway in Deltas. These beasts sported eight-foot tires, looked like a land-crawler from *Star Wars,* and had a separate passenger cabin that was not only cold but poised so high above the frame that when the machine pitched to one side, those individuals sitting on the up-side of the pitch were thrown across the aisle and landed in the laps of the down-siders.

But even this wasn't enough: some people took this daily ride to even greater heights. One day a cargo strap was found looped around the passenger cabin of one of the deltas. Out on the snow road a new sport was invented—delta surfing. The idea was to see how long you could ride strapped to the fifteen-foot-high, heaving and pitching roof of the delta.

And we had more to come. As we departed McMurdo for a Pole run one day, I carried with me a video camera for my running documentary. We flew parallel to the Transantarctic Mountains until we passed over Minna Bluff, about eighty miles out. From there, the mountains curve away rapidly to the east like an inverted *C* before slicing back toward the Pole. At our papa 1 position—our mandatory radio reporting point a hundred miles out from McMurdo—we were adjacent to the Byrd Glacier. From here, the mountains continue winding along to the Beardmore Glacier. In clear weather Pole flights are blessed with unparalleled views of this majestic, virgin range. Today, because I had a camera with me (for one day only), the mountains were covered with low, dense clouds.

The Pole, at least, was crystal clear. To my surprise another plane was just about to take off as we approached. I decided to tape their takeoff from the air. I was in the right seat and took the controls while the third pilot was in the left seat with the video camera. I descended to a hundred feet and flew down the right side of the skiway just as the second plane started its takeoff slide. It was beautiful, a once-in-a-lifetime shot. As we flew by at 180 knots, the other aircraft was climbing out at 130; no more than three or four wing tips (about two hundred feet) separated our planes as we roared past a hundred feet above and off the other plane's right side—definitely a Kodak moment. I was pleased as punch at the thought of having all this on film until I reviewed the tape: it hadn't been recorded. The 3P had left the pause button on.

At the Pole, we downloaded our load of fuel and then, to make up for missing the takeoff shot, I had a member of the crew videotape me at the Pole. We were just starting for the Ceremonial Pole when we learned of an earth-shaking event that caused us both to do an abrupt about-face and proceed to the "dome" (the geodesic dome that covers the majority of the South Pole Station's buildings): the Pole staff had received their annual batch of seasonal T-shirts. No time for filming now—it was the day to pick up our yearly, all-important souvenirs.

When the off-load was completed, we departed. The skiway at the South Pole Station was finally back in fantastic shape. No melting here. Just a smooth, flat, and fast runway. I had my off-duty copilot film the take-off. He continued to film as I gained some altitude, performed a 90-degree turn to the right, followed it immediately with a 270-degree turn to the left, dropped to two hundred feet, and accelerated to 250 knots. This positioned the plane for a thrilling high-speed, low-altitude pass of the South Pole Station. It looked great on video!

At the Beardmore Glacier we dropped down over Plunkett Point to shoot some low-level video of the Beardmore. It was a fine day to run down through the glacier, clear and calm. At times, down low like this, the katabatic winds can really kick you around as they come spilling down unimpeded, off the polar plateau on their way to the ice shelf. The glaciers act as natural funnels for these winds, like a sluice or an open floodgate in a dam. But today it was wonderful. With no chop, the plane acted as if it were flying on its own.

We crossed the mouth of the Mill Glacier and ran headlong at Mt. Patrick. I added power and scaled its peak to videotape the site of an old UH-1N helicopter that had crashed there.

I dropped down the backside of the mountain into the Endura Glacier and then rounded a corner to join the mighty Beardmore once again. Flying down the Beardmore proper, we crossed a long parallel series of sastrugi. At a distance these formations blended to give an appearance of waves on a smooth, frozen river. But up close, as we stared down from our aircraft, the sastrugi created the appearance that the ice had been run over with a rototiller. The surface was a mangled plot of wild, gleaming waves, caught frozen in midbreak, collapsing on themselves or marking the open mouth of a black, bottomless crevasse. This was the same nightmarish ground the Scott party had found themselves in on their trek to and from the Pole.

There were times when it seemed almost impossible to find a way out of the awful turmoil in which we found ourselves. At length, arguing that there must be a way on our left, we plunged in that direction. It got worse, harder, more icy and crevassed. We could not manage our skis and pulled on foot, falling into crevasses every minute—most luckily no bad accident. At length we saw a smoother slope toward the land, pushed for it, but knew it was a woefully long way from us. The turmoil changed character, irregular crevassed surface giving way to huge chasms, closely packed and most difficult to cross. It was very heavy work, but we had grown desperate. We won through at 10 P.M. and I write after 12 hours on the march. I think we are on or about the right track now.

—Robert Falcon Scott, Sunday, 11 February 1912

At the base of the Beardmore we passed the lonely snow-free peak that many people would recognize as the model for the Prudential rock. Today the sun bathed this massive chunk of granite in a warm, soothing shade of coral. I wondered if this was the same color Scott saw after his desperate encounter with the Beardmore. It had probably looked blood-red to him.

We climbed back to altitude over the inverted bowl of sugar-white snow that was Mt. Bell and headed home. After we had given our papa 1 position report, we were informed by Mac Center that we should report to Willy Field to do some flying scenes for an upcoming IMAX movie on Antarctica. At thirty miles I spotted the film crew's helo, positioned to the left of the skiway. We called on a discreet frequency, and they said they were ready to start filming.

I came in hot, 250 knots and 110,000 pounds of burning Herc. As I passed overhead, I pulled power to flight idle and wrapped the bird up in a tight 60-degree angle of bank turn and pulled hard on the yoke. In the navy this maneuver is known as the carrier break. The crew performed a rebel yell of delight. This one was for Hollywood. We lowered the flaps and gear, and I made perhaps the best landing of my life.

On deck I taxied back to the approach end and waited. The helo slowly circled our plane as the film crew worked. Once they were in position on our starboard side, we were given the thumbs-up. I gave it the gas and commenced my takeoff slide, the helo following and filming. I rotated the nose and skied to a perfect takeoff—at least I thought it was perfect, but we did a number of takes at the skiway just to be sure.

After forty-five minutes we flew to the ice runway, where the crew wanted to shoot a wheeled takeoff with the Herc heading right for them. It took only a few seconds and was nothing special, a normal takeoff. I later saw the final IMAX film: they used a three-second shot of one of the normal wheeled takeoffs. *Heigh-ho.*

The shuttle-bus ride home was even more exciting than the one out had been. At the transition between the land and the ice, a mere fifty feet from the shore, the bus driver slid off the narrow bridge and stuck fast in the slushy ice. We all piled out to help; we pushed, we rocked the damned thing back and forth, we gave each other advice, until finally in midpush the tires caught, showering me in ice water, much to the delight of the crew and other passengers. Drenched, I elected to walk the remaining quarter mile to my barracks, as soggy as my water-logged spirits.

I showered (scalded, actually) and went in search of yet more entertainment: mail. What I found was definitely not what I was looking for: a memo from the station manager stating that it had come to his attention that an LC-130 (me) had been spotted in an SSSI (Sites of Special Scientific Interest—areas that no one was supposed to traverse so they could remain pure for later exploration) a few days ago. He was calling for heads to roll. The memo was initialed by my whole damned chain of command: the CO, XO, and Ops O (operations officer). They had all seen it and were looking for blood from you-know-who.

I called Dave and showed him the memo. We studied the charts desperately, trying to piece together how we had made such a blunder and how we were going to save our asses. More importantly, we conferred over how to find out who squealed. An hour later, armed with a bundle of charts, we sheepishly knocked on the Ops O's door, thinking we had a fairly logical explanation for the snafu. He took one look at the memo and his face twitched: he hadn't seen or initialed the document. We'd been had. We grabbed the memo and beat a hasty retreat, furious to find ourselves the brunt of a cruel but clever practical joke. *Oh, yes. It was time for revenge.*

An inventory of our flight crew pointed to only one conclusion: it had to have been our sometime copilot, Bob. He had spilled the beans on numerous occasions to his practical-joker roommate, Kent (a nefarious helo pilot), and this was too big a story for him to keep secret.

We found him and Kent in their room. I put on a worried face. Shaking my head, I lamented about how we, as a crew, were going to get screwed. We were going to face formal charges over the violation of SSSI airspace. I said it looked like we would be sent back to the States to be summarily discharged. Dave stood by, looking utterly furious—he was quite convincing. He commented that he wasn't going to lose his career over some ill-informed idiot and their loose tongue. We made it quite clear that if we ever found out who did this to us, we would be merciless in our retaliation. Kent suddenly excused himself from the room. Dave and I exchanged a quick glance—we had taken a shot, and it turned out to be right. Kent hot-footed it to the skipper's room to explain the practical joke. When he emerged, red-faced, we were all there to meet him.

He had thrown a boomerang, and it came back on him. We threatened that there would be no next time or we would kick his ass, then pack him. Generally reserved for fingies, packing was the informal initiation to Antarctica. Although the ritual had been officially banned years ago, it was still widely practiced covertly by the enlisted guys, so we knew we too could get away with it if necessary. Packing entailed catching the individuals unawares, taping their arms and legs, and then packing them in the snow. How long they were left depended on what transgression they had committed. Our humiliation wouldn't have been satisfied by any less than fifteen minutes.

I was scheduled to take the first flight of the week, Monday morning at 0001 (military midnight), so our brief was two hours prior at 2200 Sunday night. With a couple of hours to kill after dinner, I wandered down to one of this year's main attractions; a diver's viewing tube stuck through the ice of McMurdo Sound. The weather was delightful for a walk, cool and crisp like a New England fall day, with a slight but steady breeze at my back that seemed to coax me gently along. I took the road that led from the back doors of 155 straight down to the sound.

Out on the ice of the McMurdo Sound, at the base of Observation Hill, I casually looked over my shoulder toward Mac Town and was somewhat surprised by my unique perspective of the station. I was so used to looking down on it from the air that it was strange to be staring up at it from sea level. From the ice it looked like a pulp mill with steam rising from every building. The incessant hum of the generators sounded like muted buzz saws. The only thing missing was timber.

The viewing tube was forty feet below the two-foot thick ice of the sound, about half a mile from McMurdo Station. As I made my way along the snowmobile tracks that led to the tube, I ran into some friends who were in the process of locking for the evening the grate that sealed the tube. They gave me the key instead.

It was a very narrow tube, barely large enough for me to cram my six-foot-four, two-hundred-twenty-five-pound frame into. It was only with a great deal of difficulty and wriggling on my part that I was able to squeeze through the cramped confines as my shoulders scraped either side. Descending was a chore because the rungs stuck out eight or ten inches from the wall at an unusual angle. My legs were almost too long to allow me to bend at the knee and free my toes from one rung before my heel dug into the far wall and my knee caught up on the rung above. The last five steps were a rope ladder. On it I could push away from the walls of the tube and climb down more comfortably. At the bottom I wedged myself into the cramped space as best I could and bent over to stare out the windows into the unknown. The windows were small, about a foot square, but still afforded a 360-degree view. The clarity of the water was astonishing. I could see perhaps a hundred yards; farther vision was limited only by darkness.

The bottom of the ice was rough, an irregular washboard of randomly spaced stalactites, all smeared with a coating of a gooey green-brown algae. The few bare spots let in just enough light to give a spectacular but somewhat spectral view of the sea life, both benthic and pelagic, beneath the ice.

Small, pale white, almost clear fish congregated near the surface, rough-housing among the algae. Intermixed with the fish were a large variety of krill, shrimp-like creatures considered to be the base of the oceanic food chain. All these animals (none more than two or three inches long) lazed in the upper foot below the ice "penthouse."

As my eyes became accustomed to the murky twilight, I began to make out small images floating by the chamber. Weird wormlike jellyfish, delicate spiny starfish, an inch-long protozoal ctenophore, and a quarter-inch urn-shaped hydromedusa—the latter two using their undulating motility organs to propel themselves through the frigid water. Many more tiny life-forms floated by, so unusual that they don't bear description, all bobbing serenely along or staying in place with a flick of a tail, fin, pseudopod, or claw.

The bottom was littered with detritus, covered with what looked like large pinecones. Several pieces of pale white coral and brittle star poked through the muck to lend an interesting counterpoint to the relatively even covering. Groups of small red starfish lay akimbo, half on, half off each other as if they were trying to stay warm. Slender-stalked plants and hydroids wafted with the flow of the gentle, nutrient-rich current.

The most spectacular detail, however, was not what I saw. It was what I heard. Out there in the darkness, surrounding me, monstrous Weddell seals produced a haunting melody. A midrange, sonorous tone gave way to a constantly descending pitch that lowered to an unbelievably low bass note, which itself faded to below what human ears could hear. The sound would hit its nadir, then ascend again till it reached a shrill pitch, then suddenly stop, leaving me in an eerie silence. I likened the sound to the tuning of an AM radio to a far-off station.

Just as I was lulled by these descending and ascending tones, they halted abruptly, interrupted by a series of sharp chirps and then a long progression of clicks. I sat for over an hour, enchanted, listening to these other-worldly conversations, peering hard into the blackness and hoping for a sight of a seal, penguin, or whale. I realized I was becoming numb when I scratched my leg and couldn't feel my fingers. Any longer exposure, and I might not have the energy to climb out. I shook some blood back into my fingers and put my hands inside my coat to warm them under my armpits. I would need every bit of strength in my hands to get out of there.

My ascent was even worse than my descent. My legs were simply too long to climb out; I couldn't bend my knee enough to lift up to the next rung. I had to struggle and contort myself to climb, lifting most of my weight with my arms. At about the first third of my climb, I felt sure I was going to wedge myself in, stuck to slowly die in a freezing tube a mile from town. I was convinced I wouldn't be found till the next day because I had been unutterably stupid. I had broken the primary rule of Antarctic travel: always, always, always let someone know where you are going and when you plan to be back.

I had no desire to wait for the next set of adventurers to happen by and find me in such dire yet laughable circumstances. Unwilling to die of exposure and embarrassment, I tapped into my last reserves and pulled myself up with my remaining strength, hand over hand, until my arms trembled from the exertion. Finally I reached the top, where I chinned myself free using the rim of the tube as a bar. I lay on a pile of snow next to the tubes, mouth breathing hard for several minutes in the brilliant sun of the Antarctic night and hoping that no one had witnessed my stunt. It's one thing to write and to laugh about these events years later over a beer, but at the time the last thing I wanted was to be the brunt of a squadron joke.

I walked home ruefully shaking my head over my stupidity. It was a good reminder for me, however. No matter how long you've been in Antarctica, and no matter how much you think you know about it, it is not a place where you can ever take anything for granted.

A few days later I had another nature-observation opportunity. Just after a brunch of a reconstituted-egg omelet, orange juice, and toast, I worked my way to the back of a crowd assembled around a visiting admiral. His speech was oddly familiar: "You're all doing the best job in the navy; we have every confidence in you," and so on, and so on. Another officer on a junket to the South Pole, somebody else who had found his way to the adventure of a lifetime, namely, spending three days in the VIP suite on base, with maybe a "fact-finding" tour of New Zealand thrown in.

Preferring a genuine mammal to this career animal, I opted for a shuttle ride to Scott Base for a photo opportunity with a newly arrived complement of Weddell seals. From McMurdo to Scott Base one travels a volcanic ash–covered road that winds up around Observation Hill and through a gap in Hut Point Peninsula, the rocky arm that stretches from Mt. Erebus. From that rise at the height of the gap, a mile away, out on the ice, I could discern the black outlines of a dozen seals, dozing in spread-out groups. Near the shore were the half a dozen lime-green buildings that constituted the Kiwis' presence on the Ice. I asked to be dropped by the first flag that marked the path to the seal herd. Each year when the Weddells arrive, the Kiwis scout and mark a route on safe ice to enable the rest of us to take a few once-in-a-lifetime photos.

As I approached the first group of slumbering seals, I was in awe. In a moment I felt a part of the natural world, not just an observer. These unique creatures have lived here for tens of thousands of years, unchanged and unchallenged by man. They showed no fear and little interest, dismissing me as if I were just another (albeit skinny) seal instead of an intruder. A few exerted just enough energy to lift a head and stare at me, but most ignored me and continued to nap.

These behemoths are gentle creatures, ten to fifteen feet long and well-larded, the largest weighing several tons. Sidling up to one of these blubberous creatures is exhilarating, like standing next to an elephant. It is difficult to imagine something so large yet so docile. I felt safe enough to actually pet one lightly on the top of the head. She made a sharp, barking sound, sniffed, and then rolled toward me. I nearly jumped out of my skin. But she simply rolled onto her back and extended her flippers as though she wanted a belly rub. It was tempting to try, but you don't mess around with two tons of seal. I opted to move on.

Most of the seals had smooth, dense, dirty brown coats, while some were flecked with white to create a mottled covering for their six inches or more of blubber. They all had massive brown eyes, the kind of eyes that greeting-card makers love to put on sappy, sentimental cards. The seals obviously enjoyed lounging in the sun, but with their great body mass, they seemed out of place on land, like beached whales.

The air surrounding me was filled with snorts, snores, and rasping, throaty barks, a sharp contrast to the eerie sounds I heard these same creatures make under water. In the water their sounds were mellifluous, flowing, almost ethereal, but here on land their noises sounded like hoarse dogs.

While I was there, I had been videotaping sporadically, hoping to edit down what I had into some kind of mini-Antarctic tour. Later that afternoon I met with a buddy named Kent, who had video-editing equipment in his room (you would be amazed what people fly in with them). I began the editing session with optimism and ended it with far-increased respect for the great film directors of our day, because what I ended up with was not the smoothly flowing piece I envisioned but a choppy compilation of bits and pieces my two-year-old nephew, Adam, could have bettered.

I skipped dinner that evening to attend the annual Ross Island Art Show. Resident artists spend free evenings producing stained-glass windows, photographs, drawings, paintings, jewelry, and so forth, all with an Antarctic theme. It was a festive evening with all the trappings that could be mustered: wine, cheese, mixed nuts, and the lilting strains of taped classical music. Bach, what else?

As I wandered through the exhibits, I mused on just how different things were now from what they were in those early days of Antarctic exploration. Here I was at an art show, sipping wine, hobnobbing with the hoi polloi of Antarctica, while not long ago in Scott's hut at Hut Point, Herbert Ponting was giving lantern-slide lectures on exotic places here that he had traveled to and photographed.[1] Could Scott's men have joined us this evening, I wondered if they would have been shocked at our calm, civilized existence on the edge of this unconquerable wilderness.

I had the day off. I went to the bathroom, wearing only gym shorts and a T-shirt, and returned to my room to find that the door was locked. Sean had removed the tape on our door (everyone kept pieces of tape over the spring mechanisms that kept the doors latched so that we only had the dead bolts to lock and unlock) and gone out. He must have had a good reason, but I sure as hell couldn't think what it was. I hoped it was worth dying for, I mused, because the next time I saw him, I would kill him. Meanwhile, I was locked out.

Now, I must admit that I was somewhat bemused, standing there in my shorts and T-shirt and starting to feel the cold. What a classic. Someday this will be funny, I told myself. I couldn't go downstairs and ask for the spare key because I had foolishly neglected to turn mine in when the chance to have duplicates made was offered. There was no duplicate. So I opted to enter via the ceiling panels.

Before you make any snap judgments (like "What a cement head!"), know that I had been *forced* into this same situation a number of times in a different room the past season and had performed this same maneuver with such frequency that I had refined the technique. In fact, I felt I was the resident expert on ceiling entries. So I borrowed a chair (as I had always done) from my navigator, Ed, then removed the eight-foot-high drop-ceiling tile just above my doorjamb. The chair wasn't quite high enough for me to pull myself over the top of the jamb, a fact necessitating that I improvise with some additional boxes. Stacking the boxes on top of one another, I was able to wriggle through the drop-ceiling cross-bars, hang over the doorjamb, and unlock the door. Mission complete.

Except there I hung, suspended over the doorjamb, when I found I was unable to get back down onto my boxes. It couldn't be true, but it was. I was stuck. Naturally, at this point I drew some attention. Ed suggested helpfully that he "go get someone." But I wasn't about to be the laughing-stock of McMurdo. I could just imagine the jokes—"Yeah, you should have seen this geek bent over that doorjamb and stuck like a squealing pig." The story would spread through Mac Town like a windblown fire through a California hillside, only faster. I imagined, years later, when I would have to go before a congressional committee to be sworn in as the director of the National Stupid Acts Board. "So tell this committee, Mr. Hinebaugh, about your experiences with doorjambs in Antarctica." And "Oh, by the way, can you do any silly walks?"

I struggled like a banshee but was unable to free myself. Twist one way, and I burned myself on a hot water pipe; another, and I'd rip my legs to pieces on the bare metal edges of the doorjamb. So I hung there. Finally I got the idea that if perhaps three boxes were stacked below me, I might be able to wriggle over the doorjamb down onto the top box so that, if nothing else, I would fall from a lower height. Sure, I might snap my neck in two places rather than three, but if I was crippled, at least I would have done it my way.

Ignoring the pain from the hot-water line, I was able to twist around and lower myself onto the top box, then slowly turn around, and hop down—whereupon I immediately acted completely nonchalant, ignoring the six five-inch-long parallel bruises across my thighs and a third-degree burn along most of my left side, which had come in contact with the hot-water line. What was a little permanent disfigurement compared to the suf-fering of peer humiliation? At least I was back in my room now. I got com-fortable and settled in to wait for Sean.

10

OVER A

FROZEN EDEN

Mt. Patrick is the most prominent peak on the western side of the Beard-more Glacier. It rises vertically from the glacier's floor to over fourteen thousand feet. I loved flying over this area. Atop Mt. Patrick is a crashed helo that had been flying in support of a nearby camp. While trying to hover at thirteen thousand feet (the helo's maximum operating altitude at its maximum weight), it strained under the load, settled, and rolled over on its side as the rotor blades tore into the ground. Those aboard the helo were lucky. All hands survived. The wreck is still visible, partly covered with windblown snow.

Flying two hundred feet above the mountain top and then dropping over that sheer sidewall, heading for the glacier floor, I felt as though we were racing the mountain itself. From just above the peak, I would descend ten thousand feet down an ice falls, "burying"—going to the full extent of—the vertical speed indicator (VSI) at a rate of six thousand feet per minute. Still, the mountain sloped away more steeply than we could descend. I slowed as we passed a thousand feet above the ground; then I leveled off at two hundred feet above the glacier floor. We wheeled just above the ice floes, bouncing slightly from the updrafts, our spirits soaring.

The Beardmore Glacier is the second largest on the continent and sup-posedly the most active, moving up to fourteen meters a day. Ernest Shack-leton and Robert Scott both used the Beardmore route on their quests for the Pole. In appearance, the glacier is marred by huge floes of active ice and monstrous crevasses large enough to swallow several Hercs, while other sections look like quarter-mile chunks of blue cheese. Most of the glacier appears as long blue-gray bands of ice, each forty to fifty miles long. This active ice inches its way, serpentine, on a two-hundred-mile journey from the snows of the polar plateau to the Ross Ice Shelf.

On the eastern side of the glacier, colossal mountains shoot up, with Mts. Kirkpatrick, Howe, and Bell stretching skyward to over fourteen thousand feet. Here in the Beardmore valley, stunning contrasts appear in a limited range of colors. The mountains lining the glacier are a study in vibrant but yet subtle shades of brown and white; light shades of brown, some nearly yellow, dulled to tan and beige, while other striations offered a vibrant counterpoint in deep chocolate brown that faded into a coal black, as if the mountain had been smeared with tar sludge.

On the slopes free of snow, exposed striations in the rock tell the mountains' life story to the trained eye. Geologists read these striations like a book, each band of lines another million-year chapter. These banded chapters rise ladderlike from the base of the glacier upward, culminating in snow-capped peaks and ridges. The mountain peaks vary widely in their appearance—some are crested with steep pinnacles or sharp precipices, others rounded and snow-capped. They reduce a large airplane to the insignificance of a gnat.

On low-level runs I never had much to say, since I always felt tiny and overwhelmed by the imposing size and complete isolation of this frozen land. As we flew, it was easy to see what Richard Byrd meant when he suggested that "This vast and secret land could only be approached and inhabited—it could never be mastered—even by the most advanced technology of any given time."[1] Anyone traveling here will understand what Byrd believed—that man will never gain anything more than a tenuous foothold in Antarctica. It is too vast an area to be conquered without tremendous support, not to mention the impossible task of dealing with the ever-changing weather.

On flights to CASERTZ over the Ross Ice Shelf, staring down at the vast plain of ice that stretched out for hundreds of miles below us, I would always be struck by the thought that nothing could be worse than to be stuck there. The entire Ross Ice Shelf is flat and littered with crevasses.

There are no cover, no landmarks, no food, and no water unless you have fuel to melt the snow. Here Scott and his men froze to death, waiting for a Herbie to blow over.

At times like this, hovering above that same desolate place, I could almost feel the desperation that must have haunted Scott and his men. The explorer wrote as the next-to-last entry in his journal: "*Thursday, March 29. Since the 21st we have had a continuous gale from WSW and SW. We had fuel to make two cups of tea apiece and bare food for two days on the 20th. Every day we have been ready to start for our depôt 11 miles away, but outside the door of the tent it remains a scene of whirling drift. I do not think we can hope for any better things now. We shall stick it out to the end, but we are getting weaker, of course, and the end cannot be far. It seems a pity, but I do not think I can write more.*"[2] My greatest fear while flying in Antarctica was that we might be forced down on the continent and have to endure similar consequences. I did everything I could to ensure that didn't happen.

CASERTZ is located in Marie Byrd Land, which borders the ice shelf. At altitude it all looks exactly the same, absolutely flat and uniformly white. Near CASERTZ the landscape changes from flat white to a tangled mass of foot-high sastrugi. These low mounds are sharpened on the downwind side and look like pointy rows of frozen waves on a frosty sea.

The weather at CASERTZ is generally poor. There were times when I'd circle the camp straining to see the skiway through the blanket of low clouds that were always the same color as the snow. Each pass became an exercise in frustration as the CASERTZ radio operator called us every time we passed over his hut at three hundred feet. About half the time, we were forced to return to McMurdo because we couldn't make anything out in that white-on-white gunk.

On a routine trip today, however, no low clouds hid the sunlight, and it was clear enough to see the snow drifting across the ground. Without natural barriers, the loose grains of snow danced and slipped unimpeded along the surface, creating the eerie effect of spirits moving through a frozen graveyard. We located the camp and the remnants of the ski drags I made only a week or so ago. The demarcation flags were still visible, but the pattern of windblown snow suggested we land in a different direction.

We circled the field several times to burn off enough fuel to land below our maximum weight of 118,000 pounds, and then we set up for a long, downwind approach. I intended for us to land to the right and just outside a long line of raised platforms that contained last year's left-over supplies. Tim, who was flying, landed us a little left of where we wanted to be, so that our landing tracks ran between the last two raised platforms in the line of the six. The off-load was quick and efficient, only five or six minutes—barely enough time for me to scoot outside for a couple of photos.

The snowy surface was an erratic and hectic series of sastrugi, blown and sharpened by the winter's seasonal wind storms. From the air these sastrugi looked imposing, but on the surface they were soft and easily crushed. The snow was perhaps a foot deep, and with every step I sank to midcalf. Footing was treacherous at best.

I wasn't afforded much time for photographs, being waved back into the plane almost the instant I left. I was mildly surprised as we prepared to taxi that we didn't need to cycle the skis in order to get moving again.[3] As Tim added power, we immediately started to slide. He made a 180-degree turn and reversed our course so that we taxied downwind about a mile away from camp to set up for takeoff.

The takeoff slide was bumpy but not nearly as bad as I had expected. We easily pushed through the two-foot sastrugi, and at 60 knots Tim popped the nose ski free of the snow and we accelerated more quickly. Throughout the takeoff Tim continued to adjust the nose attitude slightly up or down to maximize the rate of acceleration. We bounced and plowed through the soft snow like a speedboat slapping across the water, leaping from wave to wave. By 75 knots the bumping became regular so that a giant vibrator seemed to be loose in the plane. The wings rocked as the main skis lifted and plunged over the soft surface. By 80 knots both Tim and I were pulling the yokes back almost in our laps, fighting to keep the plane's nose ski from plowing back into the snow and slowing us down. At 85 knots Tim made a final swift tug on the yoke, and the Herc labored airborne. He immediately eased the nose down a little and accelerated while we slowly climbed, coaxing the plane toward the safety of air minimum control speed. A ski takeoff was always a sobering event out there in the middle of nowhere.

When we had safely accelerated above three-engine air minimum control speed, Tim selected gear up (it was wise to wait, because if we lost an engine, we'd be headed back down). But the nose ski failed to retract. Roy went aft to the hydraulic control panel (an area dubbed the "snake pit" because of all the hydraulic lines that converge there) and coordinated the effort to raise the ski. As usual, he was our Miracle Man. It took him all of five minutes to get the nose ski into the proper up-and-locked position.

The weather at McMurdo had worsened considerably since we departed six hours ago—a fact that gave our new and inexperienced copilot a chance for some valuable experience in actual instrument-flying conditions. We flew a GCA, and his first attempt wasn't very successful: he ended up high on the glide slope and lined up well right of the runway. We decided to go around and have him try again. His go-around wasn't exactly proper procedure, however. He failed to add enough power, he made none of the standard calls, he fed in too much angle of bank, and then he became so flustered I was forced to take control of the plane and get him back on track. Once I reestablished him in the proper position downwind, he took the plane and redeemed himself by flying a good approach and landing.

I couldn't blame him for getting vertigo and flying poorly. Here it happened frequently to both experienced and inexperienced pilots, but I did suggest that he review his go-around procedures. The junior copilots weren't afforded a long apprenticeship before being forced into flying in conditions that few experienced commercial pilots in the States have seen. They must get squared away quickly so that they don't become a burden on the rest of the crew. I tried to give junior copilots as much experience as soon as possible because the poor weather at season's end can be quite intimidating. I found early on that given an opportunity to fly in poor weather, they fought hard to excel. It just took awhile for them to get comfortable flying in these crazy conditions. Or perhaps "comfortable" isn't the right word—*resigned* may be more like it.

A few days later it was time for a trip to Byrd again. After waiting nine hours for maintenance to get the plane up, we were airborne half an hour before our "drop dead" time: because Antarctic air crews operated around the clock, if a crew was delayed more than six hours beyond its scheduled takeoff, its flight was automatically canceled in order for the daily flight schedule to be maintained. Normally we had a four-hour preflight before takeoff.

The flat, white ice shelf rapidly becomes prosaic to pilots, usually after only two or three flights. The novelty of flying in Antarctica had already worn off for me as well, so now all our flights over the ice shelf to Byrd or CASERTZ were a challenge of my concentration instead. Weather at Byrd today was so clear we were able to locate the skiway immediately. A few of the skiway markers were still visible, but the ski drags from my last flight had been obliterated by a recent storm. We opted to perform another ski drag to test the terrain, since it appeared roughed up by new wind-blown snow. We landed on the second pass in our first set of drags.

It was intensely cold, minus-45 with a lively 20-knot wind. As we unloaded to set up the camp, it became apparent that the station's eight-man party would not be able to accomplish all that needed to be done in the time allotted them. Luckily we were there to help. I left Tim and Dave to monitor the plane, and the rest of us helped where we could. We had two small portable heaters to warm the facility's two main generators enough to get them started. The hundred-pound heaters had to be hauled up a short but steep embankment, then fueled and started. In the intense cold, this took more than forty-five minutes.

Once the heaters were in place, I split the open-up party into three groups. While the heaters were warming up enough to be useful, one group began to dig out the door to the generator hut. Another dug down to a trap door in the ceiling, into the camp's main building, while the third group located the skiway panels and collected them in order to mark the skiway for the next flight in.

I was cold after thirty minutes, despite all my layers of clothes and my physical exertion. My copilot, Bob, commented that my face and mustache were covered with so much ice I looked like Jack Frost. I felt more like Frosty the Snowman, so I had him take a picture. I still get cold when I look at that photo.

When the generator door had been located and dug out, the heaters were put into place, warming the small generator-room in fifteen minutes. The generator mechanic replaced the glow plugs, refitted lines, tinkered, cursed, and sweated until he coaxed the generator's massive Cummins diesel engine to life. Allowing the diesel-powered generator to warm a few minutes, he then flipped on the main circuit breaker to supply electricity to the rest of the station.

Meanwhile the trapdoor that led from the roof down into the camp's main building had been located and dug out and the electric heat turned on. By the time I arrived there and clambered down the ladder into the darkened interior, it had warmed up nicely. Most of the station personnel and some of the crew had assembled in the six-by-eight-foot radio room. In ten minutes it was so comfortable and toasty, no one wanted to go back outside. All nine faces in that room suggested the blissful comfort reminiscent of a slow immersion in a hot bath. I hated to be the one to break the spell, but the cramped space soon overheated, so I reluctantly coaxed everyone back outside to finish the off-load.

We had unloaded the remainder of the supplies and prepared to leave, when the station's corpsman (the medic) approached me. She was convinced we had made a mistake and were about to leave her in the wrong spot. She stated emphatically that she was ready to return to McMurdo with us. Since she was crucial to camp operations, I had to decline her request. She tried her best to convince me that my refusal to return her to McMurdo meant big trouble. When that failed to sway me, she began to threaten me directly.

I asked what she thought we should do with the rest of the camp personnel—if I took her with us, they would have no corpsman for a medical emergency. Some unlucky soul might die. She suggested that the hypothetical patient be brought back to McMurdo too. I told her that there was nothing I could do for her, that she was staying.

I found the camp manager and related what the corpsman had said to me. I asked her if she could handle the corpsman for a few days while I broached the problem with the senior medical officer (SMO). The camp manager said that she would straighten the corpsman out, since the entire Byrd crew had volunteered for this assignment, but that she would entertain any guidance the SMO could provide. She went on to say that she was flabbergasted by the outburst, since the corpsman had lobbied hard for the job.

I laughed and told her this wasn't such an unusual occurrence in Antarctica. Last season, another crew had the misfortune to work with a really overbearing scientist. From all accounts, this scientist boasted how he had demanded the NSF allow him into the continent's interior to conduct his highly meaningful research. He had peppered the Polar Programs staff with grant proposals and made hundreds of phone calls to implore the NSF to fund his project, until he was finally accepted. His persistence and fortitude were lauded in his local newspapers, his efforts being proclaimed heroic. He and his staff methodically planned and coordinated their research trip for two years, and their efforts culminated in a flight last season to the remote Antarctic site he had personally chosen for his field camp.

The aircraft landed in the wilderness. The scientist, seeing firsthand the place that was to be his home for the next two months, promptly refused to get off the plane. He was eventually convinced to disembark by a burly loadmaster, who reportedly growled that hundreds of people had busted their humps (knowing that particular loadmaster, I'm sure that was not the exact word he used) to get him out there and that, thank you very much, he would now get off the plane. End of story.

The camp manager laughed at the story, saying that I had probably sounded like a bouncer to her disenchanted corpsman although, she was sure, I was a bit more delicate than that loadmaster had been. We made sure the corpsman was in the main building, and not stowed away somewhere on the Herc, before I agreed to leave. I promised the camp manager I would try to get a replacement sent out. She didn't want to have to deal with the reluctant corpsman for an entire season.

As we flew home, I was convinced that the white emptiness of Antarctica held a special significance only for those who could embrace it as a personal challenge. The raw beauty of Antarctica cannot capture everyone's soul. There will always be those who refuse to see beyond the cold and their own personal discomfort. Antarctica must be experienced without judgments or reservations and without regard to the overwhelming personal challenges that go along with simply surviving the elements. Only then can it thrill and capture the human spirit.

The scientist who had to be bounced into his own research site launched hundreds of letters condemning the flight crew and publicly calling for their dismissal. He had no idea he was at fault; he never felt the pull of the continent. And since he didn't understand Antarctica, his work was useless. He never unlocked its secrets. It would be the same with this corpsman. If she couldn't see beyond herself and appreciate her surroundings, she would be useless to the others. It made sense that she be replaced.

The weather gods had smiled upon us, for today was the kind of day one lives for in Antarctica—a clear, cloudless, iridescent blue sky that seemed anchored to the ground along an endless white horizon. The weather was about the only aspect of the day flight that was cooperative, however. We were to fly east of McMurdo, spanning the width of the Ross Ice Shelf to recce a couple of spots on the Ruppert Coast. The first location was in the Fosdick Mountains. Here we would choose a spot to place a science party in the field and, once that site was selected, perform an airdrop to preposition most of their supplies.[4] After the airdrop we would proceed farther along the coast to an area in the Ickes Mountains to look at prospective landing areas for a second science group.

We were often frustrated at the lack of support we received in getting missions completed on time. Today was fairly typical. We had a 0200 preflight, so at 0130 I called Terminal Operations (Term Ops), the folks responsible for preparing the cargo loads, to inquire on another matter, only to learn they had no parachutes for our airdrop, despite having known for a week that parachutes would be required. I called the ODO, and to his credit, by 0230 he had located three chutes. I suppose I should have been grateful that they were at least packed. When I arrived at the runway at 0215, I learned that our cargo could not be located; nobody, including Term Ops, knew where it was. It turned out that the pallets hadn't even been built yet.

I was given personal assurances by the officer in charge at Term Ops that the pallets would be at the runway at 0400. While we waited, my 3P asked me to go over the workings of our southcom radio. I started by explaining the theory behind the radio and the reason we carried it aboard every flight in case an emergency should force us down.[5] I took this particular radio out of its canvas carrying bag, only to find there was no handset—the essential microphone that would allow us to talk to our rescuers. We always checked out these southcoms for each flight, but aside from ensuring the battery is charged, we took for granted that we would be issued a complete set: radio, solar panel, and handset.

I checked all the other southcoms and was appalled to find that out of the five radios we used on a daily basis, three had no handsets, and the two that did have them had the wrong size plugs and were therefore useless. The handset problem was eventually resolved, but it was chilling to think of the consequences of being stranded on the continent with a working radio and no means of using it.

Our takeoff time was supposed to be 0400, so I was surprised when I learned that our cargo wouldn't be ready to load until 0420. Since we were fueled, just waiting for cargo, I asked Term Ops to send our "pax" (passengers) on out so I could brief them while we waited. I was curtly informed, however, that the Term Ops officer refused to send them early—I had a hard time understanding this since we were supposed to be airborne as we spoke. She informed me that the pax would be sent at 0500.

The parachutes arrived at 0410. We decided that we would load the pallets as soon as they arrived at 0420 (I remember hearing at 0400, "Yes, sir, those pallets are leaving right now. They are on the way") so we'd be ready to go when the pax arrived at 0510 or so. At 0500 three of the seven arrived, and at 0530 our pallets showed up. That fifteen-minute drive from Hill Cargo took a little longer than expected. As the pallets were pushed into position, our remaining four pax showed, and we finally got airborne just shy of 0730, three and a half hours after our proposed takeoff. It was frustrating to realize that late takeoffs had become the norm and not the exception.

Our flight out to the Ruppert Coast was superb, despite the uninspiring start. After we lifted off, we hugged the deck and leveled at three hundred feet. We passed directly over the spot where a huge six-ton D8 Caterpillar tractor had fallen through a crevasse and wedged nose-down in the crack. From this altitude it looked like a forgotten toy, certainly not the smoke-belching behemoth it had been the day it was swallowed by the ice. You can't take anything for granted here. Antarctica is always waiting, ready to dine on your metal or your bones if you make even the simplest mistakes. The crew was silent with all eyes on the Cat as we roared over the site before climbing on our way to the Ruppert Coast.

We spent much of the trip flying along the ice edge between the permanent ice of the Ross Ice Shelf and the jigsaw pieces of ocean pack ice that flows outward from the continent into the open water of the Ross Sea. It was here that the explorer Sir James Clark Ross was stopped by the wall of ice that now bears his name. I recalled the way Ross described his sightings in his 28 January 1841 log: "we made good progress to the E.S.E. [from Ross Island], close along the lofty perpendicular cliffs of the icy barrier. It is impossible to conceive a more solid-looking mass of ice."[6] As we flew over this area, I saw how true his statement is. The Ross Ice Shelf looks every bit of one hundred feet high, an impenetrable wall—the Great Wall of Antarctica.

Dave charted our progress outbound until we were, he estimated, sixty miles from the area of interest. We were cruising at twenty-six thousand feet, so I had Tim begin a gradual descent. We leveled at ten thousand feet. At that altitude we would keep ourselves clear of the highest local peak by more than two thousand feet.

Prior to this flight Dave and I had met several times with this science group. We learned that they were interested in comparing the geology of the Fosdick Mountains to that of mountains with similar characteristics in New Zealand. These meetings were designed to give air crews and science groups an opportunity to go over the scientists' agenda, the areas they are interested in locating their base camp, possible alternative sites, and a list of the gear they had planned to take into the field with them. Our job was to offer suggestions, such as our doing an airdrop if required or where we felt the best landing areas were. The hope was that we would all be in agreement before we ever got to the site.

Tim leveled the plane at ten thousand feet, and I called two members of the science party to the flight deck to be in communication with us while we recced their proposed put-in area, allowing them the opportunity to help select the location of their own open-field site. We agreed on a location at the base of Mt. Perkins, near the middle of the Fosdick Mountains, where they would have fairly equal access to the entire length of the range.

As we descended from ten thousand feet, we found ourselves in an overcast. I always get an eerie sensation in these conditions, especially flying into an area I'm not familiar with—you can never fully trust the Antarctic charts. Using his radar, Dave gave us a few turns and then, saying that we were clear of any threats from rising terrain, cleared us to descend to five thousand. We broke free of the chalky overcast at six thousand feet to find ourselves in nearly perfect position to commence the recce. Dave had come through again.

We were at the top of the range, in a long, wide, wind-swept valley. The loose grains of snow danced over the surface in a side-to-side fashion, as if being swept across the surface by a giant invisible broom. I initially feared these strange winds might play havoc with our airdrop, but there wasn't anything I could do about the winds. I'd have to be precise with the drops.

It was clear enough below the overcast for us to dip down into the bright gray canyon. The valley was huge, maybe fifteen to eighteen miles wide at the top but narrowing to about five or six miles as it stretched down to lose itself in the Ross Sea. We flew down the middle of the valley the length of the range, reversing our course at the bottom. To locate Mt. Perkins we flew the return trip about half a mile from the mountain peaks. Once we located Perkins, we combed the area in an oval pattern until we came to agree on two possible landing sites.

We circled the areas and looked for dark, shaded, depressed areas—the telltale signs of crevasses. Unfortunately the sun was totally obscured by the clouds, so there was no surface contrast to help us. I discussed the landing site options with the flight-deck members of the science party. They told me the optimum location for them to be inserted was at the base of Mt. Perkins. I selected a spot about a quarter of a mile from there, the one I felt had the best potential for a landing area. We flew a race-track pattern over the top and timed each leg. I figured the dimensions of the area to be one by two miles. This area was flat, relatively smooth, free of major sastrugi, and—I hoped—free of crevasses.

Once we were all in accord on the proposed landing sight, we dropped to fifteen hundred feet and then down to five hundred to once again check the surface, which looked better and better as we closed on the ground. It looked like nice firmly packed, smooth snow. I had Chris rig the back end for the airdrop. Tim slowed the plane to 140 knots as we briefed the drop and reviewed possible emergencies and escape procedures. Once Chris was ready, we opened the rear ramp and the door and descended to three hundred feet for the first run.

A jammed pallet lock forced an abort on the first pass. The second pass was successful. The pallet rolled free, and Chris reported a good chute. The pallet landed and stayed upright. Occasionally, if the snow is soft, the pallet will sink or tip over and lie on its side—which is no good if it contains fifty-five-gallon drums filled with fuel. We lined up for the second drop, released the load, and watched it fall less than fifty yards from the first. For the third pallet, Dave bet me a six-pack of Kiwi beer that I couldn't split the difference between the two previous pallets. I agreed and then promptly set that last pallet down, right in the middle—all this to a round of applause from the back but only mild expletives from Dave. It was great. All their equipment was dropped fifty yards pallet to pallet, an outstanding drop.

Our last order of business was to drop some flags mounted on bamboo poles that they would use to mark routes around their camp, our skiway, and danger areas. We had no more chutes, so we descended to a hundred feet, and as we crossed over the middle pallet, I had Chris throw the flags and poles out by hand. They landed as a group only ten yards behind the middle pallet. We had lucked out. We departed the area after one last glance at the best drop I'd ever done.

As we climbed back to altitude, we passed through the overcast and were enveloped momentarily in white, only to be spit out into clear air en route to the second recce site about a hundred and fifty miles distant on the Ruppert Coast. We located the site right off. From our discussions with this science party, we knew we were looking to place them on a plateau just beyond a precipitous cliff. It was an unusual feature, a sheer cliff some six to seven hundred feet high that reminded me of the famous white cliffs of Dover, England. Here the land abruptly stopped and then slid to the sea, a massive continental wall. The area above the cliffs posed another interesting problem because it was composed of low, rolling hills—nothing abrupt, but long, gentle swells of land. At altitude I could tell that I would be forced to land on an uphill or downhill slope. Take-off would certainly be interesting.

We departed to check on some spots farther east, allowing us to over-fly the abandoned Russian station of Russkaya. Little was left of it except a few buildings in an advanced stage of windblown decrepitude. Just another Antarctic ghost town, as eerie as any of those sprinkled through-out the American Southwest—just as lonely, only a lot more isolated.

The return trip was uneventful. Most of our pax slept. Once back to McMurdo the crew quickly completed our postflight duties so we could crawl into bed after an exhausting nineteen-hour day.

Sometimes I had one of those days when I felt like an extra on a *Three Stooges* episode. Or maybe Alan Funt would pop out of my closet and say "Smile! You're on *Candid Camera!*" One such morning I neglected to set my alarm and was rudely awakened by Dave's pounding on my door as he ran to catch the shuttle bus. In my groggy state I stubbed my toe as I got out of bed, backed into and knocked over my water bottle, which began to leak, bumped my head on my night stand as I bent over to pick up the bottle, then turned and rammed my shin into the metal bed frame. I hopped in place, holding my bruised shin and knotted head, and then fell back in bed with a strong desire to curl into the fetal position and stay there. This whole ballet took only a few seconds, but that was more than enough for me. As they say, I should have stayed in bed. But I didn't.

Mustering, only God knows how, the courage to face the day, I made it to the bathroom in one piece before proceeding to cut myself several times shaving. Rushing like a madman, I just made the next shuttle bus to the skiway. At Willy, as I slammed the door to the shuttle bus, I remembered that my wind pants (insulated overpants that protect your legs from the extreme temperatures) were still hanging on a hook, back in my room. You can't fly on the continent without them, nor would you want to.

I was already an hour late for preflight; now I had twenty minutes before the next shuttle bus ran back to McMurdo. It would be at least an hour before I could get back up the hill, retrieve my pants, and return to Willy, ready to fly. I moaned about my plight to Howie, the shuttle-bus driver, who was a pal and broke the rules trying to catch the CO's van that had just departed for the Hill. But you know what they say, "Be careful what you ask for. . . ." Howie, who couldn't officially leave Willy until the top of the hour, agreed to try to catch the skipper's van as they drove along the snow road and drop me off with them. As we bounded along the snow road, I attempted to contact the skipper on the INET (the local radio network) to tell him to stop, but he had his radio turned off.

Going forty-five miles an hour on the snow road was on a par with an e-ticket ride at the county fair. It was terrible. Frankly I'd prefer landing in a whiteout than ever repeating that ride. The road had potholes large enough to swallow trucks. I spent more time out of my seat than in it.

Some of the shuttle drivers were real characters—my friend Cindy, for example. Five feet tall in boots, ninety pounds soaking wet, she was tough as nails. You could find Cindy wheeling away, wearing her leather Harley Davidson jacket and chain-smoking Marlboros while rocking down the snow road blaring heavy-metal music into the bleak nothingness. I loved sitting up front with her, bumming smokes and commiserating as she plowed into potholes that shook our teeth loose.

The jolting, kidney-punching, out-of-your-seat-into-the-shuttle-bus-roof ride on the rutted snow road lasted only five minutes, and I was glad it wasn't any longer. We finally drew alongside the skipper's van and waved him to a stop just as I was thinking it might be a little safer to try survival in the wilds of Antarctica without wind pants than to face certain death riding in that shuttle bus, especially with Howie laughing maniacally as we bounced down the road cartoon-like, swaying and jumping off the road.

The skipper's crew had just returned from the Russian polar-research station of Vostok, with some one hundred pounds of Russian junk. We called the stuff "souvenirs," but. . . . The skipper wore a World War II leather flying cap he'd traded his polar hat for—it fit his devil-may-care personality well. Inspired perhaps by his new hat, or more likely by some of that wonderful Russian vodka they had brought back, he tore along the snow road knocking over bamboo road-marking poles with his side-view mirror. I can't completely swear to it, but I had a strong impression he was grinning as he did it.

Anyway, I got my wind pants and finally made it to Willy in one piece. The plane was ready; the crew were tapping their toes and checking their watches as I arrived. You could always expect a ribbing from the crew when you made a mistake, and I took a good one. I didn't think I'd ever live this morning down. If I was ever ready for a sedate flight, it was now.

Weather for our flight to the Pole was perfect (a forecaster's dream day, nothing they could screw up). Outbound, lenticular clouds formed over the Transantarctics to our east. Fast-moving air, forced up the mountain pressure ridges, forms these clouds, which are silky, diaphanous, delicate as hummingbird wings, and horribly misleading, for they are the harbingers of turbulence—turbulence severe enough to shake apart a wayward Herc.

Once we were at the Pole, the weather up and down—nice going in but worsening rapidly during off-load. Visibility was limited to only fifty or sixty yards. When the fueling hose was drained and disconnected, the back end of the plane closed up, and the crew strapped into their seats, we prepared for takeoff. During our taxi the clouds parted, bathing the Pole in a spot of warm light like a beam of hope. As we climbed away from the station, we made a gentle right turn, then back to the left in hopes of flying a two-hundred-foot pass over the skiway on our way home, but by the time we were aligned with the skiway, less than three minutes after takeoff, the skiway had vanished. The entire bottom of the world had disappeared under the cottony puff of our contrail. It was as if the station had been swallowed whole by a snowy quicksand.

I climbed out of the seat over papa 3 and slept till we crossed the Transantarctic Mountains, when suddenly the sensation of being on a falling elevator overcame me. We were free falling. I sat bolt upright and promptly bumped the sore spot on my head again. I wondered, *If I scream, will anybody hear me?* When my head cleared, I saw two bewildered copilots angrily pointing at and blaming each other for what had happened, each thinking it was the other's fault. The plane's uncontrolled descent then stopped as suddenly as it had started; we were in smooth air again.

Once we were stable, I explained to them that we had just hit some clear air turbulence (CAT) associated with the lenticular clouds we had seen on the way out to the Pole. Now that we were at a higher altitude, we must have run into the down drafts that were pouring up and over the mountains like waves on a rocky beach. I assured the copilots that neither of them had any control over it. They looked relieved. Unstable air that is pushed up across the plateau and over the mountains forms a monstrous, invisible arc that tries to swat you out of the sky if you hit the arc's back side. Hit the front side, you get a wild ride skyward. We must have hit it obliquely, passing through the eye of the air wave and squarely into the down side.

Losing four thousand feet in ten to fifteen seconds is just a tad unnerving, but it certainly does cure the boredom of a mundane flight. Today, however, it was not a cure that I'd wish to try again soon. With all my recent ill fortune I nearly requested a wheelchair be brought to the plane when we landed. I wanted no further responsibility for my actions. I let Tim and the 3P du jour do all the takeoffs and landings. And if I hadn't have been required to be in the copilot seat during each takeoff and land-ing, I would have strapped myself into the bunk and hoped for the best. All I wanted was a beer and a bed.

My fifth bus ride of the day was comparatively sane. Maybe things were finally turning around for me? I ventured over to the Erebus Club (one of four clubs in town) with Hubbsy, my right-hand man in the Test and Evaluation Department, for a quick drink and was coerced into staying for more than a few more. Just to get rid of my headache, you know. I got back to my room at just before noon (bars are open in the morning for us night workers), filled with stale beer and reeking with cigarette smoke, tired of bar talk but refreshed in mind and ready to tackle my pillow and then to try it all again tomorrow.

The weather had been warming lately. All the past week the temperatures had hovered around freezing, and the winds had tapered off enough to allow for brief excursions out of doors without a jacket. The summer sea-son in Mac Town was finally upon us. In fact, the weather was so fine that I was able to walk the half mile down to Penguin Ops with just a sweater as outerwear. I had received a phone call from the ODO this afternoon mentioning something about a package. There hadn't been any package mail for at least a week now, so needless to say I was intrigued enough to rush down to find out what it was.

It turned out to be two six-packs of Steinlager beer. The science party dropped it off before they departed as a goodwill gesture for our success-ful recce and airdrop. I carried my trove back to my room, where I hoped it would be safe until the next crew party.

Getting to the runway was becoming a real challenge. Finally one day instead of wading to it, the flight crews were to have the luxury of helicopter transport to the runway, at least until the thing melted once and for all.[7] The helo flight offered an interesting perspective of the town. We circled Obser-vation Hill, passed low over Scott Base, made a 45-degree turn to pass in front of Mac Town, and then choppered straight out to the runway.

Once we arrived at the runway, we were assigned a plane for the day. Today, as was generally the case, the plane was not yet flight-worthy. Usually there were minor problems to contend with—leaks, seeps, instrument problems, things that took from a few minutes to a several hours to fix. Meanwhile, the crew had to wait.

Waiting, for me, was the toughest part of my job. Luckily, just a short walk away, was Hut 20—a very special place to go. Hut 20 was an abandoned refrigerator trailer that one entered through a huge metal door like a walk-in freezer. Inside were two rooms, two couches, two chairs, and a heater that kept the temperature either just above freezing or sauna-hot. There were three World War II gray woolen blankets and one pillow, shared by a group of six. The blankets weren't much use, so everyone rested or slept sitting up.

Once every hour or so (if the wait was a long one) one of the group made the trip across the slushy street to get a maintenance update. The rest bitterly complained as the door opened, letting in a blast of Antarctic air. We called this wait the "Hut 20 Blues." We had sung them many times before; we were singing them today.

My only recourse was to bother AZ1 Japzon (pronounced *Hap-zon*). She held the rank of petty officer first class, and her AZ rating signified maintenance administration—the AZs kept the logbooks and flight times for each plane by tracking the plane's maintenance history, and they also handled the maintenance officer's paperwork. Japzon happened to be unlucky enough to have her office in the second room of Hut 20.

"J," as I called her, had the constantly questioning eyes of a mother (a fact that should have come as no surprise since she had two little boys) checking out the crews when we piled into the adjacent room. She would throw all those who came to wait in her trailer a look that said, "I won't bother you, so please don't bother me."

I found her well-grounded with the common sense and proud simplicity of a Midwesterner. She was thin as a reed and could never get warm; she used to sit huddled in her parka, hunched over an electric heater that blasted away under her desk at her feet. Despite her discomfort, she had a ready laugh and was an amazingly hard worker, with a down-to-earth practicality we all appreciated. But she had one eccentricity: she was a fellow NRBQ fan. NRBQ, for the uninitiated, is an obscure rhythm and blues band that has a cult following and is best known for such songs as "Flat Foot Flewzy" and "RC Cola and a Moon Pie." Japzon and I hit it off immediately.

Once we got to know each other, we found we had very similar tastes, so on my visits to Hut 20, we commiserated about everything and yammered away, talking for hours about nothing in particular. One frequent topic of conversation was an ongoing dispute over where the best burrito in Ventura County, California, could be found. We, the flight crews, must have been nuisances at times, but she always took pity on us bored, stir-crazy pilots and navigators who stomped around her tiny hut, waiting.

After hours of the "Hut 20 Blues" that day, we finally got our plane. When we finished our routine run, we found we had some extra gas, so the crew voted for a low-level run down through the Wright Valley. Just to be on the safe side I called Mac Center to confirm that there was no helo traffic in the valley. It was the middle of the night, and the helos normally flew banker's hours during the "day," from 0700 to 1700, but it was always best to check. We were green-lighted.

At five thousand feet over the polar plateau, I pulled back power, lowered the nose, and descended over the Airdevronsix Ice Falls, down into the chasm, arresting our descent at two hundred feet above the valley floor, where we cruised at 200 knots. Brown mountains jutted up from the valley floor, culminating in craggy peaks that seemed to claw at the sky. Directly ahead of us was frozen Lake Vanda. On the far shore, several small green huts that comprised New Zealand's Lake Vanda Station were grouped together.

It was 0430. I was sure the station personnel would still be sound asleep, so I reduced power to descend slowly and quietly. We were fifty feet above the lake bed as we approached the far shore and the station. Then something came over me. All the repressed energy of the past few days needed an outlet: as we passed directly over the huts, I cobbed on the power and raised the nose of the plane to climb right over them.

If you've ever been under a C-130 when it climbs, you know it will shake the earth below it. Basically it sounds like the end of the world, only louder. It was a gleeful moment, swooping over the huts and roaring off, a big bird with a laughing crew on board. A Kiwi friend said she nearly fell out of her rack as we plowed overhead. The station manager thought there was an earthquake. They all ran to their windows and peered out, only to see us beating a retreat for the coast. My friend didn't mention anything specific, but I'm sure they were actively planning their revenge.

We returned to the ghostly dawn quiet of the skiway, where only the controllers were awake, and made our landing on skis. Considering the mediocre day we'd had, the crew was remarkably effervescent. I felt happy, too. I guess there's nothing like a big, obnoxious plane to make an air crew jolly.

Shortly before Christmas, we carried a *Nova* television crew out to Vostock. Around McMurdo it looked like Christmas, with decorations on nearly all the hallway doors and the normally dreary lounge transformed by paper chains and Christmas banners, with wreaths and Santa and his reindeer adorning the walls. A small artificial tree sprouted in one corner. Handmade Christmas cards from Mrs. So-and-So's fourth-grade class and letters from high-school students asking "What's it like there?" also decorated the walls. A communal box of candy had appeared, and goodies sent from home—which could, in the quantities sent, have killed any human—were placed in the box for general consumption. If you had a hankering for a Snickers bar at 0400, that box was the place to look.

I grabbed a candy cane for the road and prepared to take the film crew. Unfortunately delays and screw-ups abounded. I was amazed that we got off the ground a mere four hours late. We flew directly across the sound and then over the Royal Society Range. The weather was less than spectacular—a homogeneous layer of clouds stretched over the entire plateau, following us nearly to Vostok. But even if the cloud cover hadn't obscured our view, there would have been little to see save the occasional mile-deep crevasse. We broke through the cloud cover at two thousand feet above the ground, fifteen miles from the station.

I felt for the guys stationed out there in No Man's Land. If the Pole was in the middle of nowhere, then this was Hell itself. The Russians had managed to locate themselves in the worst spot on the continent. Not only is it flat and white, it is over eleven thousand feet above sea level at what is almost the highest point on the plateau. It is a thousand miles from the support base at Mirnyy, and the Russian government still has no planes to service the personnel here as we do at the South Pole Station. Vostock has a skiway for planes that will never come. Years ago there was a Soviet plane that could land here, but it had long gone out of service. So now the skiway is maintained solely for our five or six flights a year.

Vostock is supplied (except for our small "care packages") overland by a twelve-hundred-mile snow road. The convoy is formed in Mirnyy (the Russian station on the coast of East Antarctica) and is reported to be some ten to fifteen miles long. Tractors pull sleds filled with fuel, food, and other supplies for the coming year, towing their cargo twenty-four hours a day for six or seven weeks to reach the station. The round-trip takes nearly three and a half months. The drivers spend their nights in the vehicles they are driving, so they tag team all the way, like train engineers. I never believed the stories when I first heard them. *A snow road twelve hundred miles long? Drivers out in that weather?* But I saw the road, running off to the right of the station out to the infinity of the horizon and beyond, all the way to the coast.

To obtain a landing clearance, I called Vostok on a frequency provided us by Mac Center. I couldn't imagine why this was so important, since we were the only plane within seven hundred miles (the distance to McMurdo). But I called anyway, as a courtesy. "Vostok, Vostok, this is X-ray Delta Zero Four. I'm ten minutes out, requesting a landing clearance."

"Ah, A-mer-i-caan, uh, plane, yes, bery good, da, you land, OK? You have ah, good, ah, soft landing, good?" I heard in the distinctive broken English of a Russian.

"Ahh, roger that, Vostok; Zero Four cleared to land." I supposed I was cleared.

Ed lined us up with the skiway at five miles, affording us our first clear view. It wasn't pretty. A ragtag collection of buildings that looked like they should have been condemned, two drilling platforms for their ice core samples, and—everywhere else—junk. This was no cause for alarm from their point of view; Greenpeace wouldn't be paying them a visit any time soon. The skiway was in fair shape compared to last year. It was somewhat concave, and Ed described it (using all his years of navy expertise, along with his Naval Academy decoder ring) as a Sea State of 2.[8] As we landed, we were pitched around like a small boat on an unsettled sea, proving the accuracy of his terse description. On deck we attempted to taxi to the cargo area, but it was clogged with trash, so I opted to drift the cargo there on the skiway. Once the load was off and we had the plane turned around and stopped, we were inundated with Russians.

At the time, the Soviets were our political archenemies, but in Antarctica they were incredibly accommodating and friendly. Overall the Russian scientists were very engaging people, full of life, not to mention vodka. They hugged everyone and treated us like we were long-lost relatives. Their hospitality was complete and genuine; they showered us with affection as soon as we walked through their door. Of course, they hadn't seen any other human beings for almost a year.

I took the first watch of the plane, as my troops scampered away to barter—for this was barter town, and Christmas was only a few days away. I watched the Russians drag the pallet off the skiway with one of the most unusual trucks I had ever seen. It was military looking: big, ugly, mean, austere, and ornery. It was, as I learned later, an old T-2 main battle tank chassis with a truck body bolted on top. An interesting concept.

When I was relieved a half hour later by Tim, who had had his fill of bartering, I found no lack of capitalists and good bargains to be had, as long as I was armed with greenbacks. I learned that twenty dollars American will buy enough rubles on the black market to pay for the rent on a Moscow flat for two months. For a price, we could get boots, hats, knives, cups, saucers, cigarettes, cards, pins, coats, glasses, gloves, mittens, stamped envelopes, plaques—all this and more from a number of varied sources. I traded shrewdly, giving away a patch and then grossly overpaying for some cheap pins. But no matter how much I spent, the hospitality came free.

I wandered around the camp for a few minutes before I was ushered into a well-heated room to be catered to by my three hosts. Vladimir—the giant among this group but, still, at least six inches shorter than I am—featured a bowl haircut, sparkling eyes, and a wry smile that showed his grossly twisted teeth. Alexev, a wonderful gesticulator, was squat, bearded, and bespectacled. Camille was slight, sported short blond hair, and had a ready smile.

Vladimir spoke passable English, and with some maps we were able to outline where we were all from and then talk about our backgrounds enough to favorably advance American-Soviet relations. I was offered strong black coffee, freshly prepared in an elaborate ceremony, and Bulgarian cigarettes, which were rough but had an interesting flavor when I smoked them while drinking the coffee. My hosts sliced homemade pickles, which were very tasty, and gave me some Russian candy, which was not. I was also offered a strange looking liverwurst-type meat, but being a vegetarian, I found it about as appetizing as road kill.

They offered a toast using home-brewed vodka (made from walnuts, of all things), but regretfully I had to decline since I was flying. I did accept a small bottle to sample when I got home. We talked for more than an hour, then took video footage of ourselves mugging in front of the camera, having a real hoot. I found it remarkable how much these people gave, considering what little they had. I was thankful for their hospitality, and I wished them all well.

The *Nova* film crew proved to be the most arrogant group I have ever flown. Before we had taken off from McMurdo, NSF had briefed them that they would have only two hours on deck. When I briefed them, I made it a point to mention that they had only two hours on deck. When we landed, I reiterated—two hours, no more. During all these discussions about their limited schedule, the sessions had ended with the group's giving us the thumbs-up, indicating they got the picture. I wondered why it was that I was still trying to round these people up as we neared the three-hour mark. At one hour and forty-five minutes, I had told the 3P to find the group and let them know that we had to get going. At two hours I had told them that we need to leave right now. At two hours and twenty minutes they had said it would be just another minute. But it wasn't until two hours and fifty-two minutes that they were strapping into their seats.

Roy, infinitely more knowledgeable about human nature than I, had planned for this eventuality (as he always seemed to do), so we had come from McMurdo with a little extra gas. At times like these I didn't know what I would do without him. Takeoff was smooth as silk, so we turned and flew low across the camp for the camera man; it was the last favor I would do for them. As we flew home, I asked the film crew's leader if he knew what could have happened if we had waited any longer to depart and had then experienced problems getting out of Vostok. He just shrugged; it wasn't his concern. He was right. I was angry with myself for not having been firmer. No more Mr. Nice Guy. Next time I would let them wait for the second shuttle—if it ever came.

The flight back was as unremarkable as the one out, although we saw some bizarre cloud formations over the mountains. The clouds were being swept by the winds down from the polar plateau, over the mountains like water over rocks in a stream. The effect was much like the look of the class 3 or 4 white water I used to canoe in back home. I wished that I could have surfed these clouds in the plane the way I had paddled in my canoe.

When Tim and I got back to the Willy Officers' Hooch, we met in his room to uncork the vodka from Vostock. This elixir had a definite bite and tasted a little nutty, nothing like the vodka I was used to drinking. It burned like hell going down. There was enough for us to have about two shots each (one Russian shot), and I was glad for that: any more, and we would have been pickled. It produced a radiant glow that made the backs of my eyes feel as though they had been rolled in fuzz. After two drinks, I crawled to my own room.

Looking back, I realize that I gained a new appreciation of Russian survival techniques on this trip. Those guys really needed them. The next day I saw the recently arrived Russian research ship in port. What a bucket of bolts! She appeared to be held together by rust. They were brave souls indeed who would bring such a ship to Antarctica, with or without the fortification of homemade vodka.

The ship discharged its contingent of Russian scientists, whom we were to ferry to Vostok. From what I could gather, the Russian aircraft that would normally be used to fly these turnover scientists from Mirnyy to Vostok had been phased out of the Russian inventory more than a year ago. And the new plane, which was to be mounted on skis, wasn't on line yet. So the Soviet government had formally requested that the United States assist them in the meantime. It had been suggested in Moscow and agreed upon in Washington, and now our crew would complete the task in Antarctica. We were implementers of an international agreement. I liked the sound of that. Our job was to ferry twenty-five replacement scientists to Vostok, where they would spend a few days working with their counterparts to learn the station routine before we would return to bring out the scientists stuck there now.

The passenger manifest today looked as if the typist had closed his or her eyes and hit random keys. There were only a few names I could make out or pronounce. One was the head of the NSF's Polar Programs. And another, the last on the list, was "Arthur Chilengarov, Hero of the Soviet

Union." He gave me his card. That is what was printed on it, too. Head of Russian Antarctic Research, he was accompanying his new scientists out to the field, primarily to see that none turned tail and headed for the high ground or the other side.

While the rest of the crew preflighted the plane, I gave what has to have been the strangest passenger brief of my career. There was an interpreter, but he wasn't very good. Every few words he would stop and quiz me on the meaning of a certain word or phrase, and when he had satisfied himself that he and I were in accord, he would turn to his compatriots to explain what I had said. These explanations were mysteriously long. When, for example, I said that the flight time to Vostok would be just under three hours, he turned to face his audience and with a fair amount of gesticulating apparently explained atomic theory, only taking more time. I was puzzled how a simple sentence could take on such grand proportions, but the twenty-five scientists seemed to hang on his every word, occasionally nodding their heads. My five-minute brief took nearly an hour.

Roy had taxied the plane in front of the passenger terminal in order to save time. The Russians filtered out of the building and formed in a semi-circle to gawk at the plane while, from inside, we gawked at them. The haves and have-nots of the Soviet Union made quite a contrast. It was no small chasm but a vast gulf of disparity that separated the scientists from their boss. The scientists were dressed alike with stiff jackboots worn outside thick, ill-fitting woolen trousers that looked itchy. The men's bulky, light blue parkas looked as though they were made from leftover sleeping bags, and their thick, fur-backed mittens were similar to what we used only in emergencies because they allowed for no working movement of the hand. On their heads they wore black, tight-fitting, fur-lined, stereotypically "Russian" caps, which are warm only when they are dry; once you sweat, they become useless against the cold (I know, I traded for one). But the worst accouterment had to be their sunglasses: plastic goggles held in place with an elastic band, with lenses made from what appeared to be two pieces of exposed 35-mm film.

At the other end of the spectrum was the Soviet Hero, who was bedecked in the finest Eddie Bauer down jacket, his lined pants covering top-of-the-line Asolo mountaineering boots. He sported a huge wolf-fur cap and fine leather gloves under his mittens, which he removed in order to hold his video camera. He waved to his countrymen to stand before the plane so he could capture the Kodak moment. They shuffled into position and smiled wanly. He laughed a lot. Once everyone else was aboard the plane, he made his entrance, sitting down with the head of Polar Programs on the bench seat behind us. There were introductions all around, and he shook our hands with a firm, practiced handshake. I guess politicians are the same everywhere.

Our flight out went smoothly. I had hoped there would be few clouds so that our guest could enjoy the views as we passed over the Transantarctics. But there were only holes through which one could catch a glimpse of a mountain peak or a bit of a glacier—nothing that would make sense to an uninitiated eye. Fifty miles out of Vostok, I descended until I broke out from the overcast at fifteen hundred feet; then I descended to a thousand feet above the ground for the last forty miles. The sunlight came through the clouds in spots, creating interesting patterns of light and dark that resembled a cow's hide.

Vostok Station was not very big, and with its overall dark complexion, we had difficulty distinguishing it in the shadows. After circling twice to gauge the wind, we descended to land. The entire station was on hand to meet the plane. The Vostok personnel going home were so ecstatic to see the relief team arrive that I thought they might try to rush out on to the skiway to stop the plane as we slid past them on our landing. When we had stopped, I lowered the door, and we were immediately mobbed. My greatest fear was that some fool in his enthusiasm would rush headlong into a propeller and ruin everybody's day. I had Chris run out some line from the crew entrance door to herd folks safely away from the spinning props.

There was a joyous celebration, scientists dancing about as they hugged the new arrivals, thumping them on the backs. I sat in the cockpit pitying those who had just arrived. They stood around looking shell-shocked. Nothing could have fully prepared them for what they now faced: two years of total isolation on this plain. I tried to put myself in their shoes, to imagine what they must be going through, arriving in this freezing, flat nothingness.

All around was white, even the sky. There is a thin, wavering gray line that served as the horizon, but beyond that, there wasn't much to see.

There were half a dozen small out-buildings and two drilling platforms, a few miscellaneous vehicles, the main building, which was only about thirty by forty feet, and the year's accumulated trash strewn about. This was all they'd have to enjoy for the next two years. The station was at twelve thousand feet above sea level, but with the low-pressure altitude, it felt like fifteen thousand feet.

The air at this altitude is incredibly thin, and until you got used to it, breathing is difficult. New arrivals generally get mild headaches or, in some severe cases, develop cyanosis (they turn blue from the lack of oxygen). One of the newly arrived Russian scientists walked off the plane, took two or three steps, and fell. Then, after rolling fully over onto his side and still trying to walk, pawing the air as if he were still upright, he lay there for a few seconds and then passed out. He was promptly whisked away for some supplemental oxygen while the celebration continued without him.

When the dancing and shouting tapered off, the Russians turned to the serious business of trading for U.S. dollars. This might be their last shot at some greenbacks before they returned home, and everything, but everything, was for sale. I'm not a very shrewd buyer, so I had one of my copilots do my trading for me. He purchased a Russian hat and a dozen small pins, all for under ten dollars.

On the return flight our retrograde cargo was supposed to be ninety-two hundred pounds of ice-core samples and six passengers. But, as I found out later, the weight of our load was closer to fifteen thousand pounds. Once we were loaded, we taxied to the end of the skiway and throttled up to maximum power. At that high altitude—not to mention the fact that we were six thousand pounds heavier than we had expected—the aircraft wouldn't accelerate. After four attempts I traded seats with Tim for a couple tries.

On the sixth run I had Roy work the flaps and Tim the throttles; all I did was fly and direct their actions. We started the slide with flaps up; then at 50 knots, when we stagnated, I had Roy throw the flaps out to 100 percent. With the flaps full down, some of the weight was taken off the skis, and now able to accelerate to 75 knots, we lifted out of the snow. I yanked the plane free from the snow with just enough room left on the skiway either to get the plane airborne or to abort. At the end of the skiway the

Russians had placed two twenty-foot stacks of fifty-five-gallon drums. We had to jump them.

Once we leapt (*slugged* would be a more appropriate term to use) into the air and clawed our way out of ground effect to reach 95 knots, we raised the gear to avoid hitting the cans. Even with full power, at that pressure altitude we weren't accelerating, and I could fly at fifty feet and 80 knots for only so long. I opted, therefore, to bring the gear up first.

At that point I had the feeling that our load may have been a little heavier than we thought. Had I raised the flaps to 50 percent right away, we would most likely have settled back into the snow. Once we gained some airspeed, I brought the flaps up slowly in 10 percent increments until we reached climb speed and were out of danger. It was as dicey a takeoff as I have ever experienced. I was in no mood to explore the outer edges of the aircraft's operating envelope, but my calculated chance had worked—that was all that counted now.

As we climbed, I went into the back to talk to the principal investigator, who had added up the weight for samples that we all had nearly died for. I talked to him for ten minutes, asking why he fudged his load numbers and why he refused to tell us that his samples were grossly overweight before we tried to take off—didn't he know that it would cause us problems getting off the ground? He stared at me placidly during my questioning and then gave me the universal palms-up "I don't understand" sign. He pretended he spoke no English, but his head snapped around fast enough when I called him an asshole.

Chris told me that the PI gave him a weight of the samples as ninety-two hundred pounds just after he told the PI that the most we could bring out was ninety-two hundred pounds. Chris and I counted the number of samples and then multiplied this total by the weight per sample; we came up with a figure just over fifteen thousand pounds. These jerks couldn't wait to leave, and yet they weren't willing to leave less than half their samples to be picked up in two days. I lodged a formal complaint with the NSF representative, but I never heard anything. I was just a pilot and did not get paid to think.

Since we were carrying ice core samples, the cargo compartment had to be maintained at a below-freezing temperature. One of our idiot passengers positioned himself with a thermometer shoved into the heating duct to make sure that we weren't sneaking any heat to the samples. The plane began to feel like a meat locker. It was so cold that the diverter valve used to route heat to the cockpit froze, so we all went without heat. At this point I considered having Chris show our frigid friend where he could stick that thermometer. But through it all, the Hero looked cozy and warm, dressed in his top-of-the-line American clothes.

We landed with the flight-deck temperature below zero. We didn't warm up until we exited the plane into the tepid 1 degree air temperature. We received no thanks from our passengers, but the Hero did give me his Aeroflot VIP tag. He had scrawled something in Russian on the back. It was an invitation aboard the Russian research vessel as his guests for drinks that evening.

That evening none of the crew wanted to join me in hoisting a few vodkas with the Hero, but three of my helo pilot buddies came along. We braved the biting evening air and ascended the gang plank. From afar the ship appeared to be white. Close up, however, it looked as though it might sink at any moment. The paint was peeling off everything, half the lights were broken out, the ropes were frayed, the doors fit loosely on their hinges, and rust seemed on the verge of commandeering it. The ship stank, a particularly sweet, acrid smell like urine mixed with baked bread and topped with the foul stench of stale cigarette smoke.

I told the watch officer that the Hero had invited us aboard. In broken English, using as few words as possible to complete a sentence, he informed us that Mr. C. was not aboard, that he was still in town partying. We left to check the Officers' Club, but he had vanished without a trace. We then retired to my room for consolation beers after our Russian wild goose vodka chase, having cocktails until well into the morning. I later learned that our Hero had gone to Scott Base, gotten drunk like a good Russian, and lost his wolf-fur hat.

"Caution, men, dogs, and tents, left side of skiway, clear to land." The Pole controller made it sound like an everyday experience. She spoke in that monotone they are required learn at controller school; controllers must always sound unflappable, to keep the pilots calm. I suppose this kind of precaution was a prudent measure to take.

The men and dogs and tents belonged to Will Steger's International

Trans-Antarctica Expedition. The six adventurers had been dog-sledding from the Seal Nunataks on the Antarctic Peninsula since 27 July 1990. They arrived here at the Pole 138 days later, on 11 December. As my crew downloaded the plane, I wandered into the dome to hear more about them. A brief by the expedition leader was scheduled in the gym, so I headed down to listen for a few minutes and see if I could meet Steger.

The NSF had not sanctioned their trek. As a result the team was being forced to camp across the skiway from the station and could not use any of the facilities. I mused about the team's state of mental health—what it must be like for these six to have spent the last five months seeing nothing but white emptiness, each other, and their dogs, finally arriving back at civilization only to be excluded by some bureaucrat from the comforts of the South Pole Station.

As I waited to shake hands with Steger, I overheard coleader Dr. Jean-Louis Etienne telling a reporter something very similar to what I later saw him quoted as saying: "I call Antarctica the fiance [sic] of the world. Everybody falls in love with Antarctica on the coast and is jealous to protect her. But she belongs to nobody. Very few people come inside to meet the real Antarctica. And when you enter, you realize Antarctica is not a fiance [sic], not a beautiful woman, but a monster. It has no soul. It's boring, it's flat, it's windy. And it does not like man."[9] I involuntarily nodded my head in agreement.

Will Steger was sitting down cross-legged and looked up as I spoke. He looked right through me initially, like a man who had been at war too long. Shell-shocked. Eventually he focused on my face, gave me a tremendously warm smile, squeezed my hand, and said, "Hi there, nice to meet you." I introduced myself and wished him good luck, good weather, and good snow. He grinned and nodded his head in thanks but was obviously eager to start the question-and-answer period that had been arranged for the Pole staff. So I left quickly.

NSF's official policy was to give the team a tour of the station and a cup of coffee but no food or water—no help at all, not even a hot shower. However, I believe the station folks helped the Steger expedition as much as they could, surreptitiously. I remember reading later what the Chinese member of the team, Qin Dahe, had said about his South Pole experience: "Very warm American people, but very terrible policy."[10]

When the off-load was complete, I returned to the plane. As we taxied back down the skiway past the tents, the dogs looked skittish. I hoped they were tied—it would be too strange if they started to chase the plane. As we lifted off, I turned and we flew over the small tent-city with its legion of dogs. I found it difficult to imagine that this motley group, having walked thousands of miles across this frozen continent, now faced walking across the other half. I didn't envy them, especially as I thought of returning home to my relatively comfortable bed after dinner in the mess hall and a hot-cold shower. On second thought, I wondered if they had any extra room in their tents.

11

THE GOOD,

THE BAD, AND

THE INEXPERIENCED

On the morning of December 14 the weather was of the finest, just as if it had been made for arriving at the Pole. I am not quite sure, but I believe we dispatched our breakfast rather more quickly than usual and were out of the tent sooner, though I must admit that we always accomplished this with all reasonable haste....

At three in the afternoon a simultaneous "Halt" rang out from the drivers. They had carefully examined their sledge meters, and they all showed the full distance—our Pole by reckoning. The goal was reached, the journey ended. I cannot say—though I know it would sound much more effective—that the object of my life was attained.

—Roald Amundsen, *At the Pole*

Amundsen's true dream was to be the first at the North Pole. In his journal he reveals his giddiness as he muses on the irony of his being at the South Pole instead: "I had better be honest and admit straight out that I have never known any man to be placed in such a diametrically opposite position to the goal of his desires as I was at that moment. The regions around the North Pole—well, yes, the North Pole itself—had attracted me from childhood, and here I was at the South Pole. Can anything more topsy-turvy be imagined?"[1]

Each of my three seasons in Antarctica, I requested that I be scheduled to fly to the South Pole on 14 December so that I could pay homage to the men who braved these arduous conditions to open the world's last true frontier. I had met members of the Steger Trans-Antarctica Expedition, and I considered the similarities between theirs and Amundsen's quests. Both men had plunged into the frozen unknown prepared for the worst and often getting just that—unpredictable weather, unseen hazards, frostbite, and, most dreadful of all, boredom.

We take for granted traveling to the Pole today. We jump into an airplane and, besides the weather, have little else to worry about. But with respect to ground travel, the continent is quite the same today as it was in Amundsen's time. I think that Geoff Somers, the British member of Steger's international team, put it best when he said, "We think we are better off [today] because we have radios and airplanes. But they aren't of much use when they can't reach us for days or weeks or months. The travel is the same: The dogs don't change and the tents aren't much better. It's the same as if you swim the English Channel. Whether you swim it 100 years ago or today, it's the same water." [FT: Geoff Somers, cited in "Theory Is Frozen Out in Antarctica Reality—The Steger Team Looks Back," St. Paul *Pioneer Press Dispatch,* 18 March 1990.

So here we sat, today's bold Antarctic adventurers, huddled in the cargo compartment at preflight going over the numbers again. How much fuel did we need to get to the Pole and back given the weather? How much fuel could we carry out to give them? How much did the cargo weigh? And most importantly, what were the chances the cook at the Pole would give us some lunch?

By the time we had reached our first reporting point en route to the Pole, papa 1, I knew we were in for a long day. We were still headed toward the Pole, but someone had fallen at Byrd and broken an arm, so the powers-that-be were looking at us as the rescue bird. I was always willing to help. I thought that if I ever went down, I'd want someone there for me. The weather wasn't looking promising at Byrd just now, however. I suggested that we fly to the Pole, drop off our single pallet of fresh food but hold onto our extra gas and see what the Byrd weather looked like once we were on deck at the Pole.

At the midpoint on our flight to the Pole, papa 2, I called our position report in to Mac Center and was informed that the weather at Byrd was improving. I was still cautiously optimistic but wary of forecasters who described magically improving conditions at a place where some poor soul was waiting for us with a snapped appendage.

Weather at the Pole was fantastic, with a clear graduated sky: at the surface it was a pale blue, nearly white; from there upwards, the color gradually changed to a deep royal blue and then, at the limits of what we could perceive, to nearly black. The landing and off-load went smoothly, so I proceeded inside the dome to get an update on the weather from Byrd firsthand: a heavy overcast with an indefinite ceiling of two hundred feet, poor visibility at between a quarter and a half of a mile, no surface or horizon definition. I needed to clear my head, so I wandered out to the Ceremonial Pole.

As I stood leaning on the candy-striped pole, I gazed out over that flat, unbroken, inhospitable, frozen expanse of the polar plateau. Then I closed my eyes and imagined what it must have been like for Amundsen's group to stand utterly alone at the bottom of the world—they must have been both exhilarated and frightened, knowing that they were finally at their goal but were now reduced to fighting to remain alive and to get back home. I couldn't imagine what it must have felt like to know that you were really only half of the way to your destination because you still had to walk back out.

While I had been to places on the continent that Amundsen would never see (as he had been to places that I never would), I could stand alone on some barren spot, thinking that I was where no man had ever been. But always in my ears was the sound of my safety valve, my ticket out: the low growl of four Allison turboprop engines and four Hamilton Standard props. I was never truly alone.

I was pulled back into the twentieth century by a tug at my sleeve and a cheerful thumbs-up from my loadmaster trainee; it looked like we were ready to give this rescue a go.

At about two hundred miles out from the Pole, we flew over the Horlick Mountains, the anchor point of the continuous chain of the Transantarctic Mountains that stretches from there to the South Pacific Ocean, some two thousand miles away. Off our right wingtip I could see the isolated Thiel Mountains and the almost ten-thousand-foot peak of Anderson Summit. Beyond that, snow blankets the remainder of the Transantarctics until they once again poke through the snow at the distant Pensacola Mountains.

Two imaginary lines meet at right angles at Byrd: the base is located at the intersection of the 80-degrees south line of latitude and the 120-degrees west line of longitude, and it was the last place in the world that I wanted to be then. A major storm had formed over the Weddell Sea along the Antarctic Peninsula and had gathered momentum as it spread itself across Marie Byrd Land, and that storm was now bearing down on Byrd Surface Camp, directly in its path. The storm was still hundreds of miles away, but the camp was already being hammered by high winds and blowing snows.

At fifty miles I started the descent and then made an easy left turn to put the camp off our right side. At twenty miles we descended through four thousand feet into a klag so thick that I was unable to see the wingtips fifty feet away. It was here that the buffeting began. I had to shrug my shoulders a few times to release the building tension. No matter how many times I've found myself in foul weather being thrown about the sky like a gnat in a wind storm, I've never been able to get used to it. My stomach muscles contract as my guts tumble over, screaming at me to give this up, save myself, and go home.

Ed had us lined up with the runway, but the winds had come about and were now blowing about 30 degrees off our nose; we would be landing in a crab.[2] At a thousand feet with the gear down, flaps at 50 percent, the usual polar backup banter started ringing in my headset. Airspeed, rate of descent, altitude, drift, course corrections—the focus required for me to understand and then apply corrections while straining to see anything in that maelstrom of blowing white was intense. My head ached.

At three hundred feet we could see nothing, so we went around. On the climb as we banked into our turn, the raised wing was caught by a gust and dipped the plane into an 80- to 90-degree bank, nearly flipping us onto our back. I called for Tim, and together we wrestled it back to normal. The only thing I can remember saying was "Shit!"—it had happened so quickly. Winds were steadily picking up, now at 40 knots. If we couldn't do it this time, we were going to have to bag it. As we flew downwind, we discussed our options. We could get down to two hundred feet if we used the TACAN; perhaps we could pick up a reference point there. Once we boiled it down, that was the only reasonable thing to do—except for leaving and going home, that is.

Five miles out on our final attempt, the buffeting became so bad that Tim was unable to read off the airspeeds. He was forced to lean over, his face just inches from the wildly jumping airspeed indicator, just to give me a rough guess. I bumped up the power. This was no time to get into a stall. With Tim's face pressed against the dash, Roy had to assume Tim's calls as I focused on the flying and looking for the ground. With a less experienced crew we would have all been on the way home, or six feet under, by now. Even though my nerves were rough-cut and frazzled, I drew courage from the fact that we were all nervous yet excited, pumped full of adrenaline. Man wasn't meant to be here in these elements now, but we were confident that if any one crew could pull this rescue off, it was ours. We wouldn't get pissed just because Mother Nature was toying with us. We would do this because we knew we could—and because we would expect someone else to have done it for us.

At two hundred feet I saw nothing, even though Ed said we were lined up perfectly. I gambled. I inched the power up and flew down the skiway at two hundred feet, groping for a sign, a panel, a flag, any damn reference. After fifteen or twenty seconds Tim spied a flag. I backed off on the power as he called me down. At fifty feet I had the skiway, but there wasn't much left, so I planted the plane with two thousand feet remaining. We had flown right smack-dab down the middle of the skiway for eight thousand feet and hadn't seen a thing. *Shit!* I pulled the throttles into reverse, and we stopped with fifty feet to spare. Just another day at the office.

I taxied up to the end of the skiway and turned around, only to be staring out into nothing. The visibility was perhaps three hundred feet, no more. I taxied slowly back to the middle of the field but stayed on the skiway. There was a small turnout where we would normally park, edged by sloping terrain that rose up to a fuel bladder and then continued to rise another forty feet to the camp's main building. I felt I had used up my luck for the day, so I wasn't about to get too close to that fuel bladder without being able to see.

Our loadmaster, Chris, went over the side once we had downshifted the engines. We tethered him to the back of the plane with two lengths of hundred-and-fifty-foot climbing ropes so he couldn't wander off and lose his bearings. We pointed him in the general direction of the hut and watched as he disappeared in the blowing white cloud of snow. I was immediately glad we had taken the extra precaution. Ten minutes later he returned into view, slowly groping his way back following his lifeline and helping a sagging, bundled-up figure. Watching him inch along, I could see that he was holding his head next to that of the injured man, and I was sure he was saying things to urge him on.

Time stood still as we watched the slow progression; it was obvious the injured man was in a great deal of pain as they stopped every ten feet to rest. I heard myself say "C'mon." It was taking so long that I wasn't sure they would make it back to the plane. It had to be rough out there with the fierce wind pushing at them as they plodded along in the forty-below-zero air. As they neared the plane, the engineer trainee went out and all but carried the two back to the safety of the plane. Now all I had to do was get us out of here.

We cycled the skis and started a slight right turn away from the berm. The storm was blowing so hard now that the only thing I could see with any regularity was the tracks left by our skis as we had taxied in. And I could barely make them out—our tracks had been almost completely covered in only ten minutes. According to the rules, we were supposed to take off only if we could see two panels (a thousand feet), and at this point I could barely make out one. The two-panel rule was designed as a safety measure for use at the McMurdo runway and skiway, though—there wasn't anything but prudence to direct my actions here in the open field.

I talked to Chris to find out how bad off our passenger was. His injury wasn't pretty—a compound fracture that had required Byrd's corpsman to administer a shot of morphine. McMurdo forecasters called and said the weather there was brilliant. Obviously the storm hadn't gotten that far yet. Our crew, to a man, felt strongly that we should take off despite the poor conditions and get the hell out of here ASAP. I had to agree. I thought that if I could just keep our landing tracks in sight, we had a fair shot.

We faced a stiff 40- to 45-knot wind at 30 degrees off the nose (from right to left), which would help some, and we had at least five thousand feet of prepared skiway. After that, it was all open field, nothing to hit there, so I came on with the power and a small prayer. The plane inched forward as we craned our necks trying desperately not to lose sight of the tracks. As the air-speed built, so did our confidence. At 60 knots the nose came up. At 85 we were clawing our way airborne. I fed in a little right rudder to compensate for the crosswind drift and climbed straight ahead, not risking any turns till I was well above the ground. There was nothing to stare at now but the flight instruments. It was at times like these that life in Antarctica seemed so surreal—floating in a pure white soup, staring at flight instruments.

An aircraft's attitude gyro shows an artificial plane on an artificial horizon. And to rely on that as your only frame of reference to a hostile outside world that you cannot see takes some getting used to. No matter what sensations your body might experience, you have to quell the internal mechanisms that tell you something is drastically wrong (due to the lack of any external visual reference points) and trust the flight instruments. Yet if you relax for one minute, if you fail to trust your instruments for even a few seconds, you are doing something that will most likely prove deadly. It is a tough idea to accept, let alone to remember.

Climbing through six thousand feet, still heading out toward No Man's Land, I felt comfortable enough to turn to McMurdo. At seventy-five hundred we broke into the clear. I relaxed my grip on the yoke and allowed the nose to fall slightly so that the plane drifted along the tops of the clouds. Our conquering maneuver.

We drifted slowly up to twenty-eight thousand feet as we watched the clouds fall away like a dream upon waking. Flying home, we became increasingly giddy as the skies cleared as we inched our way toward McMurdo. We had the field at a hundred miles and started a slow descent, landing on the off-duty skiway to save a few minutes. We were met by an ambulance, and our passenger was soon to be spirited away. I walked to the back of the plane and gave him a thumbs-up as he was wheeled from the plane on the gurney. I'm sure he would have thanked us if he hadn't been so doped up. So I thanked the crew for him after postflight, with a bottle of bubbly I had brought from Christchurch. Now seemed the right time to hear the melodious "pop" of a champagne bottle being opened.

An hour later under the warm spell of the Moët & Chandon, I mused that Amundsen's party, upon discovering the Pole, must have felt an elation similar to what I felt now, after our successful medevac—to have reached your goal despite the dangers, to have bested the elements for a least one more day, to live as you choose, and to laugh aloud at Mother Nature's fury. At that moment I bonded with his spirit and was all the happier for it.

Our mission was changed from an open-field put-in to an Up B cargo run. The day was beginning to brighten: all of a sudden I had three things going for me. First, I didn't have to get into a potentially dangerous situation in the open field with two unqualified guys (the operations officer had scheduled me with two raw copilots to do an open-field put-in, a maneuver that required more skills than either possessed). Second, I didn't excuse myself from the flight schedule for what Operations perceived was a weenie excuse not to fly to the open field (see above). And third, the plane was up, loaded and ready to go.

We wasted no time getting into the air. Once we were cleared for take-off, I added power, and we slid sluggishly down the skiway, then lifted ponderously into the air. The flight was boring. We flew over the wide flat expanses of the Ross Ice Shelf, searching for something that wasn't there, anything out of the ordinary. I always searched for major fissures in the shelf where it was breaking up to flow to the ocean, and I dreamed of the day I could identify a three-hundred-square-mile chunk of ice about to work itself free, touching off a frenzy of research activity around the world. Today, though, there was nothing to see but the tops of the clouds, which looked remarkably like the bottoms of the clouds.

Up B is in the middle of a massive crevasse field. Large fissures surround the camp, while smaller areas of crevasses lie adjacent to it. Even the small Up B cargo-staging area to the right of the main skiway was hemmed in by a smaller crevasse field, making it a tight squeeze for a bulky airplane like the Herc. With the exception of the few Jamesways buried under ten feet of snow, there was little more than collected bits of junk on raised platforms to let you know you were at Up B station. The area surrounding the camp is littered with broken, twisted, tumbled down, crevasse-infested strips of active ice. Looking south, one could see a low, rolling rise, like a wave of snow on a white ocean. Apparently there hadn't been any flights out here in some time.

Every person in camp was there to greet the plane. They all waited for their supplies, crowded into the small confines of the cargo area that I was supposed to taxi into. People were circling us on snowmobiles and a big Tucker Sno-Cat, which looked more like a Martian lander than something to be used here. The remainder of the camp personnel ambled around watching, waiting for something to happen.

I stopped on the skiway. There was no way I could ensure the safety of all those folks while they idled away the day watching us work. I suppose they figured that a 118,000-pound airplane could just turn on a dime or that I was so good that I could taxi without hitting someone. Not hardly, not in the snow. The second loadmaster went out, rounded everyone up, and formed them into a line at the edge of the cargo area so they could watch from a safe distance. I taxied when the coast was clear.

Our first pallet tombstoned, sliding off the ramp and sticking in the snow. As I came on with power to drift the second pallet, the first pallet, which was very light—rumored to have several dozen eggs on it—became airborne from the prop wash, completed a 360-degree flip, and landed (luckily) right side up, some thirty feet behind its initial position. I was relieved that no one had been standing behind the pallet, and I hoped that this group liked scrambled eggs. After the second pallet was away we topped off their fuel supply and took off.

We climbed to thirty-seven thousand feet, ever grasping for heaven and an elusive ghost at forty thousand. At altitude our indicated airspeed always drops off, due to the "thinness" of the air, but our true airspeed (the speed that we are actually moving through the air mass) remains nearly constant. Our ground speed (the speed at which we move over the ground) always varies greatly as it depends on the wind.

Being familiar with the interdependencies of these airspeeds is a basic requirement for anyone who flies multiengine aircraft. So when my copilot asked me why I was flying at 140 knots, I turned the question around and had him tell me why. He was befuddled, so I patiently explained that as we climbed and got into thinner air, our indicated airspeed would decrease but our true airspeed (the speed that we were moving through the air) stayed nearly the same as it had been. We learn these general principles in basic flight school, so I was somewhat peeved by his question. I thought back to this morning's arguments with Operations and their firm resolve that I take this particular set of 3Ps into the field and do a put-in. I sighed to myself as I tried to imagine how professional we would have looked during our drags as I flew and tried to explain what I was doing at the same time. I was sure that the only reason it was scheduled as such was because one of the 3Ps also happened to be the XO.

I didn't suppose for a moment my copilot had considered the fact that he might be endangering lives by pushing himself on a mission he was unable to perform. After all, this was the same man who used to state, somewhat condescendingly, that when he did the landing with me flying with him, the plane had an autoflair function (implying that he didn't need to be flying at all since I was on the controls always helping him out). He made these statements, I believe, to try to make me look bad, as though I weren't letting him fly. If we were flying anywhere else but here, I might have been less threatened by his lack of ability. But in the Antarctic we flew on the edge, and if he wasn't willing to learn the simple characteristics of the plane, he shouldn't have been flying it at all.

I let him land on the skiway at Willy. His landings were always "unique," and I always considered them a treat for the maintenance guys—something for them to laugh about that night as they partied away their blues. God knows, I needed some good entertainment tonight, but as it turned out, the evening was far from what I'd hope it would be. There was supposed to be a huge party at Willy, but I wasn't in the mood for a crowd, so I opted to stay local at the Officers' Club. That was my mistake.

I ordered a scotch neat at the bar and scanned the crowd for a familiar face. I didn't see a soul I knew, so I downed my drink and began to put on my flight jacket to leave. I had gotten one arm into a sleeve when I was grabbed by a drunken scientist who wanted to know why he hadn't been given priority to go to the Pole that day. I shrugged my shoulders and said, "I give up. Why?"

"Don't you I know who I am?" he asked.

"No, should I?"

He looked at me as if I had just coughed up a hair ball. He held me by the sleeve and began his diatribe. I wished after a moment that I had a gun. He had decided that he was *the* single most important person on the continent, that he should receive special attention and be given the highest priority. "Screw the rest of the scientists here, I'm the one," he stammered. He went on to ask me why his airplane was broken so that he couldn't be taken to the Pole, why couldn't our ground personnel keep them flying, and by God why weren't they working tonight on his airplane?

Anytime something didn't go as planned, scientists acted as if it were the pilot's fault. I dealt with this mentality all the time. I patiently explained to the researcher that this environment just wasn't conducive to flying, that the intense cold caused things to break here more often, and that considering the conditions the maintenance guys worked in, I was surprised the planes worked as well as they did. My argument made no sense at all to him. His only exposure to air travel had been in the States, where it rarely, if ever, gets this cold and where the conditions, even at the worst airport in the country, are a hundred times better than here. Yet he still expected to draw parallels.

I felt like I was arguing with the Hare Krishnas. No matter how sound your argument, how well thought out, however steeped in fact, they always will win because you're just another instrument of the Devil. After twenty minutes of listening to him ramble and trying to assuage his fear that he wouldn't get to the Pole, I left—frustrated, angry, and hoping that he'd never get there. I realized that my job was to support the scientific research that was going on here, to give 100 percent of myself and to coax the same from my crew in order to get people to the research sites safely. But I had a hard time convincing myself that I was responsible for appeasing everyone when it came to things I could not control. I guessed the next logical step in his argument was that if the weather had been too poor for us to fly, I should have been able to do something about that, too.

I've got to stop wearing this flight jacket, I said to myself as I exited the club. *It's giving me away. It's singling me out to the point where I feel like I have a Day-Glo "Kick Me" sign pasted on my back.* I had similar conversations many times during my seasons in Antarctica. I was a magnet for such behavior, or maybe I was just too stupid to learn how to avoid it.

I remember once walking up the hill from my office to Building 155 and passing a scientist staring out across the ice shelf shaking his head ruefully. I had on a civilian coat, so he had no idea who I was when he said, "Look at that idiot out there." I turned, followed his gaze, and saw the Hercules buried up to the top of its skis, straining under full power. He continued, "I just don't get these guys. How the hell did they get that plane so stuck?"

I looked at him and said, "What do you think they're doing?"

He laughed and said, "Beats me. I watched those idiots taxi over there about twenty minutes ago, and they've been stuck ever since."

"Yeah," I said, "I guess it's hard for someone who hasn't flown down here to understand this, but when we change an engine or work on one, we have to run it up to full power to check it out before we release the plane as safe to fly. In order to run the plane up to full power, they have to bury it in the snow; otherwise, at full power on the ice, it would just slide away out of control."

Looking me up and down as though I were a smart-ass, he retorted, "Oh." Then he turned and walked away, shaking his head.

There was some relief from the wind today, but we were surprised at the state of affairs at Willy when we arrived for preflight. Visibility was nil. And as we readied the plane, the weather continued to grow worse. Operations was pestering me to go, but I decided to wait to see how the weather had held for a plane that was returning from the South Pole. I figured that if I heard a loud noise, followed closely by smoke, the weather wasn't good enough for us to try to fly.

Once on deck the crew inbound from the Pole said they had no problems getting in, so we opted to go. Soon after the nose of the plane was in the air, we were sucked into the clouds. I wondered if the other crew were laughing all the way back to the Hill over the fact that we were stupid enough to believe them.

Something didn't seem right as I read through the items on the after-takeoff checklist; I had the sense that we were falling. A quick scan of the gauges told me all I needed to know; my copilot in the left seat flying the plane had lost situational awareness. Instead of being where we should be, at one thousand feet or better climbing straight ahead, we had rolled 40 degrees to the right, passing through six hundred feet, plummeting earthward at better than two thousand feet per minute. Another few seconds, and we'd have been a ball of flames.

I jumped on the controls, rolled the wings level, then pulled back on the yoke pointing us skyward, arresting the descent at two hundred feet above the ground. Complacency will kill you faster than most weather or mechanical problems combined. I tried to persuade my copilot, without much success, that the fault was entirely mine, that I should have been paying closer attention, even during the checklist. It didn't matter that I had confidence in his abilities as a pilot; watching and backing him up was my job. The only thing I was upset about was that when he had begun to get vertigo, he had shut up—he had tried to muscle it out by himself, without help. I reminded him that we fly in a multiperson aircraft, so he should let everybody else know when there is a problem. I know that I learned an important lesson, always keep one eye on the other guy, and likewise I'll insist that he or she always keep an eye on me.

We stayed in the clouds all the way to the Pole, never seeing more than a hazy, gray, cottony mass. Weather there was supposed to be as poor as at Willy, which was disheartening in that we might not have seen land again until we touched down back at McMurdo, and perhaps not even then. As we approached the South Pole, the weather reports got worse: one hundred feet, a quarter mile visibility, nil and nil, with snow and blowing snow, temperatures in the minus-40s. I didn't want to waste too much time burning fuel unnecessarily, so I talked it over with the guys, and we decided that we'd try two approaches, then head for home.

The GCA controller, looking out from a small bubble built in the roof of the GCA shack, described the weather for us as terrible, the worst she had seen since the beginning of the season. She had watched the weather deteriorate since we took off; until now, she had barely been able to make out the skiway marker that was only a hundred yards away. Chris suggested that perhaps we should just try one approach. Then at a thousand feet, still three miles from the skiway, a miracle. The skies opened so that there was but one hole in the overcast, and it was directly over the station. We marveled at the sight as the skiway was illuminated as if a giant spotlight had been centered on and then reflected off the eighty-foot metallic dome.

By the tone of her voice, it was apparent that the GCA controller thought I had lost all my marbles as I canceled the approach, to land visually. "Say again," she urged. "You're doing what?" I cajoled her into leaving her radar screen to take a look at what was happening. Her voice came over the dead calm of the radio as she reached her viewing perch, "Oh, my God." We agreed. It was truly an unbelievable sight to behold. We all knew how quickly the weather could change in Antarctica, but to watch it happen was nothing short of incredible.

Watching the skies part as we approached the Pole, I couldn't help but think that I was sitting in the front row for one of God's miracles as our clouds separated like the parting of the Red Sea. Then, as we defueled, I sat in the cockpit and watched as the clouds closed in around us, as though we were being wrapped in a thick, wet, oozing blanket. It was as if some giant mouth had yawned, and we had flown in.

When we were ready to depart twenty minutes later, the mouth of fog had closed so tight that I had to do an instrument flight rules (IFR) take-off.[3] We could see perhaps a thousand feet, just under the two-panel rule for takeoff. As we started the takeoff slide, one panel slipped beyond the windscreen and another popped into view. It was good enough for me. Once again as we raised the nose, we were enveloped by the gray-white mists, as if we stood still while time floated by. The clocks all had moved ahead, but it certainly didn't seem as though we had been doing so until the TACAN needle swung around to the south, pointing at Willy Field, now a hundred miles away.

Weather at Willy had improved dramatically, so things seemed to be looking up as we ran through the descent checklist—until we started our descent. As I pulled back on the throttle levers, the number-three pro-peller's rpm-rate began to wind down, too. This wasn't supposed to happen. The propellers are designed to spin at 100 percent rpm all the time; the engine speed will increase and decrease, but the propeller will always change the pitch of the blade to compensate and continue to spin at 100 percent—unless something is amiss, that is.

It was fortuitous that Roy happened to catch the problem as the prop was winding down through 96 percent rpm, just before the point where we would have developed serious problems. There are bleed air valves on the compressor section of the engine that allow for pressure to be released as the engine is starting.[4] These valves close when the engine reaches 94 percent rpm. If our propeller rpm had fallen to 94 percent, the valves would have opened up, and the engine would have shut down spontaneously.

The engine's rpm-rate following the throttle movement was the classic symptom of a pitch-locked propeller. We still had to shut the engine down before we landed, but we now had the option of when to do it (as opposed to having it shut down as we retarded the throttles and being forced to try to restart it for troubleshooting). We followed the prescribed procedure and shut it down and declared an emergency. I was lucky. There is hardly any noticeable yaw when an inboard engine isn't running.

The weather was good at one thousand and three, so I had no problem putting the aircraft on the deck. The fire trucks rumbled back to the position where they always sat and waited whenever planes were in the air. I often wondered if the rescue guys didn't secretly wish for a mishap—not a dangerous one with loss of life and limb, but something where they could break out the hoses and wash us down. I wondered today because it looked as though the fellow riding in the right seat snapped his fingers as we taxied by. He seemed to be saying, "Damn, I thought they might not make it. Oh well, back to waiting."

Cindy was on her last run of the evening, so I jumped aboard the shuttle bus and fired up a smoke. We sang (badly in my case) out loud to the AC/DC tape that was playing as we bounced along the snow road toward home.

On the way to the Pole, over the Transantarctics I spied three small, diaphanous, lenticular clouds floating above the stately blanket of clouds below, like specters hovering over the grave, waiting to ascend to heaven. These enticingly beautiful and harmless-looking clouds are formed as very unstable air rises rapidly over natural barriers. They appear frail as they seem to flow over the peaks below, following the contours of a mountain like water over a dam. I also can't explain why these lenticular clouds always seem to appear in groups of three. Sometimes I like to imagine that they represent the spirits of the last of Robert Scott's polar party, forever circling the continent looking for their lost comrades.

A thick cloud deck had claimed the Pole today, too. On our first approach we saw nothing. Our second found us breaking out at a hundred and fifty feet a quarter of the way down the skiway. There was no surface or horizon definition. It was impossible to distinguish between earth and sky. The whiteness melted everything together in one amorphous sea of milky soup. And in all this white soup, the dull black skiway panels floated like well-aligned flotsam. I had to do some seat-of-the-pants flying to get in. Forced to use that second sense I had developed here in Antarctica to tell me how things should be instead of how things seemed to be at the time, I dove the plane for the deck and then scooped it out at the last second.

As I landed, I remember hearing only Roy giving me any information—airspeed, rate of descent, and altitude calls. I wondered what the hell my XO copilot was doing, so I glanced over to see him wide-eyed, grasping the arms of his chair as I worked my way in. I could see him out of the corner of my eye, pale and trying to keep it together but still clutching his seat like a security blanket. I called his name to see if I could keep him in the game; the last thing I needed was for him to "check out" during this critical phase of the flight.

When we landed he blew out a loud sigh and relaxed his grip on the seat. It was a difficult landing but nothing that we hadn't seen before. Even though he was a helo pilot, he had, for some reason, taken to flying with our crew occasionally. Unfortunately as a helo pilot he did not often see this kind of severe weather—and especially not in this particular type of plane. But he still insisted that I treat him as though he were integral to the crew. I had argued against his flying a multiengine plane just for this reason: he was a part-time flyer and could freeze in a hairy situation because of his lack of experience. And today he had proved me right. He had frozen when I needed him the most. Any trust in him that I had developed was melting faster than butter on hot corn.

At the Pole one of our fuel transfer pumps wasn't working quite right, leaving us unable to completely download our extra gas. I asked Roy if we would be able to use the fuel to get home, and he informed me that it was just the off-load side that was bad; the plumbing to the plane's engines was working fine. The weather over the Transantarctics on our return trip had dramatically improved, so I decided to use extra gas for a VFR (visual flight rules) traverse of the Dry Valleys. The crew gave me a hardy assent. A hundred miles from McMurdo I called Mac Center and told them we had a minor problem and that we were going to go over the Ferrar Glacier to do some troubleshooting. Mac Center acknowledged our request and asked that we call when we were ready to come back in. Tim gave a cheery "Aye, aye." He had a penchant for all that navy talk.

As the sun sank lower in the sky, the whole continent was bathed in the soft orange hues of a perfect sunset. For me fall was the most beautiful season here, with its twenty-four-hour sunsets. I was giddy with anticipation as we reduced power to descend and level off just above the rounded crest of Minna Bluff, which stands as a natural barrier between McMurdo and the Pole. A rocky, outcropped arm of Mt. Discovery, Minna Bluff stretches east for fifty miles—certainly an imposing obstacle for those early explorers who were forced to skirt its distance on their attempts to reach the Pole from Ross Island. I've always been glad that we have the luxury of being able to fly over it.

Tonight instead of descending over that long, rounded hill to squeeze between Black and White Islands, we turned left so as to fly along the northern face of Minna Bluff and pass behind Mt. Discovery, positioning ourselves directly toward the Transantarctic Mountains and the rugged Royal Society Range. Once we were beyond the turtle-shaped Mt. Discovery, we made a slight left and began descending to the rising terrain of the upper reaches of the Koettlitz Glacier.

Near its top the Koettlitz has two other glaciers, the Foster and the Renegar. We chose to follow a course to the left, up and over the Foster Glacier, and climbed to avoid running headlong into the near-vertical falls that plunge from the glacier's roots on the polar plateau. The Foster Glacier ice falls are formed as the ice is squeezed over a saddle that lies between Mt. Moxley and Mt. Kempe, our gateway to the Royal Society Range. Safely through the saddle, we veered right nearly 90 degrees, to pass between Rampart Ridge and the back side of the Royal Society Range.

Rampart Ridge is aptly named, for it resembles a series of monstrous fortresses built one on top of the other, with a different color used for each succeeding layer. It has the appearance of the Great Wall of China as it winds in and around itself, sprouting watch towers at irregular intervals, as if it too were designed to repel attacks by marauding hordes. At its extreme southern end stands Bishop Peak, which tonight looked like a lone sentinel bathed in fading pink light, standing a silent vigil on the parapet.

On our right was the back side of the Royal Society Range, dominated by the thirteen-thousand-foot Mt. Lister. From the McMurdo side, Mt. Lister is the focal point of the range, but on the back side it seems diminutive because of all the snow that has blown off the plateau and collected over the ages, creating what appears as a shawl wrapped about the back of a proud old man. As we swung by Lister, I was afforded a splendid view of the double humpbacked peaks of Ross Island. From my vantage point they looked like twin mounds of sugar formed into Chinamen's hats.

At the upper end of the Emmanuel Glacier we sucked the power to flight idle and plummeted along with the cascading glacial ice down into the broad valley dug out by the Ferrar Glacier. We made a sharp left turn into the Ferrar, followed closely by a quick, climbing right turn to "S" our way up to pass over the yawning brown chasm of the upper Taylor Valley. We steered on Mt. Fleming, which was slightly off to our left. and is the western anchor for the Airdevronsix Ice Falls. These five-mile-wide horseshoe-shaped falls are carved from the same multicolored, multilayered rock that forms the Rampart Ridge. The various browns and tans of the mountain make a stunning contrast to the blinding white snow. The snows of the ice falls spill vertically from the plateau at half a dozen spots down a thousand-foot drop and collect in a twenty-five-square-mile pool, which abruptly ends at the upper end of the Wright Valley in an area appropriately named the Labyrinth.

We banked sharply right, away from the falls, and reduced power to drop down across the Labyrinth, straight into the Wright Valley. The Labyrinth has been cut and shaped into a swirling brown maze of blind passages cut over the ages by 100-knot winds bearing down from the great East Antarctic ice sheet through this unprotected valley. Below the Labyrinth the valley opens up to a vast flat plain with steep, sepia-stained walls that rise, almost vertically, on the south side of the Olympus Range. The north side is less steep, with slopes of gradually increasing pitch interspersed with long, broad ice tongues that flow imperceptibly toward the valley floor. Near the center of the valley the frozen, iridescent blue of Lake Vanda sits like a puddle in a sand box.

We dropped to fifty feet to snake through the remainder of the long valley as we followed the course of the Onyx River as mountain ranges loomed above us. The lower valley was cloaked in the same heavy twilight, the long shadows cast from the peaks above reaching nearly the width of the gorge as if trying desperately to swallow every bit of the remaining light. At the mouth of the valley, we were forced to climb slightly to pass over the tumbled down, jumbled mass of ugly blue-brown and white ice blocks—the crevasse fields that constituted the eastern side of the Piedmont Glacier.

A mile of this brought us to the clear-black open water of the McMurdo Sound, and with a slight right turn, we made a beeline for home. As a crew we smiled, for there wouldn't be many days like this left in the season. A fortuitous string of events had allowed us this short diversion from the everyday, and with the weather closing in, it might be our last sightseeing run. We would have to relish it.

12

KIWI COWBOYS

Christchurch, New Zealand, was our nearest true recreation spot. When I had the chance, I liked to bike in the area and look around. Sundays were especially good—not much happens in New Zealand on Sundays, at least not at 0730. The roads were always deserted, and if I was lucky, brilliant sunshine would highlight the sensational views.

One Sunday I took one of my private bike tours. The weather was too perfect, 70 degrees Fahrenheit with a slight wind. I passed through the city center and started the laborious climb up the hills that edge the city to the east. I pedaled four or five miles to a haven for thirsty hikers and bikers, the Sign of the Kiwi, where I rested and purchased some juice while enjoying the view. From this vantage point, the whole South Island of New Zealand presented itself to me.

Directly behind me was the snug port town of Lyttleton. To my right was Somerset, an unhurried, postcard beach community. From there the coast began its long slow curve to the northeast, forming Pegasus Bay. To my left was the South Island's prominent "thumb," Banks Peninsula. It was all extremely picturesque, but to my mind the finest view was the one that now lay directly below me: Christchurch, a city designed like a medieval town with the church at the hub and roads radiating out like spokes. Beyond the city to the west lay the rich, green fields and pastures that comprise the Canterbury Plains.

But the most stunning sight was the towering snow-covered Southern Alps, nearly a hundred miles distant yet looking as though I could bicycle there in just a few minutes. In a strange way, this view reminded me of America in miniature—these low, rolling hills where I stood were the Appalachians; the Canterbury Plains, our heartland; and the Southern Alps, our Rocky Mountains. Perhaps this fancy on my part explains why, although I was seven thousand miles from the United States, I felt at home here.

By the time I started back, the city was beginning to wake up, so I took my time and rode back downtown to the botanical gardens. Spring is vigorous in New Zealand. The cherry blossoms were out in full, and though they might not be as sumptuous as those surrounding the Tidal Basin in Washington, D.C., their pink-white flowers added a counterpoint to the raw bursts of vivid colors that accented the pale green of the awakening gardens.

Christchurch's botanical gardens are very English—small, well-packaged, neat. Today the garden plots were filled with jonquils, tulips, and forsythia, all vying for the title of most impressive bloom. Flowering trees sprouted rosy half-opened buds; new, translucent green shoots of grass pushed up from the dark brown soil; and while birds sang a welcoming song, the scent of life suffused the air. To my senses, everything about these gardens shouted, "I am alive!"

Directly across the street from the gardens is the old Christ's College, a boarding school for boys that was founded in 1850. Partially remodeled, the complex now boasts an array of craft shops and is home to a small group of artisans—wood and bone carvers, painters, sculptors, and weavers. These craftsmen use traditional and almost-forgotten methods to produce such items as cow bones intricately carved with ancient Maori symbols, which they create now for aesthetic enjoyment rather than the traditional ritual uses. The common area and numerous exterior passages of the old school brim with food vendors offering tastes from around the world. A heady and intoxicating blend of aromas from occidental and oriental foods fills the closed-in corridors of stalls. After my bike ride and a careful inspection of all the stands, I opted for falafel on pita bread, with cucumber and hot sauce (I carefully based my decision on the fact that the most beautiful woman I had ever seen was serving the falafel). For dessert I had a giant, freshly baked chocolate-chip and apricot cookie.

The denizens of Christchurch were out in their spring finery at Christ's College. Most of the women wore light cotton dresses and sweaters, while the men wore sports jackets, shirts and ties, and pleated shorts. Small children were decked out in pastels, young girls were in spring dresses, and young boys looked uncomfortable in white, light-wool sweaters. From the food venders hawking their wares to the squeals of the children, there was the kind of din that is unique to carnivals and fairs all around the world, distinguished here only by the shouts of "G'day, mate!" and "Cheers!" I had a pleasant ride home, now that my belly was full of food and my mind filled with the agreeable sights of the college.

The New Zealand spring is odd yet wonderful in its weather. At any moment it may cloud over and rain, then boast brilliant sunshine, then blow spitefully cold and gray, with winds that push through your jacket and chill you to the bone. The strange weather notwithstanding, my most powerful memory was the overwhelming scent of green. I know it's just air infused with chlorophyll, but the sense of that verdant luxury was wonderful. We tend to take this distinctive scent for granted until something, such as living in Antarctica, deprives us of it. My passion for summer was rekindled here in New Zealand with every whiff of newly mown grass. After the frequent thunderstorms, the air seemed to vibrate with pure life. I wanted to swim in it, to eat it up, to breathe it in.

In Christchurch I ran, drank, ate a great deal, and rested. Lounging whole afternoons away, I lay in the grass staring at the clouds, watched the boundless energy of the children playing in the park, or looked for Ms. Right in the crowd that gathered in the square at lunchtime. I shopped, went sightseeing, found a few new bars, and revisited old trusted ones. Each day ended with a festival of overeating and overindulgence in fresh Kiwi beer—just because the opportunity was there.

One year, I was in Christchurch when the annual Christmas parade passed just under my balcony. It was a strange sight. No elves, snowmen, or reindeer but instead, storybook characters, rock and country bands, and a funky kind of marching band that performed from the back of a truck. An interesting assortment of princesses, clowns, bees (probably something to do with the fact that Christmas falls in the middle of the Kiwi summer), dancers, acrobats, jugglers, unicyclists, and tractors pulling floats went by. Santa eventually made an appearance, bringing up the rear of the parade on a sleigh pulled by what appeared to be the Little Engine That Could.

But the most peculiar feature of this parade had to be the prevalent use of water bottles and squirt guns. Every once in a while a wild-eyed youth would pop through the protective wall of onlookers and get off a great squirt aimed at the back, or occasionally the front, of an unsuspecting marcher. The perpetrator would then duck back into the crowd for a quick reload from a bucket of ammunition. At first I thought I was witnessing an isolated incident, but I soon came to realize the same thing was happening all along the street. The pavement was soaked. And I was truly surprised to see a water-armed group of marchers exact their revenge, wetting a number of would-be assailants without breaking their lock-step marching.

From mid-December on, we generally flew two missions to Christchurch per week, so as a crew we went north often. However, not every trip was pleasant. One night I returned to my room to find a note on my door saying that I was to pack my bags because the crew was going to Christchurch for an emergency medical evacuation, a seizure. A contract employee had developed diabetes, and his symptoms had gone unnoticed till he went into insulin shock that afternoon. He needed to be taken to a hospital immediately.

I remembered that when I was in college, my sister developed diabetes and I was very scared she might die. Our family doctor had told my mother that all Diana had was a stomach virus and that my mother should keep pumping in the fluids. He recommended things that she might like—Coke, ginger ale, juice, lots of sugary stuff. Diana continued to lose weight until she was as bony as an Auschwitz victim. My mother continued to nurse her, hurting her with the best of intentions by unknowingly acting on irresponsible advice. While I was away hiking for the weekend, Diana went into diabetic shock. She spent a week in intensive care till she fought her way out. Recalling her fight to survive, I now vowed to get this guy out ASAP. With each radio transmission I reminded the controllers that we had a medical emergency onboard so we would be given priority handling.

The ambulance I had requested every hour on the hour during our flight north was awaiting our arrival. We taxied into the ramp area, stopped, and were immediately boarded by the ambulance crew, a nurse, and a customs inspector. Our patient went off with the ambulance crew, the nurse, and the inspector, leaving a trail of smoking rubber tracks on the tarmac as they raced away.

We continued to sit in the plane for an extra hour until we were cleared by an off-duty customs agent. The on-duty agent went with the ambulance but failed to let anybody know that the crew needed clearance. At this point it was unclear what we should do—stay or return to McMurdo. As we waited for customs, Dave, our former navigator who was officer in charge at Christchurch, called McMurdo for guidance. The news wasn't good. We were expected to return immediately. We were more than a little disappointed, especially with Christmas so close. We had hoped to do a little shopping. Dave good-naturedly came aboard and took down everybody's requests—all for commodities from the liquor store. He was to call in the order, and I was to collect the money, pick up the booze, and then dash back as the crew readied the plane for the flight back south.

When I called to hire a cab, I made sure that I asked that a van be sent to accommodate a large number of packages. The driver looked a tad perplexed as I asked him to take me to the closest liquor store and wait as I made some purchases. But he nodded in understanding as I huffed and puffed my way back, pushing my modest dolly-full of Holiday Cheer. In all, I bought eight cases of beer, twelve bottles of wine, four bottles of assorted liquors, and a very expensive bottle of single malt. The last, my own private Sanity Juice, was my own gift from Sanity Claus.

The plane was ready, fueled, loaded with nothing but Christmas mail, and the flight plan had been filed. With the weather looking good, we launched after only three hours on deck. The flight back was pure hell, sweetened only by the fact that we held Christmas in our back end. Not long after we passed PSR, the winds shifted and became much stiffer than predicted. This could mean problems where fuel was concerned. I asked Roy to run down the numbers as I figured how to work around the situation. We descended a few thousand feet to a flight level where the winds were less severe; then, through judicious use of power and timely climbs to better altitudes, we could probably economize enough to make it back to Willy. There were some anxious moments on the plane as we fiddled with the controls for four hours, hoping what we were doing would work.

Nine hours and ten minutes later, we were almost home when, during the landing checklist, the left main ski failed to indicate that it was down and locked. The gas gauge was closing on empty, so I was out of options. We did a low pass by Maintenance Control and the tower to get a visual on the ski. Both reported that the ski appeared to be down. Suspecting an indication problem, but unwilling to throw caution to the winds, I set the plane down easy on the right main ski, then eased the nose down until I ran out of lift to keep the left wing and ski up. It held.

Once both skis were on deck, I found out that we had just landed with less than three thousand pounds of gas left, enough for another thirty-five to forty minutes of flight (we were required to land with seven thousand, since the fuel gauges can often be off by a thousand pounds). The crew thought we were in Fat City, but I was ashen, convinced that sheer anxiety had somehow gotten the plane home. In a perverse way it was nice to see Mac Town again after a week in New Zealand. We spent so much time thinking about getting away from this place, yet this was where our friends were—the scene of our own personal soap opera, in which we all were the stars.

Our postflight crew debrief was conducted in the officers' hut at Willy over our Kiwi beer that had been chilling on the plane's ramp for the last nine hours. While there, we heard an interesting tale of one of our senior pilots who had partied a bit too much the previous night during the annual Christmas Eve bash. Apparently he had gone into the XO's room, opened one of his drawers, and urinated on his clothes. Feeling chipper, he had then gone to the CO, told him how screwed-up things were around here, and when the CO had closed his door on our gallant pilot, he had peed on the CO's front porch.

What bravado! What a bladder! As we were falling all over each other laughing, the door opened and Ed wandered in. He grabbed a beer, sat down, and took a long pull at the bottle as we retold the story to him. Ed then told us that a few years ago this same fellow had gotten so drunk that he urinated on his slumbering roommate. I was shocked that he had pissed on his roommate but not at all shocked to learn next that he was to be put on the first plane north for a spell in CAAC (Counseling and Assistance Center, an in-house navy program treating sailors with drinking problems). For the next six weeks our boy would be in living hell, but if he made it through, he could be put back into productive service without bad marks on his record. We were sympathetic; drinking was an integral part of a military pilot's life, and occasionally it got out of control.

Rare incidences of alcoholism notwithstanding, one of the first lessons I learned on the Ice was that you can never have enough beer. Good beer was hard to come by, and getting it up the hill to Mac Town from the ski-way at Willy Field was tough. Getting rid of it, however, was easy.

To get our beer back to our rooms, we had to place it in a collapsible box that was good for about three cases. The theory was that while we as Herc pilots had an advantage and could get to New Zealand and buy beer, we weren't supposed to flaunt it. Once the beer was in the boxes, we had to locate a sled, which we then had to man-haul from the plane to the shuttle bus, stacked high with four or more boxes, and then get up into the shuttle bus. At the transition between the ice road and the dirt road that led to McMurdo, we had to unload the shuttle, walk the four or more heavy boxes across a hundred yards of slushy snow, transfer the goods to the passenger section of the Delta, a vehicle that is ten feet off the ground and fitted with a very narrow ladder. In just under forty-five minutes we crossed the transition, that icy No Man's Land, sweating profusely and dragging eight cases of beer in five boxes, baggage, and a bike. Then, five minutes after we had completed the reverse process, we unloaded all the booty at our rooms in Building 155.

When I finally made it to my room, chest heaving for want of oxygen, I wondered if it was worth the effort, but I knew that once the beer was chilled, all my pains would seem insignificant. I found that the mail we had ferried down from Christchurch had already been separated and that Sean had gotten ours. I had a lot of letters, a Christmas box from my parents, and some cookies from my girlfriend. The good thing about being away from home was that my bed was covered with enough letters that it would take me at least a week to respond to them all. This burden, I believed, was much better than the consequences of no mail at all.

There were a few new additions to McMurdo Station. The Coast Guard ice breaker the *Polar Star* was in the sound, creating a channel of open water for our two seasonal supply ships. And today the *Polar Star* was followed by a Greenpeace ship. The NSF station manager must have been pulling out his hair. Greenpeace members showed up every other year or so, following the ice breaker and then storming ashore, rushing around taking photographs of everything. NSFA had assigned a team to follow the Greenpeacers, to watch what they photographed and to prevent them from entering buildings. The NSFA followers were themselves followed by another Greenpeace team, until we had thirty or so paranoid people chasing each other around. It was fabulous entertainment.

Until a few years ago, just outside of town was an ugly eyesore of a dump, filled with all sorts of wastes and debris. Greenpeace made a big enough stink about it that the NSF spent thirty million dollars to clean it up, shipping the junk to the States for disposal. At the same time, the NSF had implemented an extremely thorough recycling program that reduced a great deal of the garbage that was generated. Unfortunately for Greenpeace, however, McMurdo wasn't a hotbed of activity for environmental extremists anymore.

Stories circulated about Greenpeacers emptying trash cans for photograph sessions or faking similar shots for shock value. One particular shot that leaps to mind was taken a number of years ago: it shows a group of Greenpeace protesters holding up signs proclaiming that Antarctica should be a world park and that the NSF must either clean up McMurdo Station or shut it down. The protesters posed on the steps of the Chalet, NSF's command post here. The interesting part of the photo isn't the signs but the seven fifty-five-gallon drums marked "Danger! Cadmium" that dominate the foreground. Funny, those barrels weren't usually there. In back of the drums, the protesters hid their faces behind glasses, balaclavas, and their protest signs like modern-day banditos, apparently ashamed of the farce they had undertaken.

The current gaggle of protesters barged around as though we were camping out on some ancient burial ground. They acted with impunity, without regard for anyone or anything not in their party line. They sampled the water around the ice breaker (but not the water around their ship). They criticized our flight operations. Then they flew their helicopters over penguin rookeries—areas that were absolutely forbidden to us—and dumped the raw effluent from their ship directly into the bay they claimed we were polluting. Sorry, but no medals to them this round.

I will be the first to agree that overexposure of the continent to fishing, whaling, mineral exploration, and the like will alter Antarctica, immeasurably and permanently. But I doubt the "rape" of the land due to fossil fuel exploration will happen the way the protesters claim. The weather is too fickle. The amount of money required to outfit such expeditions is astronomical, and even if oil is located, extracting it and transporting it present near impossibilities. People will argue that it was done in Alaska, but I contend that the only folks who believe full-blown oil exploration is possible in Antarctica are folks who haven't set foot on the continent. The conditions are simply too harsh, the distances too great. The bottom line is money, and this kind of exploration would amount to throwing money into a deep, unending hole.

As the season progressed and summer neared, we generally flew at least two missions a week from the Ice to New Zealand, bringing in fresh food, personnel and morale-boosting mail. But best of all, we got to go to Christchurch on a regular basis.

Once in a while we flew as passengers on another crew's run north. During one of these trips we took full advantage of the eight-hour flight by rigging racks up in the cargo area and sacking out for the entire time so we would be fresh when we hit town. The down side of this was that we could almost see the cogs turning in the collective brain of the crew who flew us up that day: how could they use this against us so that they could stay in Christchurch instead of us? The PTAC even told me he already had a great plan for them to stay, so I pondered some way to counter it.

I decided to go on the offensive and play hard to get. Once we cleared customs at New Zealand, I found Chief Jack Elston, who worked for me as test and evaluation coordinator here in Christchurch and spirited him away for a beer at the Duck. Then some of us caught a cab downtown. At the hotel Tim and I changed and went for a run before lunch, and lunch itself was, of course, an extended affair with numerous beers. When we returned to the hotel, I was informed that I had had a number of phone calls from the base. I learned the other crew was claiming to be "exhausted," couldn't possibly fly, and were asking if our crew could take the plane back south. Besides the fact that we had been drinking, which meant we couldn't fly for at least twelve hours, when the skipper (CO) was called to clear their plan, he shot it down—so we were off the hook and in town for at least three days.

The entire crew met at 1800 in Kanniga's Thai restaurant, our unanimous choice for the best eating establishment in Christchurch. Tim and I bought two cases of Moncrief's beer and turned dinner into a bona fide "off the Ice" party. Dinner was a rousing success. We feasted on plate after plate of Thai delicacies cradled in mounds of sticky white rice, all proffered by our smiling and generous hosts. We shared the meal, passing each dish around the table with the reverence usually reserved for a church collection plate. As dish after dish was scraped clean by eager spoons, the empty-plate count mounted and empty beer cans magically stacked themselves toward the ceiling. Three days of fun—we were definitely on a roll.

Several hours later we waddled the eight blocks to the brick patio of the Dux de Lux, where we sat huddled under a kerosene heater in our short-sleeved shirts, gulping beer and trying desperately not to spill it because of our shivering hands. Nights in Christchurch were often cool, even in summer. I realized I had been warmer in Antarctica last night than I was right now. I drank another beer. All this suffering would surely build character.

My favorite place to stay was the Cotswold. The name alone is still enough to make me smile. It was more than just another hotel to me; it became a second home. Built in the timber-framed style of traditional English Tudor architecture with plentiful use of rough-cut stone, it exists in a village-like complex of four buildings that form a U-shape with a charming cobblestone courtyard in the center. Today a flower box filled with pansies hung under each window.

I found the overstuffed chairs in the sitting room too comfortable, nearly impossible to extricate myself from. The bedroom was wonderfully sparse, however—only a chest of drawers and a bed, but it was a pillow-soft Tyrolean bed that required only my laying my head down to put me instantly to sleep. Yet these delights paled next to the bathroom, which housed a huge tub—one of the few I've ever found that I could stretch out my six-foot-four, two-hundred-twenty-five-pound frame comfortably in. There I happily soaked away the pressures of the world.

The staff at the Cotswold became my extended family. They invited me for drinks, to dinner to meet their families, coddled me, and became my friends and confidants. It was easy to forget I was seven thousand miles away from home while I was there. In a way, I really was home. As spring moved into summer, I enjoyed the changing seasons. On my morning runs, Christchurch was cool, moist, and green. The rising sun cast long shadows from tall trees, shadows that fell across the ground like dark ladders under my feet as I ran. The morning dew soaked through my running shoes and socks to chill my toes. The spring flowers were replaced with an array of mature leaves that turned to drink in the sun's warming energy.

I crossed the serpentine coils of the Avon River frequently. Its wandering course cuts deep into already steep banks as it winds through the city. Shallow waters meander along as wood ducks cruise easily against the sluggish current. I ended my runs passing through the shady lanes lined with the neat and tidy trees and flower plots of the city garden. A fresh breeze blended the passionate scent of newly opened roses with that of freshly mown grass, a combination of smells that affected me like an elixir. I would quicken my gait, only to receive a face full of diesel fumes from the busses as I passed through a partition of wrought-iron gates, back into the heart of an awakening city.

After these runs I would usually meet my copilots at breakfast. We gathered to watch *World News Tonight* live from New York (which was ten hours ahead of us) to get back on track with what was happening back home. Then it was time for the beer run. We had this down to a science. After breakfast I hailed a cab to the base, had him wait as I bought the beer, and then had him take me to the airplane hangar to drop it off. I ran into Dave there. As the officer in charge of the Christchurch detachment, he coordinated the turnaround missions to the Ice for the remainder of the season. He seemed happy to be spending the next three months away from Antarctica. Having spent the better part of three flying seasons there myself, I could understand.

After I had stowed my beer in my locker, he briefly told me about last night's debacle. As soon as we had landed, the other crew began bemoaning their situation. They thought it unfair that they should do all the work to ferry our crew up, just to turn around and go straight back. They even called to try and convince the skipper that we, as a crew, should fly the plane back to the Ice, but he wouldn't buy any of it. I was glad I was out of the loop. Our crew had had enough to deal with in the last few weeks without this kind of noise. Dave and I continued our conversation over fish and chips at the Cotswold. Afterward he headed back to base, and I went to the Dux.

The day stayed fair. The sun was out, it was the perfect day to sit outside, drink beer, and collect a brilliant red glow on my naked pate while I watched the world go by. A number of folks at the Dux apparently felt the same way, so we all sat and watched life's slow progression together until dinner. Then I met Roy and Chris at Christchurch's attempt at a Southwest American restaurant: the Lone Star Café. Once I'd eaten there, Tex-Mex food would never hold the same special place in my heart. New Zealanders, it appeared, were made from the same mold as their English counterparts, enjoying their meals meat-and-potatoes plain. But, for Christchurch, the Lone Star was always crowded, tables full and the bar jammed. Texas posters adorned the walls along with mounted steer horns, rebel flags, and other artifacts that gave the place a feel that could best be described as Texas via Hollywood. I've lived in Texas, but I can't remember ever seeing the state so admirably represented as it was here in Christchurch. The look was classic John Wayne.

Decor aside, however, I'm afraid the food was southwest of indescribable—not good exactly, but not bad either, just some new culinary byproduct of mismatched cultures. "Kiwi cowboy," we called it. Or one could say it was chili rellenos the way Chef Boyardee would like them. If nothing else, though, the food was plentiful. After dinner we staggered over to the Loaded Hog. For my money it's one of the best microbreweries in the world, an unassuming place where the call to order is just good, fresh beer. We sat on stools made from old tractor seats, the heart-shaped kind that are about as comfortable as concrete bleachers. Now I know why some farmers have such sour dispositions.

As atonement for a day of unabashed indulgence, I spent the next morning clawing my way to the top of the artificial climbing wall at the local YMCA and then met friends across the street at the Arts Centre at Christ's College for shopping and lunch. The numerous multiethnic vendors stuffed into the close confines of narrow stone walkways always lent a carnival atmosphere to the serious facade of the college. It was a circus of delights that never failed to enchant me. We spent the rest of the afternoon in the Merrivale section of the city, doing a little light shopping before we discovered and subsequently camped out at a wonderful beer garden. It was Tudor-style, set on a tiny man-made lake, and it served a great selection of beers. A fine oak bar stretched along the entire length of the back wall. Green wallpaper with small gold designs was interrupted every few feet by a polished oak post. Smooth wooden booths lined the other walls, and high tables spilled around a central brick fireplace. The light green carpet was so deep you felt like you were walking on a golf green. And then there was the small patio, trellised and covered with ivy.

As we whiled away the splendid summer day under that natural green awning, it was difficult to imagine a finer way to spend a day before returning to the barren reaches of Antarctica. I felt as light as air. I wasn't burdened by three layers of clothes. I was free to sit in the sun and reflect on how wonderful doing nothing at all can be. All this would end tomorrow. I pushed that thought aside and enjoyed the day to the fullest.

One year we spent the first week of January in Christchurch. The weather started cool and very windy and then became warm and very windy. On occasion the wind blew upwards of forty miles an hour, which was always given on the news as sixty-five kilometers per hour, lending an increased sense of urgency to the forecasts. I didn't mind the wind as long as I wasn't biking in it—which of course, being stubborn, I was. I generally tried to ride every day while I was there, if for no other reason than to appease my conscience over our continuing (and delightful!) overindulgence.

On the first trip, I had a bad go of it trying to reach the Sign of the Kiwi, a rest house on the Summit Road, just outside Christchurch, at the crest of the Port Hills. I had just quit smoking (again) and was in less than top physical shape—that, coupled with the unrelenting wind, had me huffing like a wallowing water buffalo. I stopped at the top of the hill to rest, a really long rest, and then had the fun of coasting back down the hill and home. The next day I was able to control my wheezing long enough to make it over the mountain to Lyttleton Harbor, only to break a spoke and thus being forced to take a cab back to the city.

Finally I did succeed in making the entire forty-mile trek over the hill, around Lyttleton, back over the hill to the suburb of Sumner, and eventually to Christchurch itself. However, I wiped all possible health benefits out by stopping in Sumner for a small pitcher of beer. Once I had a predetermined reward in mind, I found a way to make the trip daily.

I thought Lyttleton splendid. It is situated on a fine, snug harbor surrounded on three sides by hills that rise from the water's edge. The inlet looks like an extinct volcano collapsed on one side, thus creating the entrance to the bay and harbor mouth. The town itself is built into the steeply rising terrain. The main street parallels the quay, which shoots numerous long piers into the bay like an octopus's tentacles grasping for ships. Along this street is a ragtag assortment of bars, restaurants, and hotels that range from fine to flea-bag, apparently built for use by sailors who would consider any room with a bed that didn't rock, pitch, and sway a parlor.

I took similar rides to Brighton on the coast of Pegasus Bay. Brighton is what I would call a sleepy seaside town. It has a mall that apparently opens only on weekends and a restaurant that took more than two hours to serve our food, even though we were the only customers in the place. And its most active resident was a big yellow dog that chased my bike, howling to raise the dead, for nearly twenty yards before collapsing in a heap to await the next foolhardy bicyclist to blunder into its way.

For the last three months of the season, we made frequent runs to Christchurch. The clarity of the midsummer mornings in New Zealand was stunning. I always enjoyed arriving there at daybreak as the sun painted the South Island in a rosy light and thin lines of clouds would materialize white and pink from the shadows of darkness to hang in the pale blue sky. At a hundred and fifty miles from the island, we would begin to be able to distinguish the snow-capped mountains of the Southern Alps. As we approached Christchurch on these clear mornings, the clouds would always grow in form and substance as the sun heated the land to become pure white against the azure sky and tower over the rough mountain peaks, puffed from the humid air that rushed up the mountains from the cold ocean.

Coming from such a barren and desolate place as Antarctica, I always felt that New Zealand was my Eden. The country was always shining, even in the rain. And there was a cool breeze, even on the hottest days. It always gave my spirits a lift when they sagged, and it made me believe in paradise.

13

WE'RE PRETTY SURE

THIS WON'T EXPLODE

One of the main projects during my Antarctic sojourn was called SERIS (Seismic Experiment, Ross Ice Shelf). It was an expedition to run a seismic line across the ice shelf, with the goal of understanding why the Transantarctic Mountains are there.[1] The plan called for a series of explosive charges to be set off at various spots along a line; this would in turn provide the seismic profile of the area, an image of the crustal structure across the front of the Transantarctic Mountains. The expedition plans were full of wonderful theories and great expectations—and revealed a certain glee at the idea of packing explosives into the ice and watching them go boom.

Somebody had to fly in the explosives, however. There were three major SERIS sites, with dozens of geophysicists, geologists, glaciologists, and the like, at each one. The plan was simple: when they gave the cue, someone would fly to these sites, prepare skiways, and then fly in the explosives. Needless to say, we pilots adored this plan. We loved it. We thought it was just jim-dandy!

Fortunately, before we had to actually kill somebody, we determined that all three landing areas were too rough for explosives. Even after grading had taken place to prepare the sites, concern remained that the unstable explosives couldn't stand up to the bouncing and jostling associated with an open-field landing. The powers-that-be speculated aloud about the odds of explosion on landing; then they asked for volunteers. Astonishingly, nary a volunteer stepped forward. Then someone had a brilliant idea. "Let's get the Canadians to do it," they said.

"Yeah, the Canadians! They'll fly anything!" we encouraged. A Canadian Twin Otter crew had contracted to fly for the NSF that season. With the Otter, a plane that can stop in less than five hundred feet, they had been known to carry just about anything. But to our disappointment, even the Canadians declined—politely, of course, being Canadians. So a new plan was worked out. The decision was made to have the tons of explosives carried out three hundred miles via land vehicles and dropped at the nearest site, where the scientists could deal with it themselves. We liked this plan, too. Everybody agreed to it—except, of course, the tractor driver and the surveyor who would direct him to the site. Here, however, one of the fundamental principles of democracy took hold: the majority ruled.

We did turn out to cheer them as they pulled out of town, driving the huge D8 Caterpillar tractor that towed a trailer piled high with explosives. I'm sure they felt ennobled as they waved back to an enthusiastic (and unmistakably relieved) group of pilots. But the expedition was ill-fated. The roaring and cheering had barely died in their ears when—about twenty miles out of McMurdo in our whiteout landing area, which is supposedly free of crevasses—the vehicles broke through a snow bridge and fell into a crevasse.

The D8 Caterpillar was sucked from the surface, and men and machine plunged down some fifty feet before becoming wedged in the narrow crack. Miraculously, both men survived; they were pulled from the crevasse by a rescue team. Eventually the explosives were recovered as well—being winched out, very carefully, with a crane. But to this day the D8 is still inching its way toward the ocean, an image I always find disturbing and somewhat haunting to consider.

I had an opportunity to talk with one of the mountaineers involved in the rescue. He told me that at one point, he was lowered into the crevasse some two hundred feet, and even then he was unable to see the bottom. It was actually a lucky break that the crevasse was so narrow; that's probably what saved the men's lives.

The accident had another unpleasant consequence. It renewed discussion of flying the explosives out. This happened during our all-officers meeting (AOM). First we had a "very special brief" from a meteorologist captain of the Pacific Fleet. I got the distinct impression he wasn't fully briefed on what we did here; he sounded ill-prepared and just a little foolish. Another VIP, just here for his trip to the Pole, lunch, and souvenir T-shirt. The indicators come early in VIP speeches. "You're doing a great job," they say, with no apparent idea of what we do at all. "You're the finest squadron in the navy." "Rah rah." And so on.

However, what these speeches lack in substance, they make up for in humor because the speaker nearly always looks the crowd over, clears his throat, then leans over to an aide and asks, "Who am I speaking to again?" I think I speak for all the squadron officers when I say that we didn't mind the Goat Ropes (a term generically defined in the military as missions or events that have a high potential for frustration since they are often ill-planned and something usually goes wrong) as much as we despised the false enthusiasm and meaningless praise.

Anyway, a department-head meeting was held immediately following the AOM. The skipper announced we had been cleared to carry the highly explosive ammonium nitrate (AN 95) into the open field via airplane. The pilots were shocked into silence. The navy had determined it was safe. Therefore, it was safe. I distrusted the way the previously acknowledged dangers were now swept under the rug. "What message are we sending the air crews?" I kept asking. "You're expendable?"

A heated debate ensued. The Herc pilots were concerned about the lack of corporate knowledge—no one seemed to know how much jostling (how many g's) ammonium nitrate could take before detonating. And worse, no one seemed too concerned about finding out. The United States Air Force considered this same explosive so unstable that transport of it was prohibited on all air force planes.

I shut up as the meeting progressed. I can smell a foregone conclusion when one stinks. Thoughtfully, the skipper had planned some advice for us. "Just be careful," he said. I could have kicked myself, for my crew and I had unwittingly paved the way for this decision by preparing a smooth landing area at one of the major SERIS sites, SERIS L, last week. Now, there was a general call for volunteers. No one stood up. Hey, we're navy pilots. We're crazy, but we ain't stupid. The operations officer, perhaps trying to negotiate a little, said that if anyone had strong objections to carrying these explosives, he would listen to them. After the meeting I told him I didn't want my crew used as cannon fodder. Tactical error, of course. My remarks landed us squarely at the top of the list to carry the boom juice.

My chief concern was how to tell the crew, for I was certain they wouldn't want to carry explosives unless I felt comfortable about it, and I didn't. I had to either lie to them or lie to myself, but I had to tell them before they heard it through the grapevine. And sure enough, within a few weeks of the meeting, the moment I feared arrived.

I went to preflight. One of the squadron planes stood alone, being loaded at the far end of the skiway. There was none of the normal hustle and bustle, the coming and going of tractors or people normally associated with every preflight. There was no power on the plane, no engineer doing a walk around, no navigator plugging coordinates into the INS (inertial navigation system), no 3P hauling the twenty-five-pound southcom. The lack of activity is what made me take note. I had a bad feeling about it. A very bad feeling.

I entered Maintenance Control and ran into Ed, the PTAC for the lonely airplane, and asked what was going on. He shook his head. "Mark, they've got me by the balls. I have to do it."

"Do what?" I asked.

"Take those goddamned explosives out to SERIS L. The front office decided that I was the best qualified and thought it best if I was the first to try." I sympathized with him in silence for a moment. "I guess they've smoothed out the skiway quite a bit since you brought the snow plane in a few weeks ago," he said hopefully. "Have you been out since and tried it?"

I shook my head. "No, I haven't been out since then." I did not tell him that it was rough as could be then. "Did they discuss with you any particular precautions to take, do anything special?" I wondered aloud.

"Not really," he said. "Just told me to land as softly as I could."

We let that one sit for a moment. "A great morale booster," I said.

"Yep. I felt all warm and fuzzy after hearing that."

I wished him good luck. It seemed insufficient, but it was all I could think of to say. I was sincere, though, because I knew we would probably be the next crew to fly the explosives.

I looked over the ADB as the rest of his crew came ambling through Maintenance Control, alone or in pairs, with their heads down, their hands in their pockets, and an air of gloom. They were guinea pigs, and they knew it. And soon it would be our turn in the barrel—how soon and where were the only questions that remained to be answered. As I prepared for what I thought was a once-in-a-lifetime mission, how little did I know that I would be answering my own question all too soon.

We pulled a flight taking a team of scientists through the broad Beardmore Valley to the Mill Glacier, an area we had flown over numerous times at altitude but had never gotten the chance to examine up close.[2] As we crossed the Beardmore, we descended through ten thousand feet. Mill Glacier, which at altitude appears flat and calm, began to come into focus as we got closer to the ground. The surface took on a horribly different look—choppy swells arranged in long, fat, sinuous furrows. These ribbon-like waves of ice oscillate gracefully downstream toward the Beardmore Glacier until, just beyond Plunkett Point, they break upon each other, causing a tumult of crevasses that are interspersed with house-sized chunks of ice.

The Beardmore and Mill Glaciers are divided by a moraine—that is, by a brown line of dirt, rocks, and sediment that have been dragged from the sheer cliffs of Plunkett Point by the rapidly flowing ice of the Beardmore. Beyond this barrier all is quiet. Mill Glacier flows smooth, clean, and clear until it rounds the moraine and is swept up in Beardmore.

Today we crossed the moraine heading straight up the Mill at a thousand feet. I flew up two miles and began a slow descent to get a better look at the surface. It was evident by five hundred feet that this was not going to be a smooth landing. The surface was pock-marked with irregularly shaped, bowling-ball-sized depressions, or "cups." I leveled the plane at two hundred feet, lowered 50 percent flaps, and slowed to 135 knots.

We were looking for some barrels that a Twin Otter crew had used two years ago to mark a proposed runway. We spotted them after a couple of passes. The scientists aboard wanted to be positioned as close to the base of a nunatak (a hill or a mountain that is completely surrounded by glacial ice) as possible. I would have to land carefully on the apex, then control my speed as we taxied down the slope toward the wall of the nunatak. The moraine would also pose a slight problem, being nearly two hundred feet high. I would have to pass over it at about three hundred feet and then dive down to fifty feet to start my gradual climb up the glacier, landing uphill. *Well,* I thought, *at least this landing will be interesting.*

I flew a racetrack pattern to align myself with my intended point of landing as we lowered the gear, wheels down, skis up. To give myself a little cushion, I extended my downwind leg of the pattern about a mile, ensuring a good lineup. Over the moraine at three hundred feet, we were looking good. I pulled off the power and descended into the natural swale, or depression, behind the moraine. At fifty feet I had to add power to climb enough to keep pace with the rising slope of the glacier. I landed smoothly, in a three-hundred-feet-per-minute rate of climb.

The surface was hell. Even though it was covered with dimples, it was slick as smooth ice. Taxiing was a chore—my brakes were useless, and the nose wheel steering was ineffective. In the balance I suppose it sounds like this wasn't much different from operating on skis, but it took tremendous effort to control the plane's speed while sliding. At least with skis, the snow provides some friction. Here, we were freewheeling on a slick and bumpy runway.

When I turned toward the nunatak, the plane started to accelerate down the sloping incline. It took full reverse thrust to keep from charging headlong into the sheer, brown cliff a hundred yards in front of us. Turning was a challenge, too. I taxied as close to the proposed campsite as felt comfortable; then I made (more like *slid through*) a right turn. The slope here was much gentler but still steep enough so that the number-one propeller came within only a foot from hitting the ground.

The loadmasters off-loaded quickly while the cockpit crew stayed glued to their seats, leaning involuntarily to the right as though we could help to balance the plane. There were some tense moments as we off-loaded a small tracked vehicle, which caused the plane to sway slightly. When all the gear was off, we raised the ramp and then taxied, this time with our nose pointing uphill and our propellers safely above the ground. The science crew were well-versed in their assignments and had the camp set up in less than thirty minutes. We said a short good-bye and proceeded with our takeoff run.

By comparison with the takeoff, our landing had been a dream. I added power, and even though we shouldn't have had any problems taking off on wheels, we accelerated slowly because of the steepness of the glacier.

As we tried to accelerate uphill over that pitted landscape, I was seriously thinking the plane might shake itself apart. It was if we were riding on a frozen cobblestone street at a hundred and thirty miles an hour. It wasn't fun. Eventually we reached rotate speed. I raised the nose, and off we went, relieved at the smooth air that carried us away from that pounding. I circled to the right and passed over the camp. The science party waved as I rocked the wings.

The mountains that defined the Beardmore Glacier were crowded with clouds, making it impossible for us to see anything except a few of the higher mountain tops peeking through the cloud layer. We picked our way through these as we climbed toward the ice shelf. Since our off-load had gone as quickly as it did, we found ourselves with enough fuel to do a little sightseeing. The crew voted to see some whales, so we took the long way home by circling around Cape Crozier and the back side of Ross Island.

This back side of Ross Island stretches for more than fifty miles from Cape Crozier to Cape Byrd. The entire length is fronted by the open Ross Sea, our best bet for spotting whales. The most dominant feature of Cape Crozier is an extinct volcano, Mt. Terror. It rises to an altitude of 10,750 feet, just 1,700 feet short of the active volcano Mt. Erebus. We descended to five hundred feet with the full height of Mt. Terror staring at us through the windscreen. Circling initially to the right to get to the outside of the vortices that swept down off the mountain, I made a broad left turn to put us directly over the easternmost portion of the island and the now-deserted inland rookeries of the emperor penguin.

As we rounded the eastern tip of the island, I could barely make out the remains of the rock igloo that Cherry-Garrard, Wilson, and Bowers built in the dead of the winter night to serve as the base camp from which they watched the emperor penguin and subsequently collected three eggs for scientific study. I recalled Cherry-Garrard's journal: "By the end of two days we had the walls built, and banked up to one or two feet from the top; we were to fit the roof cloth close before banking up the rest. The great difficulty in banking was the hardness of the snow, it being impossible to fill in the cracks between the blocks which were more like paving-stones than anything else."[3] It was impossible for me to imagine those three men building this shelter without proper equipment in the freezing, pitch-black darkness of a polar winter.

From the tip of Cape Crozier run a series of pressure ridges: frozen waves, or furrows, some fifty to sixty feet high, that look as if the area had been plowed by giants. These ridges run out from the barrier of the Ross Ice Shelf for perhaps half a mile and then abruptly end in the smooth, calm waters of the Ross Sea. It was at the edge of these icy pressure ridges and sea, some twenty miles or more from their inland rookeries, that we saw the first emperors. There must have been over a thousand of them, huddled together on or near the ice edge, some peering into the water, as if they would at any minute stick a foot in to test the temperature.

We had descended to five hundred feet about half a mile offshore and were clipping along at 250 knots, high and fast enough that we wouldn't disturb the birds that were congregated along the shoreline. Even at that altitude we could sense the majestic size of the emperors and were awed by the sheer number of them on that desolate stretch of ice. Once clear of the penguins, I slowed to 180 knots and followed the contour of the island.

It was here, as far removed from civilization as possible, that we spotted the first group of whales. Even at a hundred feet it was easy to distinguish the pod of ten or so killer whales. Their high dorsal fins cut knife-like through the clear blue water as they cruised the shoreline, looking to lunch on a juicy penguin or two. Farther along we came across a pair of minke whales swimming languidly along the surface as if they were basking in the bright sunshine.

We climbed to a thousand feet as we rounded Cape Byrd to avoid the Kiwi research site there. As we passed the site, I was glad we had climbed: next to the main building was one of the squadron's helicopters, transitioning to level flight headed back toward McMurdo. I don't think we would have run into it, but stranger things have happened.

We passed straight across Erebus Bay, skirted Observation Hill, dropped our gear and flaps, and ran through all the checklists. We were lined up on centerline at five miles out when I called for and was granted landing clearance. At four miles it looked as if there was something on the skiway, and at three miles I could clearly see the tires spinning on a stake truck, stuck fast in the snow. At two miles I asked the controller if we were still cleared to land and was greeted with a sarcastic "Yes, Zero Two, you are still cleared to land."

"I thought I'd confirm since there is a truck in the middle of the skiway. It appears he's stuck." I had the copilot add enough power to level us at a hundred and fifty feet because I knew we would go around.

"Say again, Zero Two. A truck?"

"Affirmative."

"Standby" was the reply as we approached one mile. By now I could make out the truck driver's head, bobbing back and forth as if that might free the vehicle. Maybe five seconds elapsed before:

"Zero Two, wave off immediately. Acknowledge." It was a different voice from the one before, probably the tower supervisor.

Looked like the tower had spotted the truck, too. Nice of them. "Roger, Zero Two going around. How about the off-duty? Can we get in there?"

"Roger, Zero Two. Cleared as requested. Cleared to land skiway 15."

The crew was having such a great time with this that by the time we did land, we all had tears in our eyes from all the laughter. The confusion in this scenario, if bottled, would supply the daily dosage requirements of most medium-sized countries. The failure seems to have come from a lack of communication—or perhaps, at this point in the season, from an apathy that the repeated performance of menial tasks had created. Simple operations such as crossing the skiway can be taken for granted, as an automatic act or a given situation. But that is the very thing that can cause a breakdown in communication—and a disaster. The driver of that truck had gotten permission to cross the skiway from the tower but had probably never called the tower back to say they were stuck.

Accidents happened infrequently in Antarctica, but we all had to stay sharp all the time. In fact, with all the confusion here, I always marvel that the accident rate is as low as it is. There is no time to take anything for granted: this is not at all a forgiving place.

While waiting for the shuttle bus, I noticed that I was famished. I hadn't been into the box lunch today except for a bag of peanuts. Only Ed and I lived on the Hill, so it was just the two of us in the shuttle with one of our favorite drivers, Ester. I made a special plea for her to drive as fast as she could to get me to the chow hall on time. She livened up the thirty-minute trip talking about cross-country skiing, which, she informed us, she could teach anyone, even someone as clumsy on skis as I.

Ester also told us about her summer job as caretaker of a camp at the base of Mt. Katahdin, in Baxter State Park, Maine. From May until October she worked six days a week in the woods at the base of what is not only one of the fairest mountains in the world but also the northern terminus for the Appalachian Trail. From her description her job sounded more like a vacation. In the winter she taught all levels of cross-country skiing for a guide service, also located in Maine. For the real work, she said, she came down here every other year—to keep her spirit in tune.

I looked at the wispy, long blue-gray smoke plume emanating from the snow-covered heights of Mt. Erebus. Bouncing along in the shuttle bus toward Mac Town, I didn't want to be anywhere else. OK, maybe Disneyland.

On the day we had to carry the ammonium nitrate, I noticed that the XO, a helo pilot who for the past several weeks had flown with us as a 3P, wasn't scheduled with the crew—funny, since we were flying to Mill Glacier, only the roughest spot on the continent. Landing at Mill is like careening down an ice-glazed cobblestone street.

Today we would find out if we could land there without blowing ourselves to smithereens. I also noted that today was the final flight for the AN 95 and that even though the CO, XO, and Ops O had proclaimed the explosives safe to transport by air, not one of them had been scheduled to fly an explosives flight. The NSF bubbas had seen two plane loads of ammonium nitrate flown to SERIS L, and neither exploded. Emboldened, they wanted to see if they could land it at the roughest place on the continent.

The Mill Glacier is incredible to land on. The glacier is a sheet of blue ice covered with grapefruit-sized pits—not to mention the fact that to land there, a pilot would have to fly the approach from the base of the glacier, which meant the landing would be uphill. We were to be guinea pigs and sacrificial lambs. I wouldn't have minded a nice case of mononucleosis about then.

Actually I was less angry about flying the explosives out than I was about the decision-making process. The folks in charge had determined that these explosives were safe to fly, yet they were unwilling either to fly them themselves or to ride on any plane that was carrying them. Today we would fly as a junior crew with only one passenger. We loaded the AN 95 at the far end of the skiway, well away from the general population—a mere gesture, really, because if it were to have gone off, all of Willy Field would have been leveled. This was a cheering thought. At least if I had to go, I could take this whole blasted place with me.

I briefed our lone passenger—the explosives expert, of course, sent to lend credence to the idea that the flight was safe and to give us a sense of confidence. I was heartened by the fact that he was the same guy who had driven the tractor into the crevasse. I figured his luck had to be all right. After all, it would be too ironic to survive a fifty-foot fall into a crevasse, only to be blown up two weeks later on solid ground.

He explained to us that the AN 95 is akin to gelled nitro (1 oz. = big boom) and that it had been frozen to increase its stability. His basic message to us was: "We're pretty sure this won't blow up." I asked if it could withstand the severe vibrations we would be encountering at Mill Glacier. I could see him wondering, how severe? But he put a confident face on. "I think so," he replied. I was so convinced that I gave the crew a thumbs-up, and we made ready to go. We would just float aloft on such inspiring words.

On the flight out I watched the crew's reaction to carrying explosives. They were confident to the point of absurdity, which I felt was a mask for their fears. They had absolutely no idea of what to expect, in fact no one here did, but they had resolved to staunchly support our collective abilities. We were the best, we would do it without dying, we would come back cocky just to piss everyone else off.

To ward off any jitters they may have been feeling, Roy, Chris, and our training loadmaster, Jane, actually sat on the explosives and played cards during the flight out. You've got to hand it to them for nerve. Any qualms I had evaporated in the face of their raw courage. Crazy, but endearing— that's how I thought of them then.

I hadn't been briefed about the AN 95 and didn't know what to expect, so I had each of the nonpilot crew come forward to fly the airplane for five to ten minutes apiece. Many crew members throughout the services fly for years without ever actually controlling the plane they fly in. This seemed to be the perfect opportunity for them to find out what it was like, since it might be their last flight. I was confident nothing would go wrong with the explosives in flight (and not with Roy holding three aces), but I wasn't so sure about what would happen once we hit the ground.

As we began our descent into the Mill Glacier Camp, Roy informed me we were too heavy to land. He said we needed to burn off about twenty minutes of fuel first, so we opted to fly down low through the Beardmore Glacier. Even though we've seen this site many times, the crew always made me feel like Dad on a Sunday drive with the kids screaming for ice cream. The Beardmore was our crew's favorite treat.

It's true. It's an awe-inspiring sight, with incredible ice formations, moraines, and massive snow "falls" from ten-thousand-foot peaks. The proportions of these falls must be seen to be believed, their size rendering everything else in the vicinity insignificant. To put it in context: Niagara Falls plummets a mere 167 feet (on the American side), a distance that is *sixty times shorter* than what we saw here regularly.

Seeing the Beardmore restored my sense of calm. I flew up along its northern wall as we dropped the flaps and gear and ran through the landing checklists. I made a sweeping right-hand turn to lose altitude and then turned back to the left in a slow arc, descending to pass over the two-hundred-foot-high moraine that stood between us and the Mill Glacier. At 120 knots we passed over the moraine; this way I wouldn't be forced to dive so much on the opposite side. I drifted down slowly to fifty feet above the deck and then added a slight amount of power to aid with the uphill landing.

When the main tires touched, I added just a bit more power so that we glided over the surface like a boat on a calm sea. I relaxed my grip on the yoke, and the plane settled nicely as I pulled off power. I lowered the nose gently, then added reverse slowly. We slowed to a stop without a boom, which was very comforting. With the dread of screwing things up, I made a picture-perfect landing. I still can't believe that it worked out so well.

The blue ice of the Mill Glacier was blanketed by a fine covering of snow, making the brakes useless, so we stopped using only reverse thrust. The Mill also has a dramatic slope to the right, toward the nunatak, a fact that always made for dicey taxi conditions. When we taxied back down the glacier toward our takeoff point, the number-one propeller dangled only a foot or two above the surface, and visibility was continually whited out by the loose snow that was kicked up in front of us by our constantly reversing the props to control our speed.

We stopped abeam the small camp—that is, with it off to our side, at a right angle. There was a subtle instant of relief. Then it was business as usual. Chris lowered the ramp and gently maneuvered the goods out. On that icy slope, once we disconnected our winch cable, the explosives began an uncontrolled slide toward the camp. It was about a ten on the sphinc-ter-tightening scale. I had had enough fun delivering this stuff, so I made a quick right turn and lined up for takeoff. The stuff could blow itself up, for all I cared. It was out of my hands now. We accelerated in a comic poof of snow and left the camp personnel to chase the pallet of explosives, which seemed to be gathering speed, as it careened down the icy slope toward their camp.

Tim did the takeoff, which became so violent that he cursed the entire time about how bloody bumpy it was. I'll admit that racing uphill on that pothole-infested surface wasn't my idea of fun, but I didn't mind, now that our load from hell was gone. He could have been taking off over a volcano, and I wouldn't have cared.

But it was bone-jarringly rough. After about forty-five seconds of bounding over the surface, Tim yelled, "This is bullshit!" I asked if he wanted to get out of here. He nodded vigorously and said, "Shit yeah!"

I said, "Flaps coming to 100," and I pushed the flap handle to full flaps. We instantly jumped into the smooth caress of the air above the ground. We breathed a collective sigh of relief and headed out. At a hundred and twenty miles out from home, the chips light came on, indicating that metal particles were contaminating the gearbox oil. The gearbox (spinning at 13,820 rpm) might be coming apart. *Fine,* I thought, *we live long enough to dump the explosives and then crash because of a maintenance problem?*

We were the only C-130 squadron in the navy that had these chips lights, and since the magnetic plugs had just been recently checked, we were somewhat concerned. We didn't have any secondary indications, such as low or fluctuating oil pressure, but we elected to do a cruise engine shutdown (a precautionary measure that would allow us to rapidly restart the engine in case of a more dire emergency), just to be on the safe side.

Tim directed the engine to be shut down and, forty-five minutes later, made an uneventful three-engine landing. We wrote up what we thought was a minor problem, probably some metal filings collected on the plugs. I learned later, as I boarded the shuttle bus, that the gear box was filled with metal chunks and loose ball bearings. It was within minutes of coming apart. Had we waited another few minutes to bag the engine, we would have faced catastrophic engine failure. With gears spinning so fast, the gear box would have exploded. Other C-130s with this problem have reported damage varying from gears splitting off and flying through the cockpit, to entire propellers departing the plane, some even taking with them the other engine on the same wing.

I hunched down in my seat on the shuttle bus back. Just another merry day of Antarctic adventure.

14

GOAT ROPES

One day the squadron's operations duty officer called me at 0330 to tell me I had been summoned to the NSF director's office for a meeting. I asked him what was up, but he remained enigmatic and told me that all would soon be explained. I shaved and showered, dressed in my "greens" (the nickname for the olive-drab uniforms we wear when not on flight status), and made it to the Chalet (NSF's headquarters on the Ice) with ten minutes to spare, but still rubbing the sleep out of my eyes.

Twenty or so people milled around a large silver coffee urn and a tray of fresh, hot doughnuts—pastries appeared only when something was a big deal. I grabbed a cup of coffee and a doughnut and crossed the room to find out what was afoot. The NSFA operations officer confirmed what I expected: the meeting concerned an on-continent flight for VIPs who had recently arrived at McMurdo for the dedication of the new Albert P. Crary Science and Engineering Center (CSEC), scheduled for 5 November 1991.[1] Then he threw me for a loop—my crew had been handpicked to ferry them to the Pole.

He was just going into the details when we were interrupted by the arrival of the head of the NSF's Office of Polar Programs, with the commanding officer of the Naval Support Force, Antarctica, and my CO in tow. I hoped I didn't have doughnut crumbs on my greens. We were herded en masse into a conference room for our briefing. The room ran nearly the length of the Chalet and was lined with windows that afforded me a backside view of Building 155, Downtown Mac Town.

We sat and received copies of the day's schedule of events. The blinds were lowered, and the NSF event coordinator used an overhead projector to run through the schedule of individualized wake-up calls, shower times, and breakfast and runway transportation deadlines. When it was time to discuss the day's mission, I was briefed in great detail.

The entire success or failure of VIP trips to the Pole rested on four main factors: precise timing, who sat where on the plane, whom I should address and how, and how my crew was to be attired—they wanted us in identically colored flight suits. We were tasked to fly a cabinet secretary, the U.S. ambassador to New Zealand, the head of the NSF, and twenty-one other VIPs to the South Pole for lunch. More Goat Ropes.

The NSF plan specified two crews and three planes for this particular Goat Rope, two planes for the flight plus one backup. My plane would actually carry the VIPs, so we had to have it fueled, started, and warmed by 0740. The VIPs would arrive promptly at 0745, to be loaded for an 0800 takeoff. I was then to amend my speed as necessary to arrive at the South Pole precisely at 1100. There we were to wait for thirty minutes, until we were sure the chase plane (which would pick them up and bring them back to McMurdo) had made it off the deck at McMurdo on time. When we had confirmation that the chase plane was good to go, we were to fly to papa 2 and orbit until the chase plane was on deck at the Pole; then we were free to return home.

When the brief ended, I walked to breakfast with the NSFA operations officer. He told me privately he thought that there was no way this would work as planned. He couldn't understand the need for two flights and two planes, and we agreed that two missions for one event meant double the odds for trouble.

The crew did a remarkable job on preflight. The plane was clean, warm, and ready to depart at precisely 0740. I called the passenger terminal and told them we were ready to load the passengers on time at 0745. The first of two vans arrived at 0810. Loading commenced promptly at 0825.

During the flight to the Pole, I was amazed at the unresponsiveness of our passengers. Here we were, passing over some of the most beautiful, pristine, and awe-inspiring vistas on the planet, and no one said a thing. I even invited them to come to the flight station, where there is a commanding view. No one came. I then told the passengers that the weather over the Transantarctic Mountains was the clearest I had seen this season and that I'd never seen the area look so captivating. I stressed the point that they would be denying themselves a unique opportunity if they didn't come to the flight station and see the consummate beauty of these mountains, which, to me, typified the rugged splendor of the continent. Two people came forward; neither of them asked any questions. All the others remained seated, folded up in their parkas, trying to get comfortable in the dark, cluttered, and noisy cargo bay.

I decided that they must have had too much fun at the CSEC dedication party the night before. Perhaps they were experiencing their first Antarctic hangovers. I myself had gone to that party, lured by stories of rivers of milk and honey, Kiwi beer, huge shrimp swimming in cocktail sauce, delicacies of all kinds and other wondrous delights. The reality, however, was nuts with too much salt, cheese and stale crackers, hard salami, and domestic champagne. Yes, they had all probably drunk too much, trying to mitigate the effects of having sat through speech after speech that afternoon.

The first of those speeches had concluded an hour after I arrived. Then the second speaker had produced a two-inch stack of three-by-five-inch cards and begun to recount, somewhat stiffly, the history of the continent, beginning with the first sightings in the late 1700s. When I left, the crowd was stifling yawns and he still had an inch and a half of three-by-five cards to go. Truth is, I don't even like domestic champagne. But if my VIP passengers were still in the throes of the hangover curse this morning, I would do better to leave them alone.

South Pole weather was supposed to be terrible, only a quarter mile visibility, poor and poor, from drifting snow. However, once we started our approach, the weather cleared and we caught sight of the skiway at six miles out. The sky remained clear until we touched down, but in the five minutes it took us to taxi to the pits, the weather turned completely sour. It was classic South Pole fickleness. We landed at 1059.

The cold was insufferable. I was used to it, but outside the plane even I went absolutely stiff in a minute. I got so cold I found it difficult to move; I stood transfixed, staring at the loose grains of snow blowing across the gelid landscape like sands in a shifting desert. Occasionally the wind would suck the snow from the ground, twirl it around like cotton candy, then cast the lot aside. This rush of air created twisting, pulsating, shimmering phantoms in a second, danced with them a moment, and then, as if bored, dispatched the shadowy tornadoes with alacrity. As those snow demons twirled around me, it lent an eerie feel to the place, as though I had infringed on a frozen graveyard. All about me was white, a dense white shroud that when seen from above was nearly transparent but when seen from the ground made a white, murky light without contrast. We had been extremely fortunate to land when we did; a few minutes more and it would have been impossible.

Once we were parked, the VIPs were rounded up and herded off for a photo opportunity at the Ceremonial Pole, where a three-foot-high red and white barber pole is topped with a mirrored ball about the size of a basketball. This serves as the de facto Pole. Here the twelve flags of the original member nations of the Antarctic Treaty are arranged in a semi-circle around the barber pole as a symbolic gesture of good will and cooperation.

I watched the group as they huddled together, smiling wanly for the camera, and I felt sorry for them. They were rushed about, told where to be, told with whom to shake hands, told to smile for the camera, without ever seeing anything of the extraordinary desert that surrounded them. The severe cold snapped me back to reality, so I headed down the snow ramp and through the massive twenty-foot entry doors along the ice-covered corridor leading to the bowels of South Pole Station.

Along the way I bumped into the head of NSF's polar operations, who told me he had changed his mind—which also changed our agenda. He now wanted us to wait an hour on deck and then see him before we departed. This was to be only the first of his changes: he continued to modify the plan every fifteen minutes or so during our entire stay at the Pole that day. As we talked, the now-frozen VIPs stumbled into the warmth of the mess hall to defrost slowly during another dreary history lecture about the South Pole Station, after which they would be treated to the real reason for their visit—lunch.

The South Pole staff had pulled a real coup this season, hiring a world-class chef, and it appeared that the secret was out. I had befriended this chef one evening in the McMurdo Officers' Club before he was shipped out here, so I wasn't surprised when he pressed a bowl of his seafood chowder into my hands and pointed to the radio shack. He could pass me a bowl of soup in his kitchen, but with all the high rollers around, I had to eat it elsewhere. It was wonderful. I was always amazed how well the folks at the Pole ate, since everything they had came from McMurdo Station. Same ingredients, but way different results. I harbored a dream that the chef would quit the starkness of the Pole for the relative comfort of McMurdo and cook for us there.

With soup in hand I strolled over to the Pole's radio-command center next door to the galley and learned that the second crew had taken off early and was inbound to the Pole. Perhaps I had been too skeptical, since events certainly appeared to be falling into place nicely; perhaps the plan had merit after all. With everything tracking so well, I rounded my crew and prepared to depart.

Since the weather at the Pole was still very poor, I asked the director if he would like me to wait until the second plane was on deck as a precaution. He seemed indifferent, so I reminded him of the cardinal rule of Antarctic flying: "Never wait for the second shuttle." He shrugged and told me with a mouthful of food to go ahead and depart. While I strapped in, the Pole radio operator called to say that the director had changed his mind and had ordered me to stay put. I guess on second thought he had been burned by the cardinal rule before, or perhaps he just thought it prudent not to chance it now.

Whatever his reason, we were going to have to wait another hour while the VIPs finished lunch and went to the small ship's store for an official South Pole T-shirt, so I cleared the crew to wander about, giving them the go-ahead to check on the availability of lunch leftovers. I decided to have a look around the station myself, since I had been there hundreds of times but had never had the opportunity to really see it in detail.

The most prominent feature is the large silver geodesic dome. It is 165 feet round and 53 feet high and resembles a space station in a low orbit on a sea of frost-bound clouds. Entrance into the dome is made by descending a gently sloping snow ramp, guarded by two hulking doors that stand open during the summer but are closed during the winter to protect the station from the brutal elements. Just inside the entrance, two forty-by-eighty foot tunnels constructed of tubular steel run off to the left and right. These tunnels house a variety of maintenance and engineering facilities, fuel bladders, and a small basketball court. Straight ahead from the entrance is the forty-foot passageway that leads to the interior of the dome.

Whenever I entered the dome, I always had a sense of foreboding, since the walls of the main passageway are covered with a thick layer of frost like the inside of a massive freezer. In those forty feet I felt that I had entered a white tomb and that I was descending into the bowels of the continent. As it usually happened, the openness of the dome was my reprieve, once I saw the half-dozen Day-Glo orange modular buildings that formed a small, cheery community there beneath the snow. To my right as I entered the dome was the galley, and above that, on the second floor, was the station bar. Just to the left of the galley was the station's command center, its cramped spaces filled with radios, computers, and the ever-cheerful faces of the station radio operators.

Above the command center is the recreation center, which has a room with thousands of paperbacks, a TV room, and a pool room. Here also is the one-room post office and ship's store, where many South Pole visitors spent their money on the coveted yearly South Pole T-shirt. Another building houses a dozen small dorm rooms and a tiny greenhouse. The last shack in this group serves as the station's fire house.

Today, the South Pole Station ship's store was open for business to anyone who cared to participate in the most ludicrous shopping experience in the world. The store carried a few odd bits and pieces, but mostly carried promises that, given time, they could get anything we wanted. We called it the Southern-Most Inconvenience Store. The store is tucked into a cramped six-by-ten-foot room with a large window propped open like a hungry mouth calling, "Throw your money in here!" And folks do, to the tune of some sixty thousand dollars a year.

You could buy candy (the good New Zealand kind), liquor, combs, brushes, toothpaste, patches, pins, popcorn, tapes, pennants, and bumper stickers, as well as the T-shirts. The official annual South Pole T-shirt was worth its weight in gold. I spent my money on them more than once. These ten-dollar shirts, given prudentially, garnered me uncountable goodwill rewards, making them quite the bargain.

While buying shirts that day, I couldn't help but think of the overall cost of my ten-dollar treasures. Nothing gets to the Pole unless we fly it there, yet here I was with five T-shirts wadded up in a plastic bag, flying them back to McMurdo, and ultimately back to the States. Somehow I think our precious cargo space could have been more efficiently utilized.

Purists would argue that buying a genuine South Pole shirt is a wiser karmic investment than buying one that simply glamorizes the place—as if somehow the actual South Pole molecules touch the cotton and magically enhance it. And while the idea of buying T-shirts that I myself brought here still seems silly to me, that fact never prevented me from buying a ton of them. Boredom can make a man do strange things.

Whenever I'm at the Pole, I normally stop in and chat with the duty radio operator—an individual with a job that is one of the most mundane yet, during the season, one of the most important on the Ice. The HF radio is manned twenty-four hours a day to monitor the web of HF radio traffic on the continent. At the Pole, these operators are the ears of Antarctica.

While I was waiting for the VIPs, one of the off-duty radio operators offered to give me the nickel tour of the station. I eagerly accepted. We hurried out into the dome and into the small greenhouse. It was difficult for me to believe I was still at the South Pole when I came face to face with hydroponically grown lettuce in the cool blue light of the 80-degree room. Greenhouse production was geared toward providing twenty-five people with a fresh salad once or twice a week during the winter—psychologically as well as nutritionally, an important item.

Back in the dome we wound our way down a long ice-encrusted corridor and entered a room that was noticeably warmer. Stored there were milk, lemons, soda, lettuce—items to be kept cold but not frozen. I was standing in one of the Pole's refrigerators, where—compared to the ambient temperature outside—items are kept warm. Leaving the relative warmth of the fridge, we continued along the passage to a staircase that led to the station's four-story observation tower. My guide shot up the ladder while I, fifteen years his junior, brought up the rear huffing and puffing. I usually had no trouble with the thin air at the pole, but climbing forty feet this quickly winded me.

The tower commanded a spectacular 360-degree view of the station and permitted the inhabitants to see what was happening around them without ever leaving the safety of the domed city. High above the Pole, I watched as the engines of my plane spun silently, then I scanned the horizon. Adjacent to the plane was the Ceremonial Pole, and behind the South Pole dome stood several olive green seasonal out-buildings.

The dome, a few buildings, and several antennas were all that inter-rupted thousands of miles of smooth, white snow that surrounded us. As we gazed out over that silent, vast frozen ocean, my guide said, "The pole is ninety-eight hundred feet above sea level, and ninety-six hundred feet of that is snow. It snows here only maybe an inch a year. If you want to imagine what constitutes a long time, think about how long it took for that much snow to accumulate." My lightening-quick mathematical mind pro-vided me the answer almost instantly: *a helluva long time.*

We made our way back to the communications center, where I was promptly handed the HF radio mike and informed that the inbound chase plane had a landing-gear problem. Since we had experienced the identi-cal problem in that plane a few days earlier, I suggested ways to alleviate the problem. But it was soon obvious that their plane had a significant mal-function. I was sure that they should not risk landing here. Roy, sitting in our Herc monitoring our still-running engines, overheard my conversa-tion on the HF radio. The chase plane's aircraft commander, his engineer, Roy, and I held an impromptu discussion on the problem. The engineer said he could get the landing gear down once, but he wasn't sure about twice, so between us, we decided they should return to McMurdo and let us fly the VIPs back.

The decision took the pressure off them, so they were free to con-centrate on the gear problem without the extra headache of a planeload of VIPs. I went to our plane, and I could barely make out the chase plane as it passed a hundred feet overhead. I was relieved that we hadn't left the Pole on the original schedule; if we had, we would have had to turn around and fly through this weather to come back and retrieve the stranded VIPs.

By departure time the wind had picked up to 30 knots, which reduced the forward visibility to less than a thousand feet, nil and nil. I returned to the dome, found the NSF director, and related that visibility was so poor we would be forced to wait until it cleared, perhaps for some time. I sug-gested he round up the passengers and have them standing by so that we could launch quickly if the weather broke. If we couldn't load and launch quickly, I told him, we might have to stay the night.

With the mention of a possible camp-out at the Pole, the faces of the VIPs within earshot dropped significantly. I supposed that lunch and a personalized "hero" photo of themselves standing next to the Ceremonial Pole would be enough adventure for one day. Perhaps an unusually high concentration of prayers emanated from our passengers that afternoon. In any event, visibility soon improved enough for me to see two panels (our take-off minimums) about thirty minutes later. I called for our passengers to shake a leg. It was important to take advantage of this weather window. I waited. No one showed.

Ten minutes earlier it was clear that all the VIPs wanted was to be gone from this God-forsaken place, but now it took us nearly twenty-five minutes to round up the stragglers and get them strapped in. The skiway was in poor shape, well grooved and rough from all the recent wear and tear. The slushy conditions prevented us from accelerating above 60 knots, so on the second attempt I called for flaps 100 percent, and we wallowed skyward at 75 knots, 45 knots short of our air minimum control speed. The VIPs all thought it fun. I guess they didn't know me well enough to know that I sweat only when I sense real danger. But still, it was probably just as well that they didn't see how profusely I was sweating as we climbed out.

The skies were clear as we crossed the Transantarctics for the second time that day, so I decided to give our passengers a thrill and fly down low through the valley of the Beardmore Glacier. As uninterested as our group had been on the way out, they all jockeyed for prime window spots (in the cockpit) now. I could have sworn I saw some elbows thrown; it was better than watching a hockey game. We descended to three thousand feet above the floor of the glacier, well below the mountain peaks that form the valley. For the next few minutes the cockpit bristled with animated banter, pointing, and picture-taking as we flew over some of the most breathtaking scenery on the continent.

The weather for our return to McMurdo wasn't supposed to be all that great, but naturally the Weather Shamans were dead wrong, and we saw the field from forty miles away. I was surprised because as we descended over Minna Bluff, a little better than eighty miles from McMurdo, the winds were incredibly fierce. I descended at 250 knots, and the winds (as foretold by the blowing snow) were nearly keeping up with the plane. I guessed that they were in the neighborhood of 150 to 180 knots, perhaps higher.

The rush of wind carried the snow with such force that the snow looked like a river of milk spilling over the rocky island. In the swale between Minna Bluff and Black Island, the wind formed flowing clouds of snow that looked like eddy currents suspended in midair. We were more than thirty miles away, yet we could feel the power of the wind as it rolled and kicked in the trough between the island and the bluff. With such fierce wind, I thought it prudent to inform Mac Weather, because McMurdo's weather is directly affected by the high and low pressure ridges these winds represent.

I knew they needed my input; the remote anemometer on Black Island had been blown apart at 126 knots during an early-season Herbie, which meant the forecasters had no early warning of heavy winds. They couldn't predict Herbies until the last moment. When I related what we had encountered, two forecasters called ten minutes apart to confirm my PIREPs (pilot reports). I was surprised when, as we set for landing, the tower called the runway IFR, since we had been able to see the field continually for the last forty miles.

I soon realized why as we got closer to the ground. Above twenty-five feet, I could see for miles, but with the winds kicking up at 30 to 35 knots, below twenty-five feet we were blinded by a localized fog of blowing snow. We could see the ice runway as we looked straight down, but looking ahead for landing, we saw only the fog as the runway disappeared. I knew I was on centerline as we crossed the threshold where the runway vanished. I kept the nose as straight as I could until I caught a glimpse of the runway panels on either side of the runway, at which point—even though this is considered bad form in the C-130—I jockeyed the throttles (increased and decreased power quickly) close to landing on the runway because I had lost most of my visual landing cues.

We touched down smoothly, halfway down the runway, 10 knots below my charted touchdown speed in what was technically the worst landing I'd ever performed on the Ice. Tim and Roy chided me for my inferior performance, making me feel as guilty as hell until one of the VIPs stuck his head into the flight station and offered his congratulations on such a fine landing. He said he hadn't even felt the plane touch down. I thanked him and told the cockpit crew, "I did what I did because I wanted to wow the VIPs." Yeah, right. They didn't buy it for a second.

With the flight behind us, I was extraordinarily proud of my crew's stellar effort. Considering all the delays, the problems with the other plane, and our having to tend to the flock of VIPs, we kept to the schedule and had even made it back in time for dinner with five minutes to spare—not that anyone was in a hurry to eat. Chicken cookies, anyone?

We flew passengers on many occasions, often to drop them off for research expeditions in remote locations. And on many occasions, we had troubles. On one such flight, Chris, thinking ahead, asked where the Mogas (gas with special additives to prevent freezing) for the skidoos was.[2] I searched through my paperwork and told him there wasn't any Mogas manifested. Chris confirmed this when he talked to Term Ops. They told him that no Mogas would be going. Apparently the PI hadn't listened to his graduate students when they told him repeatedly that no Mogas had been airdropped for them during the reconnaissance of the area. Usually if a remote site is going to be a large camp with tons of supplies, we will air-drop most of that science group's supplies beforehand. This saves room and weight for when we have to finally land in the open field and set up their camp.

It took an hour, but we finally convinced Term Ops and the PI that skidoos were pretty much useless without Mogas and that perhaps we should add a full four-barrel pallet to our flight today. They grudgingly agreed. As we waited, I stared into the back end of the plane. It looked like Grandma's attic. For put-ins, a tremendous amount of stuff is involved—everything that is required to sustain a group for two months: tents, rock boxes, skidoos, food, bamboo stakes with colored flags to mark safe trails, ungainly Nansen sleds, clothing, sleeping bags, and stoves. And now, four fifty-five-gallon drums of Mogas. The loading and placement of this equipment is similar to figuring out a jigsaw puzzle. Chris, as usual, did a superb job. I handpicked him prior to the season because he was the best loadmaster in the squadron. He had a keen eye for loading and was able to visualize the load in its proper position even as the junk sat on the tarmac.

Once loaded, the gear becomes a cohesive yet fragile unit; if one piece is removed, the whole puzzle falls apart, caving in on itself. Chris, in a move of genius, created a spot for the Mogas by rearranging only two ramp-mounted skidoos.

At 1100 we had the Mogas aboard, the plane reloaded, and our passengers briefed. Once we were all situated in the plane, the PI came forward to the flight deck to let me know we had to stop everything because he was missing a bag. Not any bag—a very special bag, his life. It contained his asthma medications. I wondered to myself how the hell he passed the strict physical to get down here.

Immediately he started in accusatory tones about how my crew had screwed up and misplaced his bag. Up to this point, my crew and I had bent over backward for this bozo, complied with all his requests, waited for meetings that he himself never attended, chose his working site for him without his help, air-dropped his stuff in prime condition, added the last-minute Mogas, and now we had the Bag Disaster.

I initiated a complete check of the plane, the cargo yard, the cargo holding area at the ice runway, and every other place around town the PI might have set foot. At one juncture this PI from hell was so convinced it was the cargo yard's fault that he was sure someone had placed his bag on a Kiwi Herc that just departed for Christchurch. In order to forestall his plan to recall the New Zealand–bound plane, I had Mac Center call the Kiwis, who then conducted an in-air search of their aircraft.

I noticed my crew day was about to expire; I informed the PI that our "drop dead" was 1200. I also told him I might be able to stretch that to 1230, but no more. At 1115, with no sign of the bag, I pulled the PI aside and laid out his remaining options. He could (1) go without his drugs, and once we located his bag, we could air-drop it to him; (2) give me a list of the medications he required, and I would call the infirmary for replacements; or (3) he could get off the plane so we could take the remainder of his group out and take him out later.

He refused to go without his drugs, and for some unknown reason he refused to give me a list of his medications, so options one and two were gone. Then it hit me like a bolt of lightning. It was so obvious that I was ashamed I hadn't thought of it sooner: the missing bag was a ruse. He was avoiding being put in the field today. I asked him point-blank what he wanted to do. He sheepishly said, "Stay." With a glimmer of hope that the remaining option might work, I phoned the ODO and NSFA duty officer to see if they would buy the plan. We decided among the three of us that he would stay (the PI perked right up at this prospect) and be taken out separately later.

We manned up at 1145, taxied, and lined up for takeoff. At 1155 as I was advancing the power levers toward takeoff power, we got the call from the head NSF representative to abort the mission. Hey, no big deal, just hundreds of man-hours wasted, plus a complete search of two planes, with the actual mission scrubbed just as I was in the process of taking off. Needless to say I was none too happy. Little did I know that the best was yet to come.

When I returned to town I had to see the commanding officer, then the captain in charge of the navy here, and then the head representative for NSF, to explain why I had kicked this PI off the plane. This was how pass the grapefruit was played here: since it couldn't by definition be the PI's fault, it must be mine. I spent the remainder of my day committing the incident to writing, three separate times, one for each verbal reprimand I received.

For those who can't stand suspense: after accusing the crew, Term Ops, the cargo yard, his graduate students, the Kiwis, and everybody else short of God of being the one who lost his precious bag, it was finally located. On the plane. Of course. He had placed it with the field party's food, not on the pallet for personal effects as he was instructed to do.

I recalled his look of incredulity when I had asked him if he had checked the food pallet during the search. What a ludicrous question—clearly I possessed the mental capacity of a zucchini. He rolled his eyes, let out a protracted sigh, and with the sort of patronizing tone that professors save for freshmen, snapped: "Of course it wouldn't be there! That pallet is for food!"

That science group went on the next scheduled flight. The PTAC for that flight told me later that the PI sheepishly sat in the back for the entire flight out, clutching his bag like a security blanket. In fairness, the same three gentlemen who chewed me out apologized when they learned the truth and had me write up a complete report, as if that might make me feel better. It didn't. I hate to misuse my crew's time, and this was the worst case of wasted energy I experienced in three years. The PI never apologized. He never phoned to say good-bye, either. That really hurt.

We often shuttled pallets of food and gear to various locations around the continent. We had a long mission scheduled for one particular day. We would be flying first to the Pole to drop off three pallets of food and take on enough fuel to fly to the Pensacola Mountains. There we would pick up a science party and ferry them a hundred miles to the Argentina Range and put them in there, then return to the Pole to take on additional fuel to retrieve a science party at the Geologist Range on our way back to McMurdo. I felt like the driver of the crosstown bus.

I tried to sleep the entire flight to the Pole to prevent the enervation of a long flight over the empty white expanse and to help conserve my mental energy for the open-field work that defined our day. Roy woke me when we began our descent. The weather at the Pole was similar to that at the coast, clear and calm, although much colder. Only minus-37 centigrade today, but the place was shimmering.

Our three pallet off-load and the on-load of fuel were simultaneous. The crew was so quick and efficient that we were lining up for takeoff out of the Pole after only twenty minutes on deck. Once airborne I called (and apparently awakened) our first science party, notifying them that we were two hours away. I instructed them to box up everything except their tents and then to pack and palletize their cargo according to NSF instructions. An hour out from their position I called again to make sure they were on track. I was given a resounding, "Yes, we're ready. Come and get us."

At forty miles we had the camp in view. It looked as if a tornado had just hit, with tents and gear scattered everywhere. We flew over the site at two hundred feet to get the lay of the land and to check the ski drags, since this would be our first time there. The area was suspiciously free of loaded pallets. It was worse than I had expected: not a box had been packed, there were no pallets loaded, and there was just one member of the party ambling about as we crossed overhead. He waved before he wandered back to the tent, zipping up his fly.

We landed on the next pass, only to be greeted by four hungover scientists who were stumbling out of their tent, shading their eyes from the too-bright sun. My first reaction was to turn around and go home, leave these dopes and give them a chance to sober up before the real help arrived. I called Mac Center and asked them to relay our plight to the NSF. It was obvious these folks weren't up to packing, and I didn't want to be responsible for their safety onboard while they were inebriated.

Fifteen minutes later I had my answer. We would pack their items, carry them to their next site, and if they couldn't get the camp set up, then we would bring them back with us. The crew was livid. There is an irritatingly pervasive attitude among scientists that air crews exist to serve them, which is true up to a point, but not to this extent. We will aid them in loading and unloading the plane, help with communications, fly them to the destination of their choice, even proffer advice on site selection, but we are not Sherpas; we don't pitch or strike their tents, pack their bags, or load their pallets.

Barely a word was spoken as my crew of nine—plus four stumbling scientists, who mostly heard "Get out of the way!" from my crew—took two hours to completely pack and load them. Once we had their gear packed, we palletized it, struck their Scott tents, loaded up their rock-filled sample boxes, and then dragged the lot to the back of the plane with their snowmobiles and winched the pallets aboard. We slid their four Nansen sleds on last, on top of the three pallets; then Chris drove their snowmobiles onto the ramp.

I had planned our fuel for forty-five minutes on deck here and for ninety minutes at our next spot; we were weight limited, so there was no padding in my figures. We were now running into borrowed time at the back end of the mission, so I had the crew hustle to get going. We were lucky and got off on the first attempt. As we climbed out, en route to the Argentina Range, the crew held an open discussion on the best way to aggravate the science party's collective hangover. We lucked out and found some moderate turbulence.

As we approached the new site, Ed called to say he had a blip on his radar that looked like the pallet of Mogas air-dropped here some two weeks ago during the recce. This second site in the Argentina Range was located on a vast field surrounded on three sides by jagged purple mountains, a massive cul-de-sac. I pulled the power to flight idle and dove, dropping down over a series of ice falls at least a thousand feet high, which resembled a set of stairs descending a saddle between the peaks.

We circled twice, looking at the site and discussing our options for landing. If we headed into the mouth of the valley, we would have very little room for error if a problem developed, but we couldn't just drop down from three thousand feet on the opposite end, hit the deck, and then rush out the mouth, either.

I opted for flying across and slightly into the open mouth. It was wide, and if I landed and stopped close to the entrance, we would be fine. We configured the plane and then set down for the first drag. The snow was smooth, even, thick, and soft. It was like landing on a cloud. In fact, the snow was so soft I was a little worried that we might have some difficulties taking off once we were on deck. The second drag put us alongside the Mogas by some fifty yards, and since both drags were fairly straight, I picked the second to land in. Since the turbulence had long run out, I think the crew was disappointed that this area wasn't rougher. The loadmasters in back were praying for an e-ticket puke-ride of a ski drag, as a final shot at our passengers. I was sorry I was unable to oblige them in their request.

We landed and then kicked out the science party (once again I had to disappoint my two loadmasters, who wanted to put the scientists out, and then land). The scientists took off, using the radio apparently to establish communications but really as a ploy to avoid the off-load. Only one guy messed with the radio; the rest of the party stood by "helping," looking sheepish, casting furtive glances toward the plane to see how work was progressing. They finished establishing communications with Byrd Surface Camp just as the last pallet left the plane. Amazing timing.

Once they had one of their tents up and I was sure they wouldn't freeze to death, we departed. The wind had shifted in our favor, so I nosed the plane into the wind and added power, and we were off. The surface was so smooth that we seemed to be airborne right from the start. Generally during a ski takeoff you can tell the exact moment that you become airborne. The shaking stops; lights and gauges cease to fall on your head from the overhead panel. Everything becomes still and quiet as the plane breathes a sigh of relief. Today's ski takeoff was so smooth it was like we were carried aloft by angels. We accelerated quickly to 95 knots.

As I circled to check the camp, I was hit by the figure I had unintentionally carved in the snow: a twisted yet distinguishable "H." It was beautiful to look back on that once-virgin patch of snow, seeing those drags. Here I had come from Washington, D.C., via the world to make my distinct mark in the snows of the Argentina Range, Antarctica. Never before had any plane landed anywhere near there, and now this, my temporary gouge in the snow, was my fleeting mark on history.

I continued my circle pass low over the camp before returning to the Pole. As we approached, I noticed the science party gesticulating wildly toward the plane. I thought, *What now? What could have happened in the five minutes since we departed? Please God, don't make us have to land and retrieve them!* As I pondered all the possibilities, I heard laughing over the intercom. It was low at first, but then it rose to guffaws. I was still clueless until Roy pointed toward their tent. It appeared that in their hurry to set up camp, ostensibly to get us out of there, the party had neglected to stake the tent down. When I added power to take off, I inadvertently blew their tent away.

There was justice in the world after all. Now, all I had to do was convince everybody in McMurdo that it was an accident. Accepting the congratulations of the crew, I waggled my wings as a fond-farewell gesture to those hungover, tentless fools in the Argentina Range. We headed for home, impressions of their third-finger salute fresh in our minds.

From the Argentina Range to the Pole is a straight shot across No Man's Land. We cruised along the border of what is known as the area of inaccessibility. To say this area is remote is an understatement. It's remote like the Marianas Trench is deep. It's Antarctica's desert. I feel privileged to have seen it, yet there is really nothing to see. It's a vast ocean of snow without a single distinguishing feature except the sastrugi, long waves of ice, between us and the Prince Charles Mountains at the top of the Amery Ice Shelf some fourteen hundred miles away.

One hundred miles from the Pole we were asked to do a favor for the GCA controller: she wanted to take a photo of the plane doing a low-level pass. We obliged by flying down the skiway at fifty feet. At the far end, we climbed, then made a right 90-degree turn, and immediately followed it with a left 270-degree turn, aligning the plane with the skiway. We landed.

Once we had slid to a stop in the pits, I headed into Pole Station, grabbed a slice of pie to eat, then wandered over to the radio shack. Eight or ten people were all trying to put on coveralls and jackets at the same time. "What's going on?" I asked. An inbound LC-130 was about to do a low-level pass. It was a unique photo opportunity that I wouldn't want to miss. "Really?" I said. "Was the plane coming in from the Pensacola Mountains?"

One guy spoke up. "Yes. How did you know?"

"Because here we are," I said, taking a bite of pie. The shuffling stopped, and ten sad faces stared back at me as though I had just said Christmas was canceled. Evidently the Pole radio operator heard we were going to do the pass but wasn't informed when we were ready to go. I called out to our plane and asked Roy to put on an extra couple hundred pounds of gas so we could repeat the performance. A spontaneous "All right!" rang out in the radio shack, as once again the sound of ten people getting dressed for Antarctica filled the air.

I felt like the Pied Piper as I led the throng of amateur photographers out to the plane. The crew strapped in as the motley Pole group made a beeline for the skiway. There were waves all around as we taxied by the group. After takeoff, I turned and then dropped down and made a fifty-foot pass. Christmas had been restored.

We called our next group at the Geologist Range to let them know that we were inbound and they should expect us in about an hour. As I flew over their camp, I marveled at the poor selection of the landing site. It was by far the worst place in a three-mile radius. The drag I could see looked rough. I had a bad feeling about it—but if the other crew had gotten in and out, then we certainly should be able to.

The moment we touched down I wished I had listened to my instincts and landed elsewhere. I was right; it was the worst place I had ever been on the continent. Just after touchdown (in the original drags) we were bru-tally tossed about. Anything that wasn't tied down became a projectile. Baggage fell from the overhead storage; our survival sled broke free from its nylon web binding, spilling its contents on the deck. The loadmaster was sick. It was complete chaos. The bumping stopped only when we had stopped. I asked if everybody was OK and was heartened to hear the worst thing lost was a lunch. Tim said he wasn't so sure about that landing; I was more worried about how the hell we were going to get out of here when we were fully loaded.

At least this group's on-load went very smoothly. They had their cargo palletized and their tent was struck; they had even made a batch of brownies for us. As we loaded, I asked the leader the takeoff direction of the plane that had brought them in. He pointed out a set of faded tracks that ran away from our landing track at a 90-degree angle to the left. He told me he had driven his snowmobile in that direction and it was much smoother than what we landed on. But more importantly, he had seen no crevasses.

We cinched everything down as tightly as possible, including ourselves, and added power, taking the new direction. By 50 knots I knew we were in trouble. The wings were rocking so badly I feared the outboard props would hit the ground. We were bouncing so hard it was nearly impossible for me to see the airspeed indicator. At 55 knots we hit hard enough to launch us some thirty feet. The plane groaned. I winced, and we aborted takeoff. After we stopped, I had Roy go over the side to check for damage. The news wasn't good. The nose ski had taken the brunt of the blow; it was badly bent and was leaking hydraulic fluid. He said the nose wheel-well was covered with the red fluid. It looked like the nose ski had committed suicide. Roy thought the ski would probably hold for one more attempt, as long as we taxied to an area that was smoother. He also suggested we download as much cargo as we could, to make ourselves as light as possible.

I brought the science group's PI up to the flight station to discuss our situation, leaving it up to him to prioritize his cargo. He discussed his options with his crew while we taxied to a more suitable area. We taxied east for about ten minutes, searching for smoother snow before I found an area that would suit our needs.

I don't think the PI made a very popular decision. As soon as we stopped to download the chosen cargo, the crew entrance door flew open and out came the PI and the lone female member of the party. She stormed off thirty yards or so, wheeled, and started to scream (at least it looked like screaming from that distance). She gesticulated wildly. He backed away, but his arms were at the ready, poised as if he expected an onslaught. The feud raged in full swing for fifteen or twenty minutes while we off-loaded.

The loadmasters removed the snowmobiles, Nansen sleds, a number of boxes, excess food, and a number of sample boxes. They estimated they had cut the retro cargo in half. Roy, to be on the safe side, decided to lash the nose ski to the nose gear using tie-down chains and a cargo strap. Once we were ready, I sent the 3P to get our still-grappling geologists. The PI, apparently satisfied that the argument was over, turned toward the plane. I guess his fellow geologist wasn't wholly reconciled; when his back was turned, she shoved him hard and knocked him down. I'll never forget the bewildered look in his eyes as he lay in the snow. Meanwhile the other geologist beamed, stepped on his back, and gave us a thumbs-up as she sauntered to the plane. It's always nice to see the passengers enjoy themselves.

I treated the plane like a goddess, doing everything in the most carefully calculated, the smoothest, and the most deliberate manner possible. We talked in low, respectful tones on the ICS. I caressed the power levers and eased around the mound of cargo we were leaving, carefully lining up in the tracks we had made while taxiing. I advanced the throttles slowly. At 50 knots I gently drew back on the yoke to try to cajole the nose ski free from the surface; at 75 knots I called for 100 percent flaps; at 80 knots we were flying, on our way home.

We left the skis down and flew to McMurdo slowly, trying not to exacerbate our gear problem. After an uneasy hour we were lined up ready to land. Half a dozen yellow and orange crash trucks stood poised just off to the side of the skiway. Their red lights flashed and reflected pink off the snow, giving the scene a surreal but festive look. I touched down on the main skis and held the nose high as long as possible. As the airspeed bled off, I gingerly lowered the bent ski to the deck. When it touched, I pulled the throttles sharply into reverse. We stopped quickly and, more importantly, without incident. There was no use trying to taxi; it would only further damage the plane. I shut the plane down, once we were far enough onto the ramp so other planes could get by.

I was greeted by the CO and the flight surgeon as I ducked to exit from the crew entrance door. The skipper congratulated me on a job well done, as Doc wheedled me about the emotional state of the crew. I assured him we would be fine if he could arrange for us to (1) get some sleep—we had just completed a twenty-six-hour day; (2) get a million dollars for our recent successful effort; (3) have someone take us to the club and liquor us up; and (4) be the crew going north to Christchurch tomorrow. He smiled at my folly. He would never let us get any sleep.

There was a sluggishness around the town, the preholiday blues, which seemed to have affected the maintenance cadre particularly. The maintenance effort had slowed to a snail's pace. The planes returned to the base "down" (not in flyable condition) more often than "up" now, so Maintenance Control was fighting a battle it couldn't win—the effort was merely damage control now. Briefs were pushed back hours because of airplane problems. Parts were slow to arrive, slow to be put on the plane, slow to be checked—a general malaise enveloped the station. There was nothing for us as an air crew to do now but sit back, be patient, and ride out the holidays to the end of New Year's Day, and hope for the best from then on.

We all looked forward to Christmas as our best opportunity for a week of relaxation and fun. It is always a white Christmas in Antarctica. I eased myself out of bed Christmas Day at 1030, just in time to take a wonderfully relaxing freezing-then-scalding two-minute shower before trundling off to breakfast. Christmas or not, it was the usual swill. I prayed we'd have a great dinner tonight. With no flights scheduled for the day, all I had to do now was open presents and wait.

Sean and I decided to open our gifts together, trying to make things as normal and homelike as possible. I put on some Tchaikovsky—excellent background music for wrapping-paper ripping—and we dove into our boxes. Sean had a new sweetie back home, and judging from the presents she sent, she must have missed him a lot. Foodstuffs made up the bulk of our collective cache. There were brownies, cakes, cookies, candy, pretzels and mustard (how can you have one without the other?), some semi-fresh fruit, some really rotten fruit, some former potato chips, and a bottle of scotch (thanks, Mom and Dad!). We got wreaths, Christmas tapes, cards, letters, shirts, books, posters, extra socks, and even a small artificial tree from my dear friend Sylvia.

This last gift was rather touching. Sean and I put up the tree immediately. We felt as though we had finally captured the spirit of Christmas there in our room, but it was all over too quickly. Not more than two seconds after the last bow was undone, we were snapped back to reality by a knock on the door. A spectral voice announced an AOM meeting in ten minutes. *Oh, joy.* Forced fun. They put us through this every year. Everyone filed into the lounge to the strains of "Silent Night," with the bachelors herding to the rear and the married guys going to the front, jockeying for position and smiling from ear to ear.

Why? Because it was time for the annual Walk of Shame. The skipper began with a patented Merry Christmas speech, followed closely by a great deal of hubbub as a large box was carried ceremonially into the room. With a flick of the wrist, the skipper transformed into Santa Claus and began to call out each bachelor's name to come forward and receive his "gift."

It was a standing-room-only crowd. We alternately hated and loved this. The Officers' Wives Club would spend weeks before Christmas cleaning out their collective attics and then assembling the spoils (and I mean that) into small gift bags for the unmarried "boys" in the squadron. The married guys howled with delight as they strained to see what goodies their wives had decided they didn't need anymore and therefore felt free to pawn off on us bachelors. I was lucky; my loot included a squirt gun, which I immediately filled so that I could fend off would-be persecutors from the married ranks. Others of us weren't so fortunate: gifts ranged from pulp fiction to pocket toys, the kind that have the small metal balls you try to get into the holes, and of course, the requisite candy canes and chocolate Santas. Mike Nee found that his wife had wrapped up and given away his prized collection of the *John Carter of Mars* series. He had to go from person to person to get them back (it didn't take much persuasion on his part to get mine).

With the conclusion of the afternoon's amusement (and before they could wrestle me to the ground and take away my squirt gun), we retired to our rooms to enjoy a few minutes of solitude before the rush to stand in line for dinner. But I didn't want to just sit around, so I went to my office to lay things out for my petty officer for the coming week. The heat was off; it was so cold my hands went numb in only a few minutes. I gathered together what I needed and returned home to join the enthusiastic queue for dinner.

The line was half the fun because it built up the anticipation. I waited with my friends Sharon, Lisa, and Sean, all of us standing in a line that curved around through 155, ran down several hallways, and finally led into the dining area. Since I had been to Christchurch recently, I brought a supply of wine, which we sipped as we slowly wound through our own building, taming our appetites for the impending feast.

We were rewarded for our patience. The food was marvelous. We gorged ourselves on sweet shrimp with cocktail sauce, turkey, ham (those hams looked vaguely familiar, I might add—they might have been the same ones on my flight from Christchurch just prior to Thanksgiving), stuffing, mashed potatoes, gravy, salad, nuts, pies—the works. We lingered over dinner, cherishing every bite, sipping wine, enjoying the candid conversation among good friends of varied backgrounds. Dinner was accompanied by music from a volunteer choir. They serenaded us with Christmas favorites while we unabashedly stuffed our faces. Like the gift opening, it was all over much too quickly. As I lay in my bed that evening, I wondered why the cooks couldn't cook like this every day. More importantly, I wondered if there were there any adverse side effects from taking massive doses of Alka Seltzer.

The day after Christmas, I motivated myself enough to make it down to work at 0900, just to be sure things were going as I had planned. Then I went to the gym to work off the previous night's dinner. At lunch, all traces of yesterday's feasting were gone. This brought me back to the real world. Good-bye turkeys, good-bye hams. It was routine rot on a plate again. I spent the afternoon writing letters in the lounge, where I observed an ugly display of postholiday depression. One of our female navigators stomped into the lounge, looked around, and began pulling down some decorations with a vengeance.

"What's up?" I queried.

"These are mine, and nobody noticed or appreciated them."

"Umm," I said, or something equally noncommittal. I didn't want to be cannon fodder for her next burst. But she had a point. She had probably done more to bolster seasonal morale than anyone, setting up decorations, baking cookies, wearing Christmas clothing, going all-out to lift the spirits of the rest of us under-appreciative male-pig officers. Perhaps because her spiritual goodwill had flown highest, she had the farthest to fall now that Christmas was through.

New Year's Eve we had a flight to Christchurch. The trip generally took us about eight hours, but on this night the winds were kind, pushing us toward Christchurch at a frenzied clip. At one point we were doing 450 knots over the ground, whereas we normally averaged about 300. The normal eight-hour flight sailed by in six hours and thirty-five minutes.

Practical minds might say the fast trip was due to the wind at our backs, but I know for a fact it was the mental vibrations emanating from crew and passengers, focused on getting north as quickly as possible. We landed in an intense rain squall, giving us a bouncy approach dropping to minimums before we broke free from the clouds. The rain cleared as we taxied to the hangar. Even customs was quick, so we were standing in front of our hotel an hour after we touched down, planning our patrol of Christchurch's finest party spots. From all reports Christchurch was supposed to be a hot town on New Year's Eve. We decided to find out for ourselves.

We decided we would meet for a crew dinner at the Lone Star Café, but to our disappointment, it was closed. We tried a favorite Spanish place: closed. Pizza? Closed. Plan B went into effect. We hailed two taxis to ferry us to Kanniga's Thai restaurant. We were in luck; they were open, as was the liquor store just across the road. We bought five six-packs, all different brands, and then settled in for a massive crew dinner.

Kanniga seemed fond of us, despite our history of unannounced arrivals in large groups. She always served us way too much food and showed us more attention than we deserved, inviting us to parties, consoling us with free meals if we had been late getting to the bank. Her big heart was deeply appreciated by those of us feeling lonely in a faraway place, not to mention the fact that she served the best Thai food I've ever eaten. We gorged ourselves on platters of shrimp in peanut sauce, chicken and noodles, spicy pork and beef, rice—and, of course, our beer. For dessert she personally prepared sweetened rice and served it with sliced mango. Needless to say, we made many New Year's toasts to our hostess.

After dinner we went to check out the Christchurch club scene. We headed over to Limbo's. Not a thing was happening there, so on to Babalu. It was hot. The band, called "The Camels," played funky bass-oriented dance tunes that sounded like Stevie Wonder doing Led Zeppelin. It was great. We drank beer, danced with anyone who would say yes, and talked until the festive atmosphere was interrupted by a fight.

I saw some stumbling around, and our nav, Bob Fiacco, said he saw one of the combatants break a bottle, which was confirmed when I went to the bathroom a few minutes later to find the floor covered in blood. Whoever it was that had been cut, the person had been cut badly. I couldn't imagine losing that much blood and surviving, but there were no obvious corpses to be seen, so I went back to the party.

Despite the common lore about navy guys and fights, we decided maybe we could find a better spot. In a place called Cats, we listened to all the disco songs I had hated when I was in college. The band had the music piped in; they simply stood on the stage going through the motions, lip-synching the wrong lyrics on occasion. It was embarrassing.

There was one last place in the neighborhood, Daniel's, a Maori bar. From what I've seen, Maoris are treated with a great deal of prejudice, so they tend to stick with their own kind. Walking up the stairs, however, we were greeted with handshakes all around—and genuine smiles, wishing us the best of New Year's. After that reception, how could we go wrong? We spent the remainder of the evening dancing in a crowd or being twirled about the floor like rag dolls by a number of big, beautiful Maori women.

Maybe my life was like this dance, being spun out of control by an overzealous partner, not knowing where I was going or what was coming next. It was exhilarating! We kissed the girls good-bye at about 0300 and headed back to the hotel. The new year would bring change, excitement, and no doubt its share of frustration, but after that night I believed I could face it all with a smile.

Trips to the clubs aside, I spent the remainder of my holiday fending off boredom. In Christchurch during the holidays, nobody works from the week before Christmas till the day after New Year's. Shops were closed, buses stopped running, maids didn't clean (the towels in my room threatened to block the bathroom door), and the town generally went into hibernation.

We busied ourselves with long walks in the park or pick-up games of touch football, which amused the locals to the point of uproarious laughter, and frequent trips to the outdoor picnic tables at the Dux de Lux, which I think must have stayed financially afloat from our patronage alone. It was curious that with so many shops closed, all the restaurants in town were open, yet empty. We often found ourselves alone in a posh place, catered to by snooty waiters who wouldn't give us the time of day a few weeks ago—and wouldn't again, once their tables were filled with respectable local people. I gained weight, and I enjoyed adding every extra pound.

On 6 January, word came we were to go south at 0800 the next day. It was a shame to leave. The maids had returned to work, and we could again see the floors in our rooms.

We were flying from Christchurch to McMurdo, and Ed had just swung the compasses over to grid, pointing us toward the South Pole, heading 350 degrees, almost due north. At such southerly latitudes, a normal magnetic compass was useless because of the strong magnetic pull of the magnetic South Pole, so we used a grid system. We placed an imaginary grid over the entire continent with the South Pole being in the middle of the grid, or grid north. By this means, the navigator could manually align the compasses to allow us to fly anywhere within the grid. Once we were free from the continent, heading north to New Zealand, the compasses were realigned to magnetic north and operated normally.

The Southern Alps, the last vestiges of New Zealand, were safely behind us and the weather looked good. I figured we should be landing in Antarctica in about seven hours. On this trip, we had a completely full plane—thirty-five passengers, packed in closer than kipper snacks. I was trying to figure out how to ease the congestion. People sat in four rows of webbed bench seats, shoulder to shoulder, occupying about the first third of the sixty-foot cargo compartment. Each passenger had about twenty-two inches to call his or her own for an eight-hour flight. The last person in each row was wedged in tightly against a fully loaded pallet. A stacked half-pallet sat on the ramp. Two rows of seats faced inward along each side of the plane, and two rows ran back to back down the centerline. These rows faced the outboard seats, with aisles of three feet in between, so that in addition to being crammed together shoulder to shoulder, our hapless passengers were also knee to knee. I don't know who designed this seating arrangement, but he or she must have been a true sadist.

In addition to the squeeze, the passengers were required to be fully dressed in survival gear for the duration of the flight. Most of them were sweating profusely. A hardy few, willing to upset the tenuous balance that temporarily existed in the cargo bay, were attempting to wriggle themselves free of their bulky clothing. Here was a unique opportunity to study human dynamics, to observe the reaction of the group to a few individuals squirming. As packed as they were, when someone moved, there was a domino effect, a sway among all the passengers. It was like watching one of those human waves at a football game.

Besides the thirty red-coated, sardine-packed passengers, we carried three and a half pallets of bulky junk. The pallets themselves are light, but now each was completely full, stacked to within twelve inches of the overhead. The biggest problem I foresaw was getting to the urinals through the pallets. For me to go to the bathroom from the flight deck, I first had to climb over fifteen or twenty people, then climb up the cargo netting covering the boxes on the boxes, squeeze through a twelve-inch crack between the boxes and the overhead, claw my way along the side of a second pallet by hanging onto its cargo netting, then drop down to the deck, wriggle through another slit of an opening on the slippery uphill ramp, locate the urinal, and then brace myself precariously on one foot while I attempted to hit a four-inch-diameter urinal hole.

Lucky there were no women on this flight. The pull-down toilet was completely blocked. While I stumbled my way back to the cockpit, I noticed a lot of crossed legs and pained expressions. Our new cargo compartment motto for this flight was "Make every trip to the urinal count!"

I did everything I could to alleviate the congestion in the aircraft. I had the loadmasters rig as many canvas racks as they could to free up some bench space and allow folks to sleep. I allowed three people to come up to the flight deck to sit or sleep on the two beds there. Beyond that, however, there wasn't much that could be done. I was working with a finite space.

Back in Christchurch before we left, I had argued with the cargo-yard personnel and the NSF representative that if we encountered an emergency, we would be in dire straits. With thirty-five people and the unusually bulky load, we'd be sunk if we were forced to exit in a hurry, especially if we couldn't use the up-front crew entrance door and had to get out the rear of the plane. More importantly, the way the load was packed, if we were down, we would be cut off from all our survival gear.

This was, of course, a nonissue with the cargo yard and the NSF rep—the people needed to go south; this had been the next plane heading south. End of discussion. I tried to persuade them to download at least one of the pallets, but they wouldn't budge. "After all," the NSF representative said to me as we squeezed the last passenger on, "what are you worried about? You got plenty of room up front."

So we had flown. Seven hours out of McMurdo, the plane looking like a tin of Vienna sausages, I prayed that all would go well—and that I, too, could hold it for the rest of the flight. The weather held at McMurdo, so we continued on. Once we passed Cape Adare, the entire Ross Sea opened out in front of us, a huge blue pool with bits of white floating on its surface. The seasonal ice had nearly finished breaking up and was moving out of the sound, floating passively toward the South Pacific Ocean. They were mostly massive chunks of ice; nearly all looked large enough to land our plane on safely. But now they were easing away from the continent to die by slow decay.

The field was clear. The 3P performed a flawless landing. Once we had taxied in to the ramp area and shut down, we rushed to open the crew entrance door to allow the tide of water-logged human cargo to spill out, much to the amazement of our cargo handlers. To them our plane must have looked like a circus car spewing out scores of clowns, all running for the bathrooms. Riding back up to the Hill, I relished my freedom of movement and, in a quiet moment of reflection, was grateful all had ended well.

For flights north I liked to load the passengers five at a time with the engines running. This allowed the loadmaster to give individual attention to each person and assist if there was a problem. Often passengers display a very cavalier attitude—we've just survived the worst conditions in the world, so what could go wrong now? Three passengers in the past year had to be physically prevented from walking through a prop arc; one had to be tackled and then restrained as he turned on his savior to exact revenge for what he considered an unprovoked attack. Had this same fellow been allowed to continue, he would have been turned into jelly by the twelve-hundred-pound prop spinning at more than a thousand revolutions per minute.

This evening all had been going well. Our last group of five passengers, fully dressed in their Antarctic survival equipment and loaded to the gills with souvenirs and other bootie, struggled to cross the hundred yards of open snow to the plane's ladder. But the next-to-the-last passenger was visibly swaying, obviously drunk. According to the squadron's operations manual, as the aircraft commander I am authorized to deny transportation to any passenger(s) who have been drinking excessively, and as to the definition of "excessive," I am granted a great deal of leeway.

I climbed out of my seat and met this fellow as he tried to climb the stairs. I turned him around and pointed him toward the terminal, telling him he was too drunk to fly today and that I would make calls to get him on the next flight. He refused to start back. He started to scream that I had no right to keep him from going north, that he was Mr. So-and-So and I was just another peon, that if I didn't let him board this plane, I was going to be in big trouble. *Oh, my.* I thought for a moment, then called our loadmaster, Chris—a bodybuilder who enjoyed working with uncooperative individuals—to escort this gentleman back to the terminal, which Chris was more than eager to do. The man's resistance vanished when he looked at our newly appointed bouncer. Every Herc should have one.

Once the plane was loaded with the sober passengers, I called for takeoff. As we climbed out, passing Mt. Erebus off to our right, I called the duty office to give a heads-up to the ODO of what happened. We had a good laugh over the fact that I was in big trouble. What else could they do to me after sending me to Antarctica?

As anyone who knows me can tell you, I have nothing against drinking. As a matter of fact, I have been known to take just a small sip now and then myself, but I have never boarded a plane while intoxicated. In Antarctica, things must necessarily be stricter than back home. We are all codependents here, responsible for not only ourselves but also every other person on the continent. We must watch over each other and be prepared to give aid. You can die here in a minute. The story of the stevedore who got so drunk he passed out in a ditch and froze solid is no joke. If our plane were forced down over the continent, I would personally be responsible for everyone's safety; if some drunk hampered my efforts by requiring extra attention, the situation could potentially become ugly. I received no further comments on my actions.

Up at 0700 to work out, then a little breakfast, cash a check, shower, and I was ready for the day: a Pole run with a twist. There were two Coast Guard admirals who were to be given the VIP treatment—a flight to the Pole, lunch with the chef, then a return flight with a mandatory low-level run down the Beardmore Glacier. It takes most of the fun out of a low-level flight when you are tasked to do it, but I guessed we'd survive.

On the snow road to Willy Field, it looked as though we might have departure problems. Low-lying fog hung like a pall over the ice. These convection-type fogs are a product of temperature differences between the open water of the sound and the permanent ice of the ice shelf. Over the water and on the hill, the skies were clear, but here at Willy the sky was totally obscured. We'd be lucky if we could see a hundred yards.

Ice fog is similar to fog caused by water vapor, except for its unique luminescence. The ice crystals reflect the light and magnify it so that the fog is blinding. Another unusual first for me was walking in a blinding fog. Even sounds were strange—perhaps sound bounces differently off the ice crystals.

The fog ebbed and flowed throughout the preflight, at times becoming such a bright soup that we were unable to see the plane from fifty yards away in Maintenance Control. I opted to wait it out. Generally in the mornings the temperatures are cool enough to create the fog, but as the day wears on and the temperature rises, the fog burns off. I figured we'd have about a fifty-fifty shot.

Lunchtime came and went. By 1400 I knew the fog was here for a while, so I canceled the flight. Back on the Hill, I found a new folder in my in-basket, telling me I was to be the project officer for a new satellite communications system testing next season on the Ice.

Some background: during a majority of the flights to and from Christchurch, HF communications had been hampered by solar flares. High-frequency radio waves are extremely long and are utilized for long-distance communications because they bounce off the stratosphere and can travel great distances. The solar flares changed the polarity or shape of the upper atmosphere, thereby absorbing the HF radio waves and wreaking havoc on our HF signal propagation.

UHF satellite communications are supposed to alleviate the problems associated with solar activity. Instead of relying on our HF signal to bounce off the ionosphere, we would bounce our UHF signal off a satellite. And with an increase in solar activity predicted for next season, we would need all the help we could get. I was pleased to receive the appointment. I just wished they had started the testing sooner.

A few days later it was time for another Goat Rope. Our passenger manifest for our Pole flight was a "Who's Who" of contemporary Antarctic admiralty. Our latest Admiral on Ice was the navy's chief oceanographer. He would join our two previous VIPs, Coast Guard admirals, as we once again tried for the bottom of the world. I get leery when I see this much brass.

The U.S. Navy's presence in Antarctica is minuscule, yet we seem to receive a lot of attention. I often wonder how the navy benefits from these visits to the Pole for "power lunches" and photo sessions. I understand the need in Washington for "good press," but it was difficult for me to stomach the constant public relations effort. Our mission was science support, and these kinds of flights did nothing at all to further science.

The Weather Shamans, in deference to their bosses, gave us the best and certainly the most professional weather brief I'd ever heard. They were so courteous, kind, helpful, and cheerful that I thought I had wandered up to the wrong window. As they gave us the forecast, which was for perfect weather everywhere, I kept trying to peer behind their backs, looking for crossed fingers. But the weather turned out just as they predicted—I wondered what prevented them from doing this well all the time. Maybe I should have kept this oceanography admiral on my crew as insurance.

The passenger manifest was rounded out by two marine helicopter pilots, a major, and a captain who would observe as we recced a potential blue-ice runway site at the base of Mt. Howe, some hundred and fifty miles south of the Pole. The NSF contacted the marines about using one of their CH-53 "Sea Stallions" (the Herc of helicopters) to recover the crashed UH-1N helicopter off the top of Mt. Patrick. Once they had recovered the crashed Huey, these marines would then assist in setting up the blue-ice runway at Mt. Howe. We would give them the tour and let them see what they were getting themselves into.

With three admirals on board I thought I might have a power struggle on my hands as to who would sit in the cockpit on the bench seat, which holds only two. But all of the admirals wanted to sit in the back, thus freeing the seat for our marines. Our flight outbound was ordinary, if you can use that term to describe flying through the vast white plains of the ice shelf to the ten-thousand-foot ice falls of the Transantarctic Mountains and on to the vast white plains of the plateau. Through these stunning, awe-inspiring transitions from flat to massive to flat, our marines busied themselves capturing the moment, video cameras blazing. Our admirals slept, no doubt saving themselves for the big doings at the Pole.

The weather at the Pole was so clear that the station seemed to shimmer. The snow sparkled, the metal dome glistened, the Pole personnel beamed. It seemed too good to be true. We herded our passengers into the waiting arms of the station manager. Then, our job done, I wandered off to explore.

Below the dome is the entrance to the guts of the South Pole machine. I can't recall how many times I wandered through this portal, but each time I was amazed by the doors. They looked like they weighed at least a ton each. It made perfect sense that the Pole personnel would leave them open for the summer and close them only during storms and during the dark, five-month winter. It probably took a tractor just to push them open and closed.

I made a right turn just inside the doors and wandered down past the small gym where I had met the Trans-Antarctica Expedition members, past a carpentry shop and an electrical shop, and into the cavernous expanse that serves as the vehicle repair facility. Here were two smaller versions of the front doors, which led back outside to the cargo yard. Stored in neatly stacked piles was a smattering of everything—wire, wood, food, pipes, and parts, all covered with two inches of snow.

Two hundred yards ahead of me, adjacent to the skiway, were the two small, bolted-together buildings that are the Pole GCA control center. I knocked on one of the doors and was greeted by a weary-eyed yet cheerful woman. She ushered me inside the cramped space and quickly closed the door, trying to keep her room warm. I had spoken to Susan hundreds of times on the radio, but we had never actually met. As the Pole GCA controller, she had talked us down on landings when I had thought there was no way we would make it in. I felt as though I was finally confronting the Great Oz. As the controller, she was some disembodied, all-powerful entity that could play with my fate. Yet unmasked and in the flesh, she was just like me, with similar hopes and dreams. We talked about her antiquated equipment, and she gave me a brief demonstration. It amazed me that this stuff still worked. I was even more impressed that she could decipher the blips enough to line up a moving plane with the skiway.

Next to the small GCA control room is the Jamesway that is home to her and a technician. Theirs is a cold, lonely existence, sequestered here waiting for planes or repairing old equipment (which is in constant need of tweaking and tuning), leaving the place only to eat meals in the main building or to use the shower. It didn't sound like such a good deal to me.

I returned to the dome, where my passengers were eating lunch. I grabbed a bowl of soup and sat down to go over with them the chain of events for the return flight. We would fly to Mt. Howe for a recce and then return to McMurdo via a low-level flight through the Beardmore. There were smiles all around.

The idea for a blue-ice runway to serve the Pole had been batted around for a number of years. We had already explored one possible site for such a runway at Mill Glacier, and today we would be looking at a second site. Having a blue-ice runway would be fine with us, since it would free up the LC-130s to spend less time supporting the Pole and more time doing what they were designed for, supporting science in the open field.

On the return flight we checked out the Mt. Howe site. It didn't look like much. There was a patch of blue ice at the base of six-thousand-foot Mt. Howe, but the area being considered as the potential runway was, in my opinion, too close to the base of the mountain. We dropped down to five hundred feet and put out 50 percent flaps so we could slow down and get a good look. I made a number of practice approaches. Once I felt comfortable with the landing pattern, I lowered the gear and made several low-level passes at fifty feet, each time waving off in different directions. The passengers paid close attention.

Among the crew and me, the opinion was that it would be tough for an LC-130 to land there—and nearly impossible for a C-141. First, the main runway would face a constant 40-degree crosswind component, and if the winds were anything like they were today (20 to 25 knots), they would prevent a C-141 from landing (with its low wingtip clearance, the C-141 crosswind component can't exceed 25 knots). That would force the plane to land into the wind, which raised a second problem. Landing into the wind would point you squarely at the mountain. I know few pilots who would land on ice facing a mountain as the overrun of a runway. An additional minor inconvenience was a five- or six-hundred-foot hill that a pilot would have to clear and then dive into the main runway. It would be a hell of a choice, dive over it or land into it. On a positive note the surface looked all right; at least I would have no qualms about landing there. It certainly looked smoother than Mill Glacier, which now stood as our lit-mus test of where we as a crew would and wouldn't land.

On the way home I dropped down into the Mill Glacier to make the right turn into the Beardmore. As we passed over the Mill Glacier camp, it looked to me that the entire staff was there "mooning" us. I couldn't be sure at two thousand feet, but it was either that or those guys had recently turned very ugly.

As we leveled the plane at three hundred feet, there was much jock-eying for position in the cockpit. Flying low-level through pristine wilder-ness brings out the child in everybody. It was a once-in-a-lifetime chance for them to experience the shining beauty of the continent in a way that they would never forget. Everyone was happy.

We landed without incident back at Willy. Sliding to a stop with engines in reverse, we were met by three pickup trucks, one per admiral. One signaled for me to join him, but I waved him off. The regular van would be fine for me, a chance to gossip about the day's events. Van time was our time to be alone as a crew, to roll our eyes and laugh at the world as we knew it.

As I've said, we often flew science teams to research destinations. Some of the science that goes on in Antarctica is, in my mind, the most over-sensationalized bunch of hooey I've ever come across. The science par-ties were presided over by PIs—principal investigators. Most of the PIs whom I met were arrogant, self-centered, anal-retentive bastards whose only real achievement seemed to be milking the government for money. They competed not to see who could come up with the best scientific results but to see who could write the best proposal and receive the biggest grants, for thus was established the pecking order.

Each flying season runs from October to March, but a majority of PIs will head home at Christmas, leaving their graduate students to collect data. These data may or may not be what the PI wants—but if the infor-mation base is wrong, it offers the PI a prime excuse for coming back.

During dinner one evening I chatted with a marine biologist who was in Antarctica for his twelfth year. He was studying seal herds. He admit-ted there was no accurate way to count the number of animals or to deter-mine if they were truly declining as he postulated, but he was doing his research anyway. I asked how he was able to get continued funding for such a long study with such dubious results.

He stated—with an air of self satisfaction that seems prevalent among the PIs I have come in contact with—that it was merely a matter of rewriting the grant request differently enough from last year's to get the NSF to buy the "improved" project. But he just did the same basic thing—diving with seals. After twelve years, his group was still far from obtaining substantial data on the seals.

Another group had been coming down at least as long as this, studying the sponges that inhabit McMurdo Bay. At a science lecture, their PI admitted point-blank that they couldn't tell whether the sponges they studied were still alive, but the funds were forthcoming anyway. And yet another achievement in misinformation: groups studying the hole in the ozone layer made their discovery known, touching off a worldwide ban on fluorocarbons. Gradually it emerged that these same scientists and others suspected the hole might always have existed, but the scientists studying this phenomenon convinced the media that their findings had earth-shattering implications. I'm sure they all got funded through eternity to stave off our cataclysmic death-by-ozone-depletion.

During my time on the Ice, I saw literally dozens of such projects being funded every year by us taxpayers. Government misspending, it seems, is alive and well in NSF Polar Programs.

15

FLYING IN THE
MILK BOTTLE

Whales! I went to work for a few hours before the brief today to find a pod of twenty or so killer whales not ten yards offshore. I stared, fascinated, as they moved gracefully through the dark blue water. There was a curious instant when the group came to an abrupt halt, and one of the larger members (judging by the size of the dorsal fin) raised its head from the water and looked around. Satisfied, it sank beneath the water, and the pod headed off in a new direction, thinking, sentient mysteries that I wished I could understand.

I must have stared after them for at least an hour before violent shivering sent me to shelter. I made my way to my office, which was as hot as a sauna, to thaw out.

This morning, the tanker ship was preparing to get under way. She was riding high in the water after pumping her tanks free of JP8 (the fuel we used both to operate the aircraft and to power the station). Our half-dozen storage tanks had been refilled; the town was set for next season. For the past week there had been fuel lines running from the tanker along the outer streets of McMurdo like black rubber tentacles from some giant squid. They were gone now, rolled up and back in storage, and with them had gone the overpowering smell of diesel fuel. The only odor left was the dreaded bouquet of the mess hall's daily menu.

Our mission today was a straightforward put-in on the plateau. We were taking a group of four Kiwi scientists out to the polar plateau to study virgin snow. Any flight to this area of the plateau promised to be mundane at best. We flew these brave souls to a spot where there was absolutely nothing, save snow.

The sky pressed blue down upon the snow, compressing the sastrugi into low, narrow pancakes. The wind then sharpened the edges of these sastrugi to fine points. The area was a homogeneous white, entirely flat, and extended for five hundred miles in every direction. I had a strange sense that what we were doing was somehow wrong. I felt we should be trying to rescue people who had been forced down into this vast ocean of snow, not leaving them here on purpose. I felt like I was making these scientists walk the plank. Since they planned to stay and collect samples for two months, I secretly hoped they had packed a *lot* of beer.

We set up in a racetrack pattern at three hundred feet over our intended point of landing and depressurized. I had Chris drop a smoke grenade to learn the wind's direction and speed, as well as to mark our intended point of landing. The smoke fell in a spiraling purple arc. As soon as it was clear of the plane, we banked sharply to follow its trajectory. The grenade landed and bounced twice on the snow before it spewed out its remaining dye, marking our landing zone with a purple haze.

The wind was blowing with the snow drifts—a good sign. There's nothing like lining up on the predominant drifts, only to find the winds have shifted, forcing you to do a crosswind ski drag. I put Tim in the seat for his first operational open-field landing, where he would select the site. His touchdown was good, but the minute-long drag really knocked us about. The surface was tightly packed snow, covered with a clear glaze of ice. It didn't give.

The drag was the roughest I'd ever flown. We bounded along the surface like a child's wagon bumping out of control down a steep hill. We were just barely able to stay ahead of the plane's dips and dives, waggles and rocks, as it pounded over the surface. It felt as though the skis might fly off at any moment, as we charged headlong at about a hundred miles an hour into windblown sastrugi, which had hardened like sharpened stakes.

We normally dragged the surface for one minute, but today we hit a large sastrugi at fifty-four seconds and were vaulted airborne. It was as if we had hit the end of a ski jump: in a split second we were thrown clear of the surface and were once again flying. I was relieved to be in smooth air, away from the clutching, grasping hands of the wind-whipped, rock-hard, swaying surface below. And I certainly wasn't thrilled with the prospect of doing a second drag.

Tim maneuvered the plane to place his drag down my side as we flew its length to check for crevasses. There were none. By using the first drag as a benchmark, we unanimously decided that one ski drag was sufficient on this surface and that since we didn't want to be stuck out here with a broken ski, we would land on the next pass. Tim set up for a short, half-mile final, then landed in his drag, and stopped the plane in about two thousand feet. We taxied for another half a mile, rocking over the rough, undulating surface until we were about at the midpoint of the drag.

The scientists went off some fifty yards from the plane to establish communications with Scott Base as we drifted their supplies. They were stout fellows, bringing only eighty-seven hundred pounds of equipment for their two months out here in the open. It was a paltry amount compared to the stockpile of some parties, who complained that they could take only eighteen thousand pounds of gear.

Once the field party had established communications, set up their tent, and were fanning the flames of a Coleman stove, we taxied to depart. The takeoff was only a tad less daunting than our ski drag had been, since we now had a fairly packed set of ski tracks to use as a makeshift runway. The packed snow made for quick acceleration, so we were off in less than three thousand feet, which was fine since the less time we spent rocketing over that surface the better.

Our return trip was quick but dull, so we decided on a low-level run through the Dry Valleys. Since we had all seen the Wright Valley numerous times, today we opted for a run down the Balham and McKelvey Valleys to the south of the Wright. Dave briefed Tim and me as we descended to avoid the Barwick Valley, which was strictly off limits. The Barwick was listed as a Site of Special Scientific Interest (SSSI), an area that the NSF has set aside as virgin territory to be explored later as a completely pristine wilderness where no man has walked.

We passed over the Upper Wright Glacier, and the Airdevronsix Ice Falls on our left, and descended along a ridge line that ran down into the Balham from Mt. Electra. At five hundred feet above the valley floor we turned sharply 90 degrees to our right and blasted right down the middle for a few moments before we came to the break in the Insel Range. We saw little of the Balham, but it was enough for us to know that it was completely unspectacular. Had I known just how unspectacular, I gladly would have avoided it and revisited our old friend, the Wright Valley. The Balham Valley was long and broad and defined by low, rounded mountains that were as plain as ice milk—not nearly as spectacular as the sharp peaks that define the valleys of the Olympus and Asgard Ranges. If it weren't so cold and barren, the Balham would be a perfect place for raising crops.

We made another sharp, climbing right turn to knife our way through the break in the Insel Range and then almost immediately made a shallow, diving turn down into the McKelvey Valley. We leveled about three hundred feet above the floor of the McKelvey and pointed the nose at Lake Vida. Lake Vida looked remarkably like a larger Lake Vanda. Its frozen surface was splotched with an opaque gray-blue color and covered with cracks that ran across the surface, giving it the look of a large jigsaw puzzle.

We exited the valley flying two hundred feet above the Wilson Piedmont Glacier and made a shallow left turn to parallel the ice edge now located less than forty miles from McMurdo Station. As the seasonal sea ice breaks up from the McMurdo Sound and moves out to the ocean, the ice edge moves closer inland toward the permanent ice of the Ross Ice Shelf. The high wall of ice that James Clark Ross so aptly describes in his journal is the natural, permanent line of demarcation between the seasonal ice of the sound and the permanent ice of the ice shelf.

We flew along the frozen boundary between ice and open ocean and quickly lost count of the thousands of emperor and Adele penguins and Weddell seals lounging at the water's edge. Flying along the boundary, at around a thousand feet and 200 knots, we must have been an imposing sight for the penguins. As the plane approached, they headed for the safety of the ocean, leaping into the water and then magically reappearing on land only seconds after we had passed. The seals, on the other hand, seemed so unconcerned by our approach that they did little more than look up to see what was disturbing their naps.

As we approached Cape Byrd on Ross Island, we began a slow climb toward the base of Mt. Erebus to locate the wreckage of an Air New Zealand DC-10 that had strayed off course and crashed into the mountain in December 1979, killing all 273 people aboard. We failed to see any of the wreckage, but we did circle the large cross memorial that bears witness to the tragedy.

Cleanup after an aircraft accident is always a laborious and painful task. Here, it must have been a horrific ordeal—the distress the team experienced in trying to recover bodies that were strewn great distances in all directions as well as the hardship and danger they endured in having to contend with the harsh environment. The accident not only shocked the world but also stoked the fire under environmental groups, who immediately called for a cessation of all tourism to Antarctica.

For me it was a grisly reminder that Antarctica isn't taken seriously enough. Groups fighting to exploit the vast resources in Antarctica underestimate the power of the continent. I cringe when I hear of anyone's digging wells or mining here, since I know those who propose such schemes have no concept of the conditions their workers would face. Many men and women might have to suffer and die before that point ever gets driven home.

The remainder of the flight was respectfully quiet. But the sobering reality of this place is that death always perches on your shoulder here.

In McMurdo, off-load of the *Greenwave*, the container ship contracted to replenish the town's depleted supplies, was in full swing. Most of the piled-high containers were empty, waiting to be loaded with retrograde cargo for the States or New Zealand. The process was streamlined so that cargo traveled both directions at once. A constant parade of trucks rumbled through town twenty-four hours a day, ferrying cargo to and from the ice pier. At the pier the trucks lined up adjacent to the ship, where their loads were plucked off at one end and something new was loaded at the other. All the ship's cranes ran simultaneously, digging deep into the bowels of the vessel, loading and unloading without cessation.

The weather at McMurdo was turning decidedly colder every day. Temperatures were creeping down to the minus-30 degrees centigrade range at night as the sun slipped to circle behind the mountains of the Royal Society Range. Bad weather always returned with a vengeance, with a raw feeling to the air and a piercing cold that was able to snake its way beneath your clothes and nip at the core of your soul.

Thursday, February 1. ...Wilson's leg much better. Evans' fingers now very bad, two nails coming off, blisters burst.
—Robert Falcon Scott

Weather caught up to Scott and his men in 1912. Still far out on the ice shelf, miles from safety, they found their situation changing from bad to worse. Edward Edgar Evans died in his sleep seventeen days after Scott made that February journal entry. It is hard not to think often of Scott and his men when one is confronting the same conditions they faced.

Our weather was turning foul. Clouds were gathering, and the wind flowed in a peculiar circular pattern, changing direction every hour. Moist air from the open water on our doorsteps was carried aloft by the circling winds and, colliding with drier air above the permanent ice, formed dense clouds that covered our little basin of civilization.

The sun drooped, circling lower in the sky each day. As it ringed the Royal Society Range, forty miles distant across the sound, Mt. Lister and the other peaks cast long shadows that reached out like icy fingers to claw at the station. Sun breaking through the clouds created a mottled effect in town that we usually saw only in the open field. Odd-shaped patterns of white and gray left me rubbing my eyes to focus. This mottling matched the sky, where white melted at the horizon into the background of snow. It was impossible to tell up from down, side from side, as if we were under some sun-dappled stream, looking upward through the water. These are vertigo-inducing conditions. One learns to be wary of them, especially during flights.

It began to snow. It came down quietly and vertically at first, a gentle snow, but an hour later, as the wind began to gust and swell, it became horizontal and driving, a virtual wall of snow pushed ever forward by the icy blasts of air. "Condition II" was announced, indicating it wasn't safe to travel outside alone. Our flights were canceled in anticipation of another full-blown Herbie. High winds hurled snow against the station. Drifts mounted as the wind shook and tugged at the buildings; old 155 started moaning as if hunkering down against the onslaught.

Just before 2300, "Condition I" was set—it means *stay where you are.* The shuttle bus stopped running. The station folded its arms and curled up like a seal with its back to the wind. We were in a certified Herbie. Winds raced through town at 60 to 70 knots, hurling snow and limiting visibility to only a few yards.

Sitting at the lounge window watching the boiling white tempest outside was a remarkable experience. Less than a mile away, weathering the same storm, was a diminutive hut, the museum-piece of Scott's first expedition to the Antarctic. I tried to imagine what the early explorers who faced these storms in wooden bunk houses, heated by coal-burning stoves, must have felt. No amount of coal could stave off this bleak and bitter cold. I thought of Victor Campbell and his Northern Party.

Lieutenant Commander Campbell accompanied Scott on his second trip to Antarctica. While Scott was dying, fighting blizzards and hunger in the cold, boundless reaches of the Ross Ice Shelf, a stranded Campbell and his party were burrowing in for the winter at Evans Cove, at Campbell Bay on the coast of Victoria Land. Scott's ship, the *Terra Nova,* had deposited Campbell at Evans Cove to carry out a six-week sledging program. When it came time to recover the party, the *Terra Nova* was unable to penetrate the ice pack. Campbell and his men were thus marooned.

Campbell—with no hut, only thin summer clothing, and less than a month's worth of rations for six men—was left to his own devices in the fast-approaching winter. When gale-force winds, exactly like the ones I was now watching, tore their tents to shreds, they were forced to dig an ice cave out of snowdrift on the edge of a granite outcrop they called Inexpressible Island. When completed, this rough igloo measured nine by twelve feet and, at its highest point, only five and a half feet. None of the party could stand fully upright in it. In this cave, six men passed six months in Antarctic winter darkness, in complete solitude.

They heated the igloo by burning seal and penguin blubber in tins they made from old food containers. Soon their clothes and hair and faces were coated by the greasy, foul-smelling smoke, which they called "smitch." They lived on seals and an occasional penguin and learned to relish eating blubber, which is normally considered revolting. To augment their meager rations of seal meat, they allowed themselves one hard biscuit a day (two on birthdays), twelve lumps of sugar on each Sunday, and an ounce and a half of chocolate each Saturday and every other Wednesday, and on the last day of every month, twenty-five raisins.

For days on end in the black of winter, they were confined to their sleeping bags while blizzards of horizontal snow raged outside. They distracted themselves with readings from Dickens's *David Copperfield* and the New Testament, and they dreamt of food.

They barely survived attacks of acute diarrhea, where they were forced to crawl on hands and knees through a narrow winding tunnel to a foul thirty-six-foot latrine. At winter's end, a thirty-seven-day trek back to the base hut awaited them. Miraculously they all made it safely back, alive but terribly emaciated. Campbell gained thirty-five pounds in six days after their return. Later on, one of the party, a petty officer named George Abbott, went mad.

At times, when I begin feeling pent-up and frustrated, I look around at my modern, well-heated quarters, at the TV, radio, ample food supplies, and, most importantly, my beer, and I remember what Campbell and his men faced. I remember, with respect.

It had been snowing in McMurdo, and it was still snowing now. Whirling drifts had accumulated fast on the sides of buildings. Visibility had increased somewhat, to perhaps two hundred yards, but no more. At Willy Field rope lines reappeared, from barracks to mess hall and bathrooms. Stray off the line, and you could be lost in the storm. On days like today, waiting for the storm to abate, folks mostly retired to their rooms to read, watch videos, or do needlepoint, or they gathered together for what was the rage of this particular season, playing games of "Risk."

In the lounge, there were usually half a dozen people, and the TV was on. Some folks were reading magazines or papers while keeping an ear cocked for something interesting. Today, four people were at the foosball table, swatting a ball across the smooth surface with pivoting men on a stick. The pool table was empty for now; someone had confiscated the cue ball. The dynamics of this common room were unique—the constant comings and goings make it like a strange version of musical chairs. Many people, like me, would come in here because of the windows, to sit and observe the world outside.

Today we were staring at the bleak wintry scene that masked the station in a blustery veil of white, placing bets as to when it would end. The flight schedule had been canceled until further notice. Days like this, I wished I were the operations duty officer: cancel everybody, and then kick back and read without a single phone interruption. Bliss. It continued to snow heavily, and then the temperatures dropped, fluctuating between minus-15 and minus-18 degrees.

Around noon on the fourth day of the storm, however, the winds ebbed and the flight schedule was resumed. Visibility was still poor when we arrived at Willy, but the forecaster once again promised a thousand-foot ceiling, seven miles visibility, and—just for the heck of it—sunshine for our return. The plane was fueled and ready to go, having been prepared for a flight that was canceled because of the storm. He lucked out and took off early.

Our weather was supposed to be poor at the Pole, but when we arrived, it was clear as ice. Landing without the aid of an instrument approach was a welcome occurrence. The off-load of fuel went smoothly, and we were in the air again in less than twenty-five minutes. Hourly weather reports while you are airborne are standard procedure; a special observation ("ob"), however, is nearly always bad news. Just past PSR, where we could have gone back to the Pole, we got a special ob of desperate conditions (often called "dog squeeze" weather conditions by Antarctic pilots) back at Willy Field. Our noble forecasters were at work again. What had been forecast for our return—a thousand and seven, fair and fair, with sunshine—was now being modified: two hundred and one, poor and poor, with blowing snow. Tim said, "They're screwing us again, man."

We entered the clouds as we began our descent, once we were sure we had cleared Minna Bluff. Not only was it now snowing silver-dollar-sized flakes, but there was moderate turbulence coupled with wind shear. The GCA radar operator gave us headings to align us with the skiway. At ten miles we were given a turn heading inbound that didn't make any sense— it was angling us away from the skiway. I questioned the call, only to be chastised. That was the heading; that's what you'll fly.

Ed's opinion differed from the radar operator's. I trusted his judgment, so we followed Ed's heading calls as we got nearer to the field. We crossed the extended centerline at two hundred feet but heading a few degrees off to the right (considering how the controller had mishandled us, I was surprised that Ed actually got us anywhere near). As we crossed, we spotted the rabbit lights glowing through the fog. Had it not been for these high-intensity approach lights, I don't know if we would have found the field.

We then made a slight left turn and descended into the foggy abyss. I fought with the plane to bring us in. From the onset of the approach, the wind and turbulence made the aircraft a headstrong animal that seemed hell-bent on exacting revenge on us for putting it in such a predicament with such horrid weather. The Herc buckled and fought, twisted and moaned, dived when I wanted it to climb. Everything seemed out of whack as we plunged toward the deck.

We broke free of the clouds at maybe two hundred feet and half a mile from the skiway; we were too high for landing. At one hundred feet and a third of a mile from the runway, we saw the faint glow of the rabbit lights that led to the runway lights. Not wanting to try another approach, I took my chance and dove for the deck, landing firmly just past a point midway down the skiway. It was no masterpiece of a landing, but we were on deck at Willy and, better yet, safe.

The snow was swirling about us in big, solid flakes that hurt when they hit my face. In Maintenance Control I called the forecaster to find out why they had painted us such a rosy picture when it was obvious, even to a novice meteorologist like me, that there was no way the weather would clear. I was patiently talked down to about satellite imaging and told how they hadn't had a decent satellite shot of the weather in forty-eight hours.

"You guys based my forecast on weather information that was more than two days old?" I cried.

"Well, sir, it was all we had, and you guys needed to go, so . . . ," he replied.

I took a deep breath and hung up the phone. From now on I would restrict all my decisions concerning weather to information I could gather myself. Hell, I could have called the Pole and gotten a better guess at the weather here than the information I received from the people who were supposed to be helping us.

We recorded our Pole fuel off-load figures with the duty officer, made the shuttle, and headed home, beaten up by this crazy weather. We made it to the Hill just in time to close down the Officers' Club. In this line of work, it paid to keep one's priorities straight. After all, last call was last call.

It was Thursday, 22 November 1990. The skies were closed-in and gray as we filed our flight plan to SERIS L to pick up a snow plane. I specifically asked the forecaster what the chances were that the weather would drop to whiteout conditions. I asked because there was just a strange feeling around the station, in the air—the lull before the storm. But the forecaster assured me that all would be well—not that his confidence assuaged my fears; I could have sworn I heard a slight cackle in the background on his end of the phone. The hair started rising on the back of my neck.

As I was walking to the plane, there were spits of snow, but the cloud deck was about five hundred feet, the visibility seven to ten miles. For our takeoff, the weather folks were calling for a thousand-foot ceiling with overcast skies, seven miles visibility, poor and poor. So I had the right weather to go, but my concern was what it was going to be like in three hours when I returned from our pull-out of SERIS L.[1] The forecasters said that all this weather would clear out by the time we returned. They said that a cold front was moving through, increasing the visibility, and that God would reach out to part the heavens for us. They thought that touch about the heavens being parted was so hilarious. God, how I loved the Weather Shamans.

After departing the ice runway, we were immediately in the klag. The clouds were firm, dense, and a sickly gray color. Honestly, they looked like impending death. We shook free and popped into blue skies and brilliant sunshine at a thousand feet above the ground—the same thousand feet where the forecasters told us the base of the cloud deck would be. Those gray clouds still hung pall-like over the entire sound. As we were climbing out, we answered a radio call from my friend Sharon, who was coming south from Christchurch and was debating whether she should pass her PSR with the current weather. I told her what the conditions were when we had just taken off, and I added that the forecasters had promised us that the weather right now was as bad as it would get all day. On my word alone, she continued heading south. I was soon to regret what I'd told her.

The clouds stopped just beyond Minna Bluff; from there we were in the clear. At SERIS L we landed without incident. It certainly wasn't the best spot on the continent. The snow was soft and sticky, an ugly, milky-white slush. The ground looked like a mogul-filled ski slope, with gentle but discernible foot-high snow mounds covering the area. We shook to a halt two hundred yards from the camp and taxied over the undulating surface the remainder of the way. Now to load the blasted snow plane.

This thing had given another crew all sorts of troubles when they loaded it at McMurdo to bring out here two months ago. Its awkward shape, height, and length made it a nightmare to load. At least at McMurdo, there had been a forklift to assist them; here we had nothing but the winch aboard the plane.

It was a slow, laborious process. We looped rope around the snow plane and gently pulled at it from several angles with snowmobiles. We had to be careful not to hit the open rear-cargo door, so every few feet we'd stop, raise the ramp a bit, reposition the hulk of a snow plane, and repeat the process. In this manner we were able to teeter-totter the damn thing in.

The radio call hit like a shot out of the blue. Our guest navigator for the day, Carol, had been updating our forecast back at McMurdo when she emerged from the flight deck with furrowed brow. She thought I might like to hear the latest weather forecast. I scrambled back to the flight deck and listened to the forecaster.

The dopes had changed their minds forty-five minutes after we departed; they now were calling for a partially obscured ceiling (one that starts on the deck, a fog), two miles visibility, nil and nil, with conditions deteriorating rapidly. Oh boy. I've been asked why I was in such a hurry to get back to McMurdo—why not just wait the weather out? The conditions the forecasters were describing were indicative of a Herbie, and when a Herbie gets going, it's anyone's guess as to when it will peter out. Simply put, we had only enough supplies to last a week and only enough fuel for a few hours. We were only forty-five minutes from McMurdo, and with the weather still above minimums, I thought it prudent to try and get the plane and crew back before the storm hit.

I had Roy figure up the fuel situation, and it wasn't good. Unless we could collect this damn snow plane quickly, we'd have enough gas for only one or two approaches. I gave the news to Chris, explaining that each minute of fuel wasted here unloading was a minute less for our trip home. With the snow plane only halfway in, I'd effectively asked him to do the impossible, but we were in this together, so we helped while he directed.

We worked feverishly, hauling for all we were worth and adjusting the cargo ramp continuously until we completed the remainder of the on-load.

Normally that would have taken about an hour. We did it in only twenty minutes. We had wasted no motion; there had been no idle chatter. Nothing but the business at hand. We all knew the score: screw up now, and we might not make it back home before the weather closed in entirely—or we might not make it back home at all.

With the snow plane loaded, all we had to do was get out of here before the weather hit. We taxied immediately back to our landing tracks. But the snow, an ugly adversary, turned on us. The first run we couldn't get the nose to stay straight. Bob, the copilot doing the takeoff, got sideways a number of times. The second takeoff run was infinitely better, but we simply couldn't accelerate in the soft, slushy snow.

Roy did some quick figuring and said we didn't have the gas to stop, turn around, and taxi back. We had to get airborne this time. We started with the flaps up, accelerated to 50 knots, and then lowered them to 50 percent, normal for takeoff. We accelerated to 65 knots but stagnated there. I pushed the flap handle all the way down to position them to 100 percent, the plane shook and rose a little higher on its skis, and we sped up to 75, then 80 knots. We pulled with all our might, burying the yokes in our laps, as if sheer force of will would pull this hulking beast out of the snow and skyward. I remember hearing someone on the headset say, "C'mon, baby, fly" as we popped free of the snow and into the air. There was a collective sigh of relief.

We wasted no time cleaning the plane up and figuring out a maximum-range flight profile, one that would give us the best gas mileage back home. We would need every drop we had. Roy figured we would be on top of the field with about nine thousand pounds of gas, enough for three good approaches, maybe four if we were lucky. Once we were at altitude, we could see Mt. Erebus at a hundred and eighty miles out. It was reassuring. I said to myself, *How bad could it be?* Once we passed Minna Bluff, however, I knew how bad it could be. The whole area was covered with low, dense clouds that looked like a death shroud. It stretched for hundreds of miles. There was no getting around it, so we had to punch through.

Tim called the tower, then Maintenance Control for conditions. Both verdicts were bad. There was no ceiling, no visibility, no surface or horizon definition. The maintenance chief did say he could see thirty, maybe forty yards, sometimes. At least we had that going for us. I put all the first-string players in the seats. This approach would tax us, push us to fly the plane with all our wits about us, to stay cool as we dove into that pea soup fog at 130 knots to search for the ground. As we descended to sixteen hundred feet, Roy gave me the numbers. He figured we had at least two but no more than three shots at this before the gas gave out. We set up for landing. The plane was working well, everything functioning as advertised—no malfunctioning gear, no engines to shut down—so that was encouraging.

I sensed that the first GCA was good, on course and on the right glide slope, but we never saw a thing—no panels, no ground, no tower, no planes, nothing but white. We were flying in the milk bottle. When we had descended below eleven hundred feet, we went into a fog so thick that we could barely see the orange paint on our own wing tips. At one hundred feet Tim yelled, "Wave off." I added power to go around, to try another approach. As a pilot I can state that there is nothing worse in the world than being less than a hundred feet above the ground, supposedly centered over the runway but seeing absolutely nothing. I pulled back on the yoke, and the plane nosed back up into the sunshine. The controller gave me instructions and headings to fly to realign the plane with the runway.

I turned on our final approach. It was now or never. The runway was out there directly in front of us at eight miles. All we had to do now was find it. This is where we earned our money. I pulled power, slowed to approach speed, and settled into the clouds again. It started to get busy in the cockpit. We were now in the hands of the controller on the ground. He called my heading and rate of descent by telling me whether I was on, above, or below glide slope.[2]

Normally we don't make major heading changes on the final-approach course for a GCA, but that day the controller had us fly all over the sky, back and forth across the extended runway centerline. The controller on the first pass had done a good job, but now we were listening to the supervisor, and he wasn't well practiced at the controls of the GCA radar. He called heading changes of 8 to 10 degrees—too gross a correction when one is trying to fly a precision approach. And the crew continued to make their own calls, adding to the noise. I was concentrating on flying the headings and glide slope, so the crew gave me a polar backup. Tim called my airspeed and rate of descent. Roy called out absolute altitudes of two hundred, one hundred, seventy-five, fifty, and ten feet. And Carol gave me drift information—that is, telling me which way the wind was pushing us. It sounded like a talk show, with an obnoxious host trying to talk over his guests.

Ours was a practiced crew, so the backup took on a cool efficiency, each member stating his or her information and then shutting up. "One-twenty-five down, three." "Two hundred feet." "One left." And then the controller: "On course, heading two-fifty, on glide slope."

The controller was giving me confusing heading calls. He was zigzagging me across the extended runway centerline, but the crew hung in there. At a hundred feet we peered out into the opaque whiteness, to find nothing. I let the plane settle some, to get an edge, to see if we could see anything at seventy-five feet. Tim called, "Wave off," and again I added power to go around. But this time as I banked, I inadvertently dropped my guard to look out the window, allowing the plane's nose to drop slightly. At seventy feet in a 20-degree angle of bank turn, with the wingtip now probably only twenty-five or thirty feet above the ground, Tim yelled, "Mark!" Together he and I pulled back on the yoke to get us more of that ever-precious commodity, altitude.

The fact that we had seen nothing after two passes only increased the tension. Seat cushions went wet with our sweat as our stomach muscles tightened involuntarily. When we broke free of the clouds, I turned to Roy, who assured me we had one more approach, before retiring the uncertainties of the whiteout area. The whiteout area was always the absolute last option, especially since that area, which was supposed to be free of crevasses, was found to be full of them. I was determined to land anywhere other than the whiteout area.

Carol spoke up. Having followed the last two approaches on her radar (which was inferior to the radar the controller on the ground had), she said the controller had screwed up, lining us up well to the right side of the runway. She asked me if I would give her a shot at it. Absolutely!

As we settled in for the third approach, we all knew that it was our last chance before we ran out of gas. We would all have to back each other up if we were going to make it. We decided that Carol would call the course as I flew, listening to the glide slope calls of the controller, Tim's airspeed and rate of descent calls, and Roy's altitude calls. Now all I had to do was ignore the controller's heading calls, find the runway, and land the plane. Piece of cake—like finding a dropped contact lens in deep grass after a light rain.

I tried to lighten the mood by telling a joke before we entered the clouds, hopefully for the last time today. It received only nervous laughter, but I forced a smile and winked at Tim and Roy. Right now, I needed to relax. We descended into the whiteness. When the controller made his first call to turn left some 5 degrees, Carol said, "No, Mark, he's not right, stay right here—you're looking fine."

Tim then said, "One-twenty-eight, down four."

Roy said, "One thousand feet."

And the controller said, "On glide slope."

"OK, Mark," Carol said, "he's saying right 10 degrees. I think we need to come about 4 right. OK, good. Steady up. Looking good."

"One-twenty-six, down five."

"Five hundred feet."

"Going slightly above glide slope."

"What is he looking at? No way! Disregard that 5 degrees farther right. Kick it over 2 degrees, no more," Carol said.

"One-twenty-five, down three."

"Two hundred feet."

"Going below slightly below glide slope."

"Mark, we should be right over the threshold!"

"One-twenty-four, down three."

"One hundred feet."

"On course over landing threshold."

I let the plane sink to seventy-five feet and kept the wings level. "Now?" I asked. Tim said nothing. I eased the power back a little more and let the plane dip to fifty feet, "Anything?" Silence. I added power to go around, but as I did, a beautiful black panel raced by out of the corner of my eye. I concentrated on it and eased the power back till we settled to forty feet. I caught another panel and drifted over to it. At twenty-five feet I had enough lateral visibility to see panels on either side of the runway. They hung in the white air, so I centered the plane between the panels as best I could.

At ten feet I eased back on the yoke, started to flair, and pulled power to flight idle. We hit the deck. The crew let out an explosive sigh of relief as the tires touched the ground. As for me, I relaxed enough to let the half of the seat cushion I had sucked up my sphincter back out again.

Home! It was a fantastic feeling. I brought all the power levers into maximum reverse to stop as quickly as possible. I still had no idea where we were on the runway, with only a hundred feet of forward visibility. We stopped adjacent to the "4" board (four thousand feet remaining on the runway). We had landed a little less than half way down the runway. As I brought the throttles out of reverse, Roy, Tim, and I all high-fived and started to laugh.

I turned around and there was Carol, her face ringed with a red welt from pressing her face so hard into her rubber radar hood. She chuckled, and that led us all into fits of hysterical laughter till we all had tears rolling down our cheeks. We were OK. We had beaten the white night, but she would have that red mark for at least an hour. Our mirth was interrupted by a call from tower to ask where we were and if we were all right. Tim laughed hysterically into the mike just enough make the controller think we had all gone mad at some point during the touchdown.

As we taxied in, I called Sharon on the HF to let her know what we had gone through to get in, apologizing for steering her wrong. She had been monitoring the weather and had figured as much, but since she was beyond PSR, she had no choice but to continue. Her navigator and engineer ran through their fuel numbers and found that they had enough to divert to Byrd. They ended up staying four days at Byrd waiting till the weather at McMurdo cleared.

Once we had completed all our checklists and shut the plane down, we unstrapped quickly and hugged. We had made it through as a team, each of us playing our own integral part under fire. Words can't describe the elation of the moment, the emotional high of cheating death—we had stared into the sucking maw and extracted ourselves through raw determination. We then assembled en masse in my room to clean out my supply of liquor. We drank, laughed, lived with the fullest measure of life, ichor coursing through our veins. We were alive. Tonight we felt like gods.

•

McMurdo Dome is located just beyond the top of the Taylor Valley on the polar plateau. The flight to the dome is a quick one, about forty minutes, which gives us a chance to fly low through the dry valleys toward the plateau and climb, as the glacier rises, on the way out to the site. We normally fly this route from the opposite direction—that is, from the plateau and down into the Ferrar Valley—so today would be unique.

We were tasked with pulling out the Taylor Dome Ice Core Project: some fifteen people and several tons of supplies in two or three flights. When we arrived at the site, I knew we were in for a long day. The entire area had been chewed up and worked over by the half-dozen skidoos assigned to the project. The snow was exceedingly soft.

As we touched down for the first ski drag, the nose instantly pitched down into the snow and we decelerated quickly, so I came on with maximum power immediately, thinking that we should try to find some firmer snow. I yanked back on the yoke, but nothing happened. We were at flying speed, at max power, but we stayed glued to the deck, bouncing along in the pasty, slushy snow. After two minutes we were still bouncing, and both Tim and I were both tugging furiously on our yokes. I was glad the surface was at least smooth—I shuddered to think what our situation would have been if it had been rough. At three and half minutes we succeeded in breaking free of the mire and leapt skyward. We reversed course and passed along the entire length of the drag, all thirty thousand feet.

The science party was efficient. In forty minutes, they had the plane loaded with the first round of gear. Ready for takeoff, I now taxied back to the end of the drag, since the snow seemed to be a little firmer and a lot less sticky there. Two minutes into the takeoff slide, I wasn't so sure anymore. We weren't able to accelerate, stagnating at between 30 and 35 knots. We tried again in a different direction, hauling as close into the wind as we could, but with the same result.

By the seventh takeoff try, I knew I needed a new tactic. I sent all the passengers and extra crew to the back of the plane to sit on the ramp. The loadmaster pulled all the extra stowed gear out of its storage area and placed it on the ramp as well. If we were going to get out of this place, we would need to have the plane's center of gravity (CG) as far back as possible; this would be the only thing that would allow Tim and me to get the nose out of this sucking snow. If we could get the nose up, we at least had a shot at accelerating.

Seventeen tries later, we were still stuck—and beginning to run low on fuel. I kept thinking about a crew a number of years ago who had taxied for eight miles before they were able to get airborne. At least we were close enough to home so that we could probably have taxied all the way there— but I didn't think it would look dignified to taxi an airplane eighty miles. We got off the ground on our twenty-second attempt.

After a brief discussion about what the conditions at the camp had been, the cockpit grew silent. There wasn't much to talk about; we had tried every avenue that any of us could think of. Were we losing our touch? We had never done more than four or five runs to get out of any-where, and although the snow was certainly softer at McMurdo Dome than most places, twenty-two tries was a bit much. The flight home was short compared to the time it had taken us to do all those takeoff runs, but it seemed an eternity.

I realized what our problem had been as soon as I touched down on the ice runway. The moment the nose wheel hit the deck, there was a sharp pull to the right. I compensated by adding near full power on the two right engines. We drifted farther right. Then suddenly the plane headed abruptly back to the left. I retarded the throttles to flight idle and then went immediately into reverse. But as we slowed, the plane veered and I again added power, leaving the two left engines in maximum reverse. I then had to push the two right engines into the flight range (about 40 per-cent thrust) to stay straight.

When we finally slowed to taxi speed, I thought we were out of the woods. I had attributed all our earlier sliding around to the slickness of the ice runway, but I realized now that there was something wrong with the nose wheel steering—it seemed to be stuck to full-right throw. It took a great deal of throttle coordination to slide the damaged plane back into position on the ramp.

Maintenance troops were looking into the nose-wheel well as we shut down, checking the steering mechanism. What they found was a blown O-ring in the right actuator arm of the nose-wheel steering mechanism. The left arm, unchecked, extended and thus caused the plane to veer con-stantly to the right. In the field we hadn't able to accelerate because of a cocked nose ski. I was surprised now that we had gotten off at all. The best I could figure was that I had finally gotten the ski straight enough on the last run to be able to accelerate to takeoff speed. What bothered me, though, was that we could have been undone by a fifty-cent O-ring. We had been operating on pure luck.

As the end of the flying season approached, serious discussions always took place among the science types over how to extend the season by a week or two. I guess we would have to crash and kill a bunch of people (scientists, hopefully) before these folks could see what a huge mistake an extended season would be. They wanted empirical proof that it couldn't be done. Unfortunately that proof can come only in the form of an accident. The whole idea is insane.

Mother Nature had had about enough of us, and by the time we did leave the continent, she would have tested us again and again, pushing us to the limits of our abilities and challenging our every takeoff and landing. As far as the air crews were concerned, every successful day we spent on the Ice past the second week in February was a lucky break. During the season, we could rarely predict the weather, but in February every day would be truly a wild guess. And with fog dominating our lives, the situation wouldn't get any better.

For preflight today the fog had shifted somewhat, moving a little farther out to sea, but the visibility was still less than a mile. At 1520, twelve hours and change after our original briefing time, our skis broke free from the skiway, and we were winging our way to Upstream Bravo to pull the camp out for the season. I was positive the folks at Up B were getting antsy after waiting twelve hours—they wanted to get out before a winter storm hit.

Weather was going to hell everywhere. At Up B we flew down to two hundred feet and just barely made the field at half a mile. It was a sticky approach and a generic landing. There was no defined horizon, and the snow surface was obscured due to the lack of direct light, so I had no external references to help gauge our speed or rate of descent, no indication of where the surface and the sky met. We could see only a gray blend of dead light that poured from the sky like rain, mixing with the ashen snow and forming a death-colored diorama.

Our schedule called for us to spend two hours on deck, but the Up B personnel had prepared well and were ready to leave in fifty minutes. We had no more than popped the nose ski skyward, however, when we lost all sense of surroundings. There was no longer any ground below or sky above, just a milky mass of white with a toy plane motoring around within.

Concentrating on keeping the wings level and the plane climbing was a challenge. I had a gnawing feeling in my gut that I was climbing too fast, that my nose was too high, that something wasn't quite right. I had vertigo. I asked the copilot to take the controls, but he was worse off than I was. I had to fight for twenty minutes as we crawled slowly toward the pale blue sky.

I felt a flood of relief as we broke free of the clouds and climbed in a slight right turn, headed home in the light—always in the light. At Willy the fog was waiting, hanging out like a thug on a street corner. We could see the field at a thousand feet, but it faded in and out as we pushed through thin layers of the icy outstretched fingers of the fog, finally breaking free at two hundred feet. I went straight home to bed; twenty-four-hour days were a bitch. I was asleep before my head hit the pillow.

The temperatures around town were now hovering about 30 degrees below zero, the winds continuing to blow cold and steady. Waiting outside for the shuttle was tough, so we huddled at the back door of the building and then dashed across the street when the van pulled up. There was that wintry feel to the place again—a feeling that suggested it was time to leave.

When I checked the flight schedule, I wasn't surprised to learn that we were once again slated to fly fuel to the Pole. The daily schedule was so littered with Pole flights that I only looked at the briefing times and not the missions. There was still the occasional camp pull-out, but those still mysteriously fell in the skipper's time slot. The plane was ready for departure when I showed up. The crew before us had preflighted, fueled, and then waited eight hours for an avionics technician to troubleshoot a malfunctioning radar.

The radar was now working fine again—just after the previous crew's flight was canceled. I was reviewing the ADB when the other crew filed through Maintenance Control, snarling at us as they picked up their flight gear to head back home. I couldn't blame them; the same thing had happened to me several times. You spend all day baby-sitting a plane, waiting to fly, singing the "Hut 20 Blues" in the most uncomfortable chairs on the continent, only to be canceled when the next crew shows up. I tried to console them by promising them we wouldn't have a good time flying. "No, sir, we won't enjoy ourselves one bit!" They didn't buy it. We were off to the Pole in less than an hour.

The flight out was automatic. Everyone did his or her job mechanically—logs, weather and position reports, walk-around inspections. All this information filtered through the headset, and I listened to each report without comment. I heard what was important and ignored the rest. It was an interminable wait before the TACAN needle swung and pointed due north (grid), while the DME (distance-measuring equipment) indicator locked on at a hundred miles out of the Pole. Power back, nose over, into the clouds. Nothing to see but white for the next twenty minutes until we broke out and, we hoped, saw the ground.

At twenty miles the South Pole GCA controller had us on radar. She gave us a call to turn right, heading 020, descend to 10,500 feet (the pole is at 9,800); we saw nothing but white. At five miles we were given minor course modifications and heard her say, "Cleared to begin descent, on course, on glide slope. Do not acknowledge further transmissions." At three miles, slightly above glide slope, four hundred feet above the ground, we were still on course, still surrounded by white. At one mile, two hundred feet above the ground, still on course, on glide slope, staring into a brilliant white vaporous muck, straining to pick out any surface feature. One-half mile, one hundred feet, still on course, on glide slope. If the runway were not in sight soon, I would have to execute a missed approach. Tim powered up as I continued to try to see anything beside the white. A panel!

"Ease back on the power. Start a slow descent at two hundred feet per minute. Easy right," I said. And the engines followed suit as Tim slid the throttle to flight idle. "Stop turn. Skiway is dead ahead. Looks like we're at the '2' board."

Tim chimed in, "I got it now, Mark." The engines wound up and down as Tim jockeyed the power, seesawing us toward the ground. At twenty-five feet he pulled the throttles to flight idle and raised the nose, and we hit. He allowed the nose to fall through; then he pulled the throttles up and over the hump, paused, and pulled them into full reverse. We were immediately surrounded by blowing snow. Visibility went to zero momentarily as the reverse pitch of the props kicked up the snow even more. Tim pushed the throttles back to the ground-idle position. Time to take a break and give the Pole our load of gas.

It had been a sticky landing, but we were becoming hardened to the fact that nearly all our landings would be like this now. As the storm clouds gathered for the ensuing winter, this is what we faced. Once the winter season hit and the initial storms of the season ended, the weather would clear up. For the next few weeks, however, life here for pilots would be difficult and frustrating.

Twenty minutes after touchdown, liberated from our forty-three hundred pounds of fuel, we tooled down the skiway for takeoff, trying hard to make out two panels two hundred fifty feet apart on either side of the skiway ahead of us—without much luck. We could definitely see one on either side of the runway. So, we reasoned, that made two, right? We climbed into the clouds as the nose ski left the snow, but we continued to see nothing until we shook free of the cloud cover at twenty-seven thousand feet. A beautiful full moon gleamed above us as we drifted up toward forty thousand feet. At 1816 local time, we officially hit 40,230 feet—my personal record. I danced a little jig.

Descending into the clouds again at thirty thousand feet, we accelerated to 260 knots to get out of the stuff fast and get home. At twenty-five miles we could see the ground below, but the view ahead was still fuzzy. When we were lined up to land at ten miles, the surface definition had disappeared, but we could see floating panels in the distance.

My recently assigned 3P was attempting his first landing with no surface definition. I coached him down, and he was looking good until the very end when he choked, sucked power off, and bounced on the snow back into the air, perhaps thirty feet. Beginner's luck. He wrestled the plane back down so that we bounced in successively smaller hops down the length of the skiway, stopping just before we slid off the end into the main street of town. He smiled and gave me a thumbs-up. Me? I say any landing we could walk away from was a good landing. The question now was, could I walk?

There was a sense of urgency in the air this morning as we preflighted. The air seemed charged with the morbid waiting-on-pins-and-needles dread of an anticipated crash at a stock-car race. Ice fog had blanketed the field, and there was a southbound flight from Christchurch twenty minutes out with minimum fuel. We nervously awaited their arrival in the cockpit of our plane and hoped that this fog would suddenly lift.

The weather office had painted a rosy picture for their entire trip south—clear skies with visibility unrestricted—and it was only when they were well past the point of safe return that they were informed that there was a possibility of fog. Now, at McMurdo, the fog was only a hundred feet thick, but it was so dense that I couldn't see anything except the two skiway markers directly ahead, less than fifty yards away. As the seasonal ice breaks out of McMurdo Sound, ice fogs always become a problem. These fogs close in quickly when there is only a slight temperature deviation between the moist air over the water and the dry air over the ice shelf.

On its first pass, I heard the southbound plane wave off, but I never saw it. On the second attempt, I caught a glimpse of the skis as the pilots added power. I radioed them on squadron common and let them know that I had seen them and that if they just let down another few feet, they might be able to catch sight of the skiway. As they added power the third time, I saw them again. They appeared to be directly over the skiway, so I radioed and told them to pull off power immediately. They continued down and caught sight of a panel at twenty-five feet and landed with about three thousand feet of skiway remaining. It was strange to be able to hear an airplane so close while not seeing anything other than the main skis in that milky whiteness.

Once they had secured the plane I met with Gary, the PTAC, in Hut 20 to listen to his story. He said that Mac Weather hadn't said anything about the rising dew point but had concentrated on the CAVU weather forecast. He thought he might register a formal complaint, and we had to laugh. Where would it go?

All of us as pilots took offense at shoddy weather forecasting, cargo yard delays, the often poor state of the skiway, and poor performance on the part of the tower controllers. Every complaint about these problems is logged in the PTAC's leg-load reports, but they are generally shrugged off as pilots' bitching. Today the weather had nearly ruined the day, permanently, for a fellow pilot of mine and his crew—not his bitching.

My crew was ordered to wait out the fog. The hope was that when the temperature warmed, the fog would burn off. It did—four hours later. With the temperatures forecast to remain constant for the rest of the day, we felt safe flying to SERIS L to complete the camp pull-out. At our initial point we descended to a hundred feet and 250 knots. I often thought it would be great to see our airplane cross low overhead from ground level. A big, fat plane like that bearing down on you, right above your head—it is an impressive sight.

With the number of flights required to pull this camp out, the whole area had been reduced to a soft, slushy mess. I taxied to a position that looked as if it might be somewhat firmer (it wasn't) to load the last two remaining pallets of supplies, one skidoo, and three camp members. As Chris was winching in the first pallet, the camp manager climbed the crew-entrance ladder with a small box. Holding the box under my nose, he asked, "You want me to bring this or leave it?"

Being an astute scholar of human nature, I asked, "What the hell is it?"

He peered into the box and said, "The leftover explosives, blasting caps and wire."

I spun him around and assisted him down the stairs and off the plane. I told him, "You can do whatever you want with it, just as long as it doesn't come on my plane." He looked perplexed for a moment but perked up, scampered off, and hopped on the skidoo. He raced away as we finished folding up the remainder of the camp.

Once we had loaded everything but the skidoo, Roy thought it wise that we pull forward a few feet since the Herc appeared to be sinking a little. We strapped into our seats, and I cycled the skis. The skis came up, and the plane sank up to its belly into the soft snow. I lowered the skis, but we didn't rise up. The moment the skis indicated down and locked, I added max power, but we didn't move an inch. I reduced the power and cycled the skis again, this time adding max power as the skis were coming down. We were officially stuck in that frozen morass of snow that held us like quicksand. I tried rocking the plane by adding and reducing power, even by setting max power for two minutes—all to no avail. The plane merely strained against the icy grip. I turned to Roy, shrugged and asked, "What do we do now?"

"Looks like we'll have to use Plan D—dig her out." During my polar training, there was only casual mention of digging a plane out, so I never considered it an option. As it turned out, this was the first time that any of us had tried it. Roy, Chris, and I grabbed shovels. Roy headed to the left main ski, Chris to the right, and I to the nose. As we dug, I heard a loud *ka-wump* and turned to see a thirty-foot fountain of snow springing from the ice. I yelled, "Oh, shit!" Then I started to chuckle as I thought, *That bastard decided to blow up the rest of his stash.*

I watched as the snow gently wafted to the ground as I continued to dig. With the next stroke, I rammed my hand into the nose wheel-well fairing. Even with flight gloves on, I had skinned two knuckles. I bled quit a bit before I had the nerve to peel back the gloves to view the damage. I was missing an inch of skin on my middle and ring finger of my right hand. I patched myself up by winding approximately five feet of gauze around each finger, which I somehow still managed to bleed through.

We shoveled snow away from the first third of the skis, creating three-foot trenches that the skis would fall into when we added power. The thought was that we would keep going after that. Although my fingers throbbed, I had to smile when the camp manager returned to the plane covered with snow. With an egregious smile plastered on his face, he signaled a jaunty thumbs-up as he rounded the wing and maneuvered his snowmobile onto the ramp.

I told myself there must be something in the air here in Antarctica that turns us all into a bunch of wild men when we hit the continent. For the pilots it was flying a hundred feet off the ground as we snaked our way down through broad glacial valleys at top speed. For the scientists it was trying to pretend no one saw you sneaking off at night on skidoos to have a romantic tryst in a fishing hut ten miles out of town. But for some it must have been the secret desire to blow things up.

When we were finished digging and were seated, ready to go, I didn't cycle the skis—I just cobbed on the power. The plane shook for a long three seconds, slipped into the trenches, and then pulled free from the frozen sludge. We attempted the first two takeoff slides in our landing drags, but we abandoned them when we were unable to accelerate above 50 knots. I decided to try the old skiway, but instead of using the complete skiway, I obliqued it, sliding parallel to the rows of sastrugi to take full advantage of what little wind there was. The plan worked, and we were airborne on the first takeoff attempt.

We had an uneventful return to base, but what a day it had been! My first explosion, my first time digging out a plane, and then bleeding all over the pure white snow. They were magical moments, all. Back at the Officers' Hooch, I had a strong desire to drink, so I rounded up Sharon. She and I closed down the Officers' Club. No doubt we solved the problems of the world that night. When she and I got together, that's usually what we did. Unfortunately we never remembered the solutions the next day, and it was probably better that way.

The days ahead mostly held additional Pole tanker runs; however we got to do the pull-out of Byrd Surface Camp. It seemed only fitting, since we put them in some four months ago. *Had it really been that long?*

As usual the weather over the ice shelf and Marie Byrd Land was forecast to be poor, although Byrd Station wasn't too bad, reporting an eight-hundred-foot ceiling and two miles visibility. Since we would just be pulling people out today, there wasn't anything to carry. After a quick preflight we blasted off.

We went into the clouds less than a thousand feet out of Willy, and we didn't see the ground again until we touched down at Byrd. At twenty-five thousand feet we had a spectacular view of nothing. We were swept along in the bowels of the overcast. Flying long distances in clouds is the most boring aspect of a pilot's job. There are no thunderstorms in Antarctica, no lightning. And there were no mountains along this route to distract us—just three hours of white, diaphanous nothing. I was thrilled when Ed told me we were a hundred miles out; at least now we could move the controls a little.

At the beginning of the season I was assigned Tim as my 2P, but as if a penalty, to balance the scales of good and bad, I was assigned a second 2P. He had flown with the crew perhaps half of our flights this season, and I usually considered him the 3P, someone to teach and to watch closely. I rarely gave him chances to do work in the open field because, frankly, I mistrusted him. He wasn't a bad pilot, just reluctant to work at it. He was a schemer, a teller of tall tales, an individual with enthusiasm and spunk as long as it was for his personal gain, but he was loath to do any real work on another's behalf. He lived and operated on the fringe of acceptable behavior. I can't recall or imagine now why I let him have the landing at Byrd.

Ed lined us up with the runway with an internal approach until I called the field at three miles and eight hundred feet. My second-2P copilot told me he had the field in sight and initiated a descent. At two miles I told him he was a little low, and he added a touch of power. At this stage, with his experience, I shouldn't be talking him through the landing, but he seemed confused. He settled even further. "You had better add some more power," I suggested.

He snapped back, "I'm flying this approach, Mark. I'm a qualified 2P. I know what I'm doing. Just shut up and let me fly this the way I want to, OK?"

I said, "It looks to me that you're going to land short of the skiway." Then I shut up.

He wiggled in his seat. He jockeyed the power levers back and forth. He swore at me under his breath and blew his breath out in long, protracted sighs. None of this worked, however. He still touched down fifty feet short of the skiway. We bounded up onto the skiway and slowed to a near-stop. I had to add power so we didn't get stuck. Since this was the ideal place to perform such a less-than-ideal landing—everything was covered in snow—there was little danger. And the plane was not damaged. Only his ego suffered.

I could tell the rest of the crew was straining to control their chuckles—they cleared the flight station soon after we slid to a stop. I asked the 2P if he was OK, but he just looked off into space and asked me if he was still doing the takeoff. I told him I saw no reason why he shouldn't. He smiled and told me that was probably the worst landing he'd ever had. I was sure it was. I dropped the subject as I unstrapped to help with the camp pull-out. He sulked all the way to the pits, a long mile away.

There wasn't much to do at the camp—turn off the lights, shut down the generators, close and secure the doors against the inhuman winter that was steadily approaching, and get everyone aboard the plane. The last piece of plywood was being nailed into place as I made my way up the snow mound to the camp's main building. Eight station personnel and three of the crew stood and stared at the secured door, a symbol of the end to their time here. A certain sadness touched them, as if they had just buried a new friend. But after only minutes of mourning, they were all racing down the hill toward the plane to go home.

I invited the camp manager to sit up front with us. She watched from the window as we accelerated past her station, and she stayed there until we climbed into the clouds at eight hundred feet, obliterating the world beneath us. She settled back into her seat, smiled, and then, with all tensions eased, fell asleep. She had done her job, suffered through four months of the worst weather in the world with all the problems associated with running a small camp in the middle of nowhere, and here they were now, on their way home. All her folks had made it through, and the collective weight of their responsibility was off her shoulders now; she deserved to sleep. Now it was incumbent upon me to get them back. The weight of the responsibility had shifted; the torch was passed. The main objective now, for her at least, was rest.

With the closing of Byrd, we had only the South Pole Station to service, bring them up to the required fuel level, and the occasional flight to Christchurch to make. We were slated to be the last crew off the Ice for the season, so we wouldn't be seeing Christchurch anytime soon. But I still celebrated—alone, with a beer, when I was back in my room.

The howling of the wind through the rigging formed one of the wildest and most awful scenes imaginable, one that will never be forgotten by any one on board, all expecting that the last days of the earth had come.
—First officer's logbook aboard the *W. H. Besse*, 27 August 1883, as volcanic eruptions destroyed the island of Krakatau fifty miles away.

These words aptly describe circumstances that often exist in Antarctica, too. So when we were tasked with flying a Pole tanker today, I was shocked that we were asked to fly at all. Stiff winds whipped up a frenzy of snow and small bits of rock, blowing so hard that the fifty-yard dash to the shuttle was tough going. When I called the Weather Shamans and asked about the wind, they said it would die down as the evening progressed.

Even as we talked, the conditions at the field were deteriorating: ceiling and visibility had dropped from eight hundred feet and two miles with blowing snow, poor surface definition, and no horizon, to three hundred feet and one mile with no surface or horizon. I was somewhat skeptical when the forecaster told me that the weather for our return from the pole would be fine at a thousand feet and three miles—which, rather suspiciously, was the exact figure we needed in order to be able to fly.

I phoned the ODO when I hung up from the Shamans, arguing that I felt the weather would continue to worsen and that I thought our flight should be canceled. He agreed. A few minutes later the phone rang. The NSFA duty officer had overruled and wanted us to get on with it; he'd already cleared it with our executive officer.

I found the XO lounging in his room, eating cookies. I offered my opinion concerning the weather and explained that I wasn't comfortable flying in it, that the present conditions were well below minimums (at two hundred and a quarter mile), and the forecast was, I felt, a little shady at a thousand and three. I asked him if he himself would fly. He wasted no time in reading me the Riot Act, explaining that I should use the rules to fly missions, not to cancel them, and that, yes, of course, *he* would have flown, so I should get out there!

On the ride to Willy it was obvious that the weather was only going to get worse. The wind blew unimpeded across the ice shelf at better than 40 knots, kicking up dusty clouds of fine snow. Over the icy surface the snow collected into long ribbons that undulated like waves, breaking apart and forming new bonds as they raced along.

Over INET, the local McMurdo communications radio, the weather controller, obviously feeling pressured to come up with an accurate forecast, called our shuttle-bus driver for a report. She looked at me, shrugged her shoulders, and said with a smile that she could see sixty-eight flags (red and green flags that marked the snow road to Willy, which are unevenly spaced but are generally three to five feet apart), whatever that meant. The forecaster acknowledged the report and dropped off the line.

I was beside myself. Forecasters wouldn't trust a report from a pilot, someone with at least a smattering of meteorology, but they seemed perfectly happy to receive a totally arbitrary report from a shuttle-bus driver about sixty-eight flags. But worst of all, I was going to fly in this crud because of a random number that had popped out of that driver's mouth! There was much grumbling amongst the crew as we preflighted. Tim, never one to mince words, kept saying, "This is total bullshit!" He was right.

By instruction, McMurdo was always our final destination. We always took off with enough fuel to fly to an intermediate stop and then return to McMurdo without any additional gas. Since it was our destination, if we had at least a thousand and three miles forecast for the time of our arrival, we had the green light to fly, even if the weather at our intermediate stop was poor. Today, the forecast for the Pole was calling for poor conditions also. It sounded like a great day all around. When the plane was ready, I signed the ADB as the senior Maintenance Control chief shook his head and said he wouldn't be caught dead flying in this weather. I handed him the book and said I hoped we wouldn't be either.

The winds were right down the runway, so at least the takeoff was easy—we were off in less than two thousand feet. We climbed through the brewing maelstrom and hit clean blue air at six thousand feet. The winds flowed over Black Island like a spring flood waterfall pushing a wall of white onto the ice shelf. I didn't like to think about it, but I knew it wouldn't be getting any better soon. When we got back, we would be in for some real drama.

Out on the ice shelf proper the winds didn't seem as malicious, but they certainly couldn't be called calm either. Masses of clouds were swirling, forming what appeared to be a hurricane. I called Mac Center and asked to talk to weather. When the forecaster came on the line, I explained what I was seeing below me. He answered me as though I were an annoyance to him, acknowledging the information I'd given him but saying that it was no big deal and that the forecast he had given us for our return wasn't going to change.

On the hour the news grew worse as we made our way for the Pole. The actual McMurdo weather went from two hundred and a half mile, to two hundred and a quarter mile, and as we made ready to start into the Pole, it was called one hundred and half a mile. At least the visibility was coming up. I wondered how many flags that shuttle-bus driver had counted for each hourly observation.

The ceiling at the Pole was right at two hundred as we broke through the clouds, some three-quarters of a mile from the skiway. There was a very obscure demarcation that barely passed as a horizon line, but there was no surface definition. We touched down hard some halfway down the skiway after fighting with the power, trying desperately to judge where the ground was.

All the time we were off-loading fuel, we monitored the weather at McMurdo. It didn't sound as if we would get the weather the forecasters were calling for. I had Roy keep some fuel on the plane so that we would arrive over Willy Field with ten thousand pounds, as opposed to the normal seven thousand, and be able to shoot a couple of extra approaches if we had to. No harm in being prudent. Mac Weather updated our forecast just prior to our departure out of the Pole. They weren't optimistic, calling the weather six hundred and two for our arrival, with poor ceiling and horizon definition. Floating panels again. At least the winds had calmed down to a mere 30 knots.

To an Antarctic pilot contrast is everything. Once the sun is hidden by clouds, shadows are nonexistent. The white of the clouds blends with the white of the snow to create an effect that renders all landings best guesses. We filled our time on the return trip today by cursing the forecasters as each hourly observation had the ceiling and visibility dropping and the winds picking up. We were consoled by the fact that at least there was a ceiling and some visibility, even if it was limited.

As we were over Black Island in our descent, in the GCA box pattern, the news was grim. The weather had dropped to zero and zero. There was no visibility. It happened suddenly, so they said. The wind has picked up to 38 knots, driving the snow into a frenetically moving fog. We opted to try a GCA landing. Close to the deck at two hundred feet we were surrounded by swirling white; the windscreen was being pelted with monstrous flakes. The wind kicked at us, pushed and pulled, hitting us on all sides at once. The plane jumped and shuddered, plunged and rose. One second we would be a hundred feet low on glide slope, the next three hundred feet high.

Airspeed was a best guess, altitude a joke. At any moment the wind could have thrown us into the ground and stomped on us to keep us there. But the biggest fight I had was keeping the wings level, or as close to level as possible. Gusts hit one side, throwing the wing straight up; in the next moment they pitched the other wing down. Sometimes it felt as if the whole plane were trying to spin about the longitudinal axis. My hands trembled on the yoke; I was sure that I had soiled my shorts. It had been bad enough seeing nothing at all, but to be tossed about like a rowboat in stormy seas was adding insult to injury. I have rarely been afraid while flying; however, this was one of those times. My head hurt, and I had to fight back the foul, bile taste of vomit. We were all shaken; we were all very quiet.

Once we powered up and started skyward, the winds helped lift us on our way—the only positive thing the wind did for us all day. I called the weather forecaster to ask about this state of affairs. Well, the weather didn't clear as expected (*no shit*), but it should clear enough to land within thirty minutes; could we hold? I guess he needed to contact the shuttle-bus driver to discern the weather from her flag count—weather guessing at its finest.

Roy worked the numbers as Tim called the tower and asked them to call us the minute the weather lifted so we could try another approach. We climbed just above the tops of the clouds at eight thousand feet and cir-cled. It was comforting to see the sun. I slowed the plane as we flew a max-imum-endurance profile.[3]

An hour later it was painfully obvious that the weather wasn't about to change. With five thousand pounds of fuel left, there was nothing to do but put her down in the whiteout. We lowered the flaps to 50 percent, put the skis down, arced our way around to the TACAN final-approach course, and then started down, into the belly of the beast.

Passing through a thousand feet, we started on our wild ride, the winds batting us about like a cat does a mouse. The wings rocked, the nose pitched, the engines clawed at the air. Our airspeed jumped wildly. Everyone held on and held off vomiting as I wrestled with the controls. The calls came from the darkened cockpit: airspeed, altitude, rates of descent, drift. I could hear them, but they seemed foreign, out of place, wrong. Unconsciously I made the corrections. The pieces fit. We still flew, almost as if by magic. I certainly didn't feel I was doing much good. I tried to think about anything else. *Is my car OK and still parked at Tim's house in California? What did I have to drink back in my room? Have I remembered to update my will recently?*

The TACAN needle swung from one side to the other till we passed the transmitter. It trailed off pointing to the left as I did the best I could to stay to the right, at three hundred feet, 135 knots (or as close as I could stay to those numbers under the circumstances). Abeam the transmitter, Ed started timing. Thirty seconds later, he gave me a heading into the whiteout area. The wind wavered back and forth blowing from 280 degrees to 300 degrees, still at 40 knots. This was fortuitous—it meant that we had only a small correction to make before we aligned ourselves with the longest section of the area.

Splitting the difference, trying to hold 290 degrees, we zeroed out most of the drift. We stared straight into the wind now. I inched the power back to slow to 125 knots. The procedure calls for 120 knots, but the way our airspeed was bouncing around, I wanted to take no chances. Carrier pilots have an axiom: "Airspeed is life." It looked like we were about to test the truth of that assumption. I started to descend at what was supposed to be two hundred feet per minute, but in reality I didn't think we could get that close. All I could say for sure is that we were headed down.

Once I had set up for the landing, I relinquished control of the power levers. Tim would have to keep the airspeed close. I had my hands full wrestling with the wings to keep them level. I felt I was fighting a snake that twisted and turned, hell-bent on my destruction. My arms were getting tired. We had twelve miles in which to land the plane. Beyond that, we ran the risk of running into a crevasse field or, if we drifted too far right, White Island.

The calls were coming through my headset again. Methodically, rhythmically, automatically. I couldn't respond. I could only fight to keep the wings level. I didn't want a wing to touch down before the skis, cartwheeling us to a fiery end.

Tim said, "One-thirty-five knots, three hundred feet down" (per minute, rate of descent).

Roy said, "One hundred feet." (All of these numbers were ballpark figures; with all the bouncing, the best we could do was to get close to what they should be.)

Ed said, "Zero drift."

Tim said, "One-forty knots, level" (no descent).

Roy said, "Seventy-five feet."

Ed said, "Zero drift. Seven miles till we're out of the area, Mark."

I was thinking, *Shit!*

"One-thirty knots, down two hundred."

"Fifty feet." The wings are jerking. I'm flying as if I'm milking a cow, with all the up-and-down motion.

"Five miles to the edge, Mark."

I said, "Anybody see anything?"

"No."

The tower controller called: "Are you on the deck?"

"Turn off that goddamn radio," I snapped.

"Twenty feet."

I was thinking, *Where's the fucking ground? I can't see shit!* I can only describe the experience of waiting to hit the ground as being like jumping off a cliff into a fog, knowing there's water below you—somewhere.

"A hundred-and-twenty-five knots, level."

"Ten feet."

"Three miles to the edge of the area, Mark. Better put this sucker down."

Zero feet on the radar altimeter, and we're still not—*Boom!* We hit. On the ground. I couldn't see a thing. We were sliding and slowing. The wind kicked at the tail as we slowed, so we began to "weather vane," our nose swinging around into the wind. We slid sideways the last ten seconds.

The power was at flight idle when we jerked to an abrupt stop. I looked around and wondered if I looked as ashen as the rest of the crew staring back at me. The loadmaster in the back crawled from his seat to vomit in the trash can. My hands were numb from gripping the yoke, but I felt elated. We beat the storm.

There was a general up-welling of emotion, starting as some swearing and laughing with relief, then building to high-pitched hysterical laughter. We were saved—we had just landed an airplane without seeing a damn thing, and we had lived to tell about it! Now we just had to taxi back to Willy Field, nine miles behind us, and hope we didn't run out of gas. Wouldn't that have been perfect? To survive the whiteout, only to get lost and freeze to death trying to find the skiway.

I got the plane turned around and pointed at the TACAN. The wind pushed us along, hurrying us like a mother hen, toward a white oblivion. Thirty minutes later, we were so low on gas we were sucking fumes, and still we were unable to locate the bloody skiway. Then, outside my left side-panel windows, I spotted a small light. It was so close that I was sure I had run over it (I had). Once we had taxied across the main skiway, we could see the faint outline of another plane. I maneuvered behind it, just a few feet from the door at Maintenance Control, and stopped. Our day was over. If anybody in that office wanted the goddamn plane parked on the line, they could do it themselves.

The wind was kicking up snow so badly that had the lights not been on in Maintenance Control's building, fifty feet away, we might have walked the wrong way and become lost in the blizzard. At that building the shuttle-bus driver soon picked up eight exhausted crewmen and ferried them to the Willy Officers' Hooch, a hundred and fifty yards away. Whereupon, we all got stinking drunk. *Amen!*

16

STIR CRAZY

To survive the six-month deployment to Antarctica it is crucial that you keep yourself on an even keel. You can go crazy dwelling on other people's motivations or behavior here. And Antarctica is not a place where you can give in too much to sentimentality—I've seen people go over the edge doing that, especially during holidays. The isolation on this continent is a crucible, burning off the surface personality and leaving only the core character of an individual. Whatever you are inside, here you become more so. The strong get stronger, but the weak get weaker, too. You must exert your will to minimize mood swings and to focus on the person you want to be. No one leaves here unchanged, but whether one is changed for the better or the worse is entirely up to the individual.

To find examples of this "solitude insanity," I didn't need to look very far. One year, about midway through the season, the guys at Willy started to notice that no matter when they turned on their TVs to the local Williams Field channel, there was a satanic horror movie on. After a week, they dubbed it the Satan Network. After a month, they slowly came to realize that the movies were controlled at the galley by the mess specialist who ran the galley (and prepared their food). When a few of the officers approached him to ask "What's the deal with these movies?" they noticed he had drawn pentagrams on the backs of his hands. The broadcasts had become his pulpit.

Many of the air crews dealt with the constant pressure by drinking whenever they weren't flying, and especially during what we called "Saturday night live!" A night like no other, where the possibilities were end-less—unless, of course, your plans required either warmth or good beer. Since the beer on the Ice was always "skunk" beer (cooled and heated so often it tasted like formaldehyde), the Willy Boys found novel ways to be able to serve fresh Kiwi beer all season long. Smuggling beer became an art form.

The first furtive attempts were two kegs wrapped in bubble wrap, cov-ered with flexible aluminum sheeting, and stowed on the ramp. This was always a little dicey since a keg, no matter how it's wrapped, still looks like a keg. After some thought, one of the chiefs had his troops in Christchurch build a four-foot-square wooden crate that would hold four kegs. Stenciled on the outside of the crate in eight-inch letters was "AIRCRAFT PARTS." It was always easy to get this crate on the plane without inspection since we fer-ried parts to the Ice on nearly every flight. Getting the kegs to Willy was another story, however.

In the early part of the season, when we were still using the ice runway, we would ask tower for a slide and go at Willy before a full stop at the run-way. At the skiway we would taxi as close to the Willy Officers' Hooch as we could and "freight train" (lower the ramp and taxi out from underneath the load) the beer. Before we had even closed up the ramp and taxied away, someone would be out the back of the Hooch and burying the beer.

In this manner we were able to have six kegs on hand for the Annual Helo Party. Near season's end, the helicopters stop flying and the helo crews get ready to head back to California, so the Herc pilots put together a big bash as a send-off. The season's helo crews arrive in McMurdo about two weeks ahead of the Herc crews, so when all the Herc pilots arrive, the helo pilots throw a party to welcome us down. The annual helo bash is our reciprocal merry-making.

As naval aviators, Herc and Huey pilots get along, but there is always a little good-natured competition between the two groups, more teasing than anything else. I don't think there is a Herc pilot who could fly with the helo pilots very long without thinking them a little crazy, balancing, as they do, on one skid on the top of a mountain to put a science party in. And likewise, there's probably not a helo pilot who could fly with a Herc crew for fear of dying in a whiteout or on a high-speed low-level run. And that fact brings me to the main reason we were happy to see the helos go:

we wouldn't have to wait until the wee hours of the morning to do our low-level runs down through the Dry Valleys.

The helo party was always a true Antarctic party: kegs of beer, assorted liquors with mixers, and the inevitable salted nuts and cheese. Besides that, it was all loud music and lots of guys. Even with good Kiwi beer I called it a night at 0100. I wandered over to the Officers' Club. It wasn't thrilling. Several drunks lounged along the length of the bar, a couple was dancing, two guys were playing darts. Over in the corner a drunken swearing match was proceeding, the issue being whether or not a Ping-Pong shot had been good. There wasn't an officer in the place. I turned directly around and left.

Back into the bright night light. Opening the door, fumbling for glacier glasses, dodging the door on its return swing. It had become second nature to me. Not long ago I could perform only one maneuver at a time. I was getting too used to this routine; it was time to leave Antarctica.

The late-shift shuttle tonight was driven by Ester. She was waiting to depart for Willy with no passengers, so I hurried across the street to claim the front seat before she pulled away. Across the street, in the dorm where the helo party was still raging, a door slammed open, and Glen barged outside holding one hand on his stomach and the other over his mouth. He grabbed the porch railing with both hands and bazooka vomited.

"Gee," I said, "I bet that felt great."

Ester watched the spectacle and let out a disgusted "Uuuuuuugh!"

When he had finished puking, he looked up at us, smiled, waved a jaunty salute at us, pushed his hair back, and returned to the party.

Glen was one of the CAD Brothers—CAD being short for "Naval Cadet." At that time the squadron had two of the most infamous CADS in Antarctica, Glen and Gordo; together they were known as the CAD Brothers. CADS are former enlisted men who have been accepted into the flight program; once they earn their wings, they are given commissions. It's a wonderful program that allows the navy to reward its finest sailors. But these two guys must have fallen through the bureaucratic cracks. To say that Glen and Gordo were rough around the edges isn't sufficient—*jagged* is a better word. They lived to annoy the front office, and they were adept at it, moving in perfect unison, doing everything together—two halves of the same totally psycho whole.

Yep. It was definitely Saturday night. Later, Glen explained that he had been guzzling tequila *Animal House* style—no hands, bottle held between clenched teeth, head tilted all the way back. You'd be amazed what sounds fun when you're midseason on the Ice.

The Willy Boys, as the officers who lived at Willy Field called themselves, usually had a poker game going late Saturday night. Actually, they had a poker game going late just about every other night of the week, too. It seemed as though whenever I went over to check it out, there was always a game in full swing. Occasionally I would toss in a few dollars and play until FSA decided it was time to play Mexican Sweat, a game that is more than I can handle.

In Mexican Sweat, seven cards are dealt face down to each player. The top card on the remaining deck is turned over, and the player to the dealer's left starts turning up cards until he or she beats the card showing. Then all the players bet on their own hands, even though they can't see their down cards. This continues and the pot gets huge, sometimes into the hundreds of dollars. Players at the end have to keep betting on their unseen hands and "sweat" out their turns. When the players started to turn to Mexican Sweat, I weighed anchor.

On my off-days I tried to catch up—on sleep and on paperwork. I spent such restful days clearing out my "in" basket and moving papers along to Kim Hubbs, the petty officer who served as my chief of staff; he would then forward them up the chain of command. Sunday was the best day to do desk work that required real concentration. The Test and Evaluation Office was located on the second deck of the supply warehouse. The supply guys, I'm nearly certain, have the largest stereo on the continent, and they are not afraid to crank up the volume for their favorite heavy-metal tunes. On Sundays, however, it was just me and Mozart and an eight-inch stack of paperwork.

Boredom usually forced me to take a break at about 1700. After that day's stint, I stretched and shouted, "Give me the front seat of an airplane, the noise, the danger, the excitement any day instead of this mind-numbing mental drudgery." Satisfying, but perhaps not as good as bazooka vomiting. I left my cubicle and climbed the dark circular stairs to the roof. I squeezed around the radar dish, unlatched the hatch, and stumbled to the deck atop the building. Hubbs had shown me this semi-secret route, and I was grateful because, less than fifty yards in front of me, a minke whale was cruising leisurely along the surface of the ice floes. I stood for fifteen minutes watching the whale swim slowly back and forth in a three-hundred-yard-long pattern before I was forced to retreat for my coat. By the time I made it back to the roof, the whale had gone, leaving only its imprint on my mind.

Wildlife watching was a favorite pastime of mine. Occasionally I would check out a small aquarium that contained a number of holding tanks for Antarctic cod caught for research. If you've never seen an Antarctic cod, you might be surprised—these fish are monsters, four to five feet long, bony, and as ugly as sturgeon. I sat transfixed at their gaping yaps as they circled the tanks slowly, like sharks in waiting. It seemed to me that their cold stares said, "Please, please, stick your finger in here. We won't bite. Honest." Never trust a thinking fish, that's what I say. Monday a storm hit us, rising from behind the walls of Minna Bluff and descending on the station with all the wrath of a jealous lover. Clumps of wet snow the size of golf balls exploded against the sheet-metal buildings like small fire-crackers. Meanwhile the ceiling and visibility fell to zilch. The flight schedule was canceled piecemeal as the day progressed. More waiting. My office was shut up tight, and all but one of my petty officers had left with the helo contingent, so there was nothing to do even if I went to work. God, I hated inaction.

Since we were nearing the end of the season, personal items I couldn't carry home were either sitting in cold storage or steaming across the Pacific on the *Greenwave,* leaving me with only a few books as entertainment. So I read and tried to ignore the storm. Our room was threadbare. Sean's stereo was packed up and ready to go north with him tomorrow, all our posters and charts were down, the desk was bare of the usual junk, the TV had been returned, our food coffers from home and from New Zealand were empty save for a few bags of microwave popcorn, and I was working on the last of the beer as I read.

With each flight north, more of our friends were going too—until there were just a few support personnel and crews enough to support the Pole close-out. A dull, routine flight to the Pole would at least allow me to spend my time productively, not idling it away desperate to think of something to do to waste more time. Time seemed to move so slowly, inching along like an arthritic tortoise. I tried to keep my mind off of the situation by staying busy, yet the yearning to leave and go home was getting stronger, and my resolve to wait was weakening.

It continued to snow through the night and into the next day, with the storm gaining momentum every hour. Then the ODO called to tell me we were canceled again at 1000, but would I mind a job? Maintenance needed a pilot, an engineer, and a loadmaster to make a few high-speed taxi runs up and down the skiway to check out an airspeed gripe. I accepted the offer quickly, grateful to have something to do. The gripe was a 10-knot split between the pilot's and the copilot's airspeed indicators, which is scary. The maximum split is only 6 knots, and even that is a little high for me.

We jumped into a preflighted plane and raced up and down the skiway at up to a hundred knots, skiing on rocket-powered skis. Despite the poor visibility, this was fun! At one point the tower lost sight of us completely in the dense snow, but we raced back and forth anyway until I was convinced the problem had been corrected—and a couple more times after that, because we were just plain enjoying it.

Then Chris, who stayed in the back, convinced Roy that he would be able to "surf" the cargo deck while I gave the gas to the plane. Naturally Roy had to try, and try again, so that by the time the plane was running out of fuel, these two were just getting the hang of sliding the entire length of the cargo deck on a piece of plywood shoring as I streaked the Herc back and forth along the packed, frozen surface of the skiway. They were rolling all over themselves with laughter as we deplaned to give maintenance the thumbs-up.

As Roy tried to sign off the gripe, still wiping tears from his eyes, he received encouraging shoves from a smirking Chris—and they both received the "Are these guys high?" look from the Maintenance Control senior chief. I tried to ignore them, shrugging my shoulders as if I had no clue what was up. I dialed the duty office to report the plane was good-to-go.

The ODO told me the weather should clear in a few hours and wondered if we would accept a flight to the Pole. I declined his offer: I had just skied in this stuff for over an hour and I thought the Weather Shamans were nuts, as usual. I didn't think it would clear up any time soon. My antithesis, a female pilot who refused to listen to reason, decided she would go. I told her, as she read through the ADB, that the weather was here to stay and that she would do well to stay put.

Little good it did. She said that if I didn't want to go, fine; *she* wouldn't let a little weather stop her crew. So they went. As I predicted, though, the weather never cleared, and they were forced to remain at the Pole. They ended up sitting on deck there for more than six hours, waiting for a break in the storm and finally taking more gas from the Pole to get home than they had delivered in the first place—and setting our efforts to refuel the Pole back by at least a day.

It's childish, I know, but secretly we were all pleased as could be that she had screwed up. I wanted to thumb my nose at her and say, "Told you so!" In fact, we were all acting a little childish—I'm sure it had something to do with winding down at the end of the season.

The infamous CAD Brothers were particularly active now that the season was drawing to its close. Their jokes and general misbehavior became the norm. If the keys to the skipper's van were missing, or if someone received a mysterious phone call in the night, or if someone's undies had been hoisted up the flagpole, you could bet the CADs had a hand in it somewhere. And drink? They were always first at a party and last to leave, mischievous sprites with the boldness for pranks the rest of us wouldn't dream of. But they kept the rest of us smiling during the grueling six-month-long deployment, just by being themselves. The mention of their names was always followed by a grin and a question: "What did they do now?"

I recall one night during our first deployment, when the officers of VXE-6 were berthed in an older dormitory where each room had a window, I awakened about 0330 on Sunday morning by a loud noise that sounded like someone had fallen into metal trash cans. I sat up, opened my blinds, and saw the other CAD Brother, Gordo, sitting but yet weaving, on a porch that ran from the adjacent building ten yards away. He was "gooned"—that is, utterly and completely drunk. Holding a bottle of Jack Daniel's in one hand, he was using his other hand to steady himself against the railing. He sat there on the porch for a couple of minutes, still weaving, then turned toward me, put his face over the railing, and threw up. He puked long and hard. When he was done, he politely dabbed his mouth and chin with the back of his sleeve, stood up, steadied himself, looked at the remaining Jack in his hand, shook his head ruefully, then tilted his head back, drained the bottle, and went back inside to the party.

The CAD Brothers were always the last ones to leave a party, and if the party ended too soon, they would entertain themselves. Early one morning after an all-night binge at the Officers' Hooch, some folks—who were there trying to sleep it off—apparently thought that the Brothers were making a little too much noise, and so they kicked them out. "You want us to leave?" the CADs asked. "OK, but we'll be back." They walked across the street to the Willy Galley, where they drank some more; then they wandered back across the street and pissed all over the doors to the Hooch, a not-so-subtle gesture of their annoyance.

Another night the CADs "borrowed" the CO's private van for a "goonex," a vigorous drinking binge. At the Willy Officers' Hooch they were whisked out the back door as the CO walked in the front. The CO asked one of the maintenance master chiefs, "Was that my van outside?"

"Hell no, skipper, that was Public Works, come to check on our heating."

The CADs were so well liked because they kept us in stitches. They were able to get away with things that would have done in the rest of us. They just didn't care what anyone thought. They wanted a good time. If you wanted to come along for the ride, hop in—if not, then stay the hell out of their way.

In Antarctica eccentricities weren't limited to people. It seemed that the farther one traveled from Mac Town, the more anomalous the situations became, and it was odd how folks adapted to these incongruities and accepted them as normal. For example, the ice runway. Here was a major airport by any standards—with dozens of flights per day, millions of tons of cargo, hundreds of thousands of gallons of fuel, thousands of pounds of mail, and over three thousand people for the season. And yet at this million-dollar air facility, the maintenance people had to eat two meals a day from paper cups and plates, with plastic utensils, in a temporary diner, getting leftovers from the Mac Town galley—chicken cookies, Jell-O, and Kool-Aid.

Or take the bathroom facilities at the ice runway. For years this was an unheated outhouse built over a hole drilled in the ice. It wasn't unusual for someone to use the facility and find themselves with the cold snout of a seal in a place where one doesn't usually expect a seal to be. To solve this problem, and to answer the environmentalists' concerns (apparently these environmentalists had seen the meals that the maintenance guys were eating), a hundred-thousand-dollar state-of-the-art toilet facility was brought to the ice runway. Dubbed the "supershitter" this five-hundred-square-foot heated behemoth with its own water supply sat for the entire season on site without any steps having been put up to it. It was never used. And worst of all, no one ever questioned why.

17

HAPPY LANDINGS

As the season neared its end, the strain began to show on everyone. There was a sense of breaking up, literally as well as figuratively. The Coast Guard icebreaker *Polar Star,* its work nearly done, was on its way home. Its crew's last task of the season was to dispatch the old ice pier, in what seemed like a lonely and poignant act.

During his expedition to the Pole in 1901, Scott picked Ross Island as a prime location for his base hut for several reasons, but a major factor was the natural, deep-water anchorage at the area. To accommodate the larger ships of today, an ice pier was constructed on the shoreline of Ross Island at McMurdo Station. Fresh water was pumped in to freeze on the surface; iron rebar was then set into position and more fresh water pumped on top to freeze and settle until an oblong ice structure fitting snugly along the shoreline had been created. Finally, bollards were set and frozen into place to receive the ships' mooring lines.

Every few years, however, the ice pier starts to disintegrate and must be replaced with a new one. But before the new pier can be built, the old one must be removed. This year, to break the old ice pier loose from its tenuous attachment to the earth, lines had been run from the *Polar Star*'s bow to two bollards on the pier. I watched for an hour as the ship strained full astern to pull the frozen pier free. To see that tiny vessel tugging at such a sizable chunk of ice was quite a spectacle, like watching an ant drag a leaf ten times its size.

Once the old pier was completely detached, the ship backed into McMurdo Sound and reversed her lines so that she was now towing out what amounted to a small iceberg. She would tow the pier far out into the sound to ensure that it would be carried out to sea, to a slow melting death in the currents and warmer seas. I could imagine how ready the ship's crew was to head north. The weather was going to hell. High winds, which characterized the beginning and the end of the summer season, were now our constant reminder that we should be heading north, too.

In about a week, at the beginning of March, the sun would—for the first time this new year—set for seventeen minutes. The day after that, it would take forty minutes, and so on, so that by the end of March, all would be darkness until August. The wind had kicked into gear for this morning's preflight, forcing us to come in and warm ourselves every fifteen minutes. It was a brutally raw, cutting cold that no one who has endured it ever forgets. It seeps into your joints and crawls deep into your internal heater, trying to shut you down. Last night the temperatures had dropped to 40 below zero and hadn't warmed up much since then.

Over the ice shelf it was partially cloudy. Bits and pieces of all-too-familiar scenery floated through gaps in the clouds like a disjointed dream. Today was our last flight to the Pole; through the holes in the clouds I was heartened to see the familiar scenes that had long impressed me. Peaks, ice falls, nunataks, and glaciers were as awe-inspiring as ever. For the first time in two weeks, I was able to see the twin peaks of Mt. Markham—in my opinion the most ruggedly beautiful mountain on the continent.

The winds had picked up at the Pole. For our approach they were over 40 knots, but luckily they were also right down the skiway. While waiting to off-load our fuel, I wandered to the red-and-white-striped Ceremonial Pole for one last, quick walk around the world. Here all longitudes converge, as if pulled together by a string, and a stroll around the globe takes only a few steps. Unfortunately the scenery is the same all around. I was out of the plane for perhaps ten minutes, bundled up in all my Antarctic gear, but I became shivering cold in no time. I returned to the Herc and asked for a temperature from Pole GCA. It was 99 degrees below zero with the wind chill. My feet felt as though they were stinging blocks of ice.

We boxed up the back end, seated our seven return-trip passengers, and headed home. Once the checklists were complete, I ripped off my shoes to shove my three-layer-stockinged feet as far into the heating duct under the dash board as I could. I thawed them there until I had to put my insulated flight boots back on for the descent into Willy Field three hours later.

We arrived to find another plane had headed north in our absence. That left just two planes out of five still to go north. With one more flight tonight, the Pole's fuel tanks would be filled to capacity, then the final close-out flight would occur to pull out all the folks who would not be wintering over there. That event marked the end of the flying season on the Ice. As it turned out, we would be heading north too, sooner than I thought. I was given a deal, of sorts.

Each of our airplanes had its own peculiarities, flying slightly differently from any of the others and having its own special problems. For example, the aircraft with serial number 160742 (our XD-01) had radio problems; aircraft 160740 (our XD-02) had ski problems; and aircraft 159130 (our XD-05) had fuel leaks. During a routine inspection, a downing discrepancy (a gripe that necessitates a fix before the next flight)—a major fuel leak—was found in one of the inboard tanks of XD-05, necessitating a one-time waivered flight north for repairs.[1]

For some reason our crew always seemed to leap to the operations officer's mind when there was a "special" mission afoot. We were no strangers to flying with the skipper's waiver, nor to flying planes with major fuel leaks, but at some point our luck was bound to run out. I wondered if the crew was feeling lucky today. I pooled the guys; to a man, they were all for taking the risk and going because they knew this was a definite ticket north. Once north, we would more than likely stay north, so this meant that we all had a thousand things to do before we headed out.

Packing, sweating, lifting, heaving, swearing, writing notes, locating the errant TAC-PAC, confirming fuel loads, reviewing logs, filing flight plans, leaving keys and notes with friends, forgetting things, locating things, phoning, picking up stuff from shuttle-bus drivers, arguing with shuttle-bus drivers who were going down the wrong road, more swearing and sweating, saying last minute good-byes to friends who had become dear as life and whom you might never see again, and then a massive fuel-venting problem while the aircraft's engines were turning as it was being fueled—all these things confronted us as we readied to take off. But it was all right because we were going north!

We filled the outboard tanks to capacity, left the leaking inboard tanks dry, and had a fuselage tank installed to carry enough gas to make it to Christchurch.[2] And just like that, we left the frozen south, with the interim assignment of two weeks' worth of turnaround flights to and from Christchurch, pulling the summer contingent off the Ice and leaving McMurdo Station in the capable hands of the two hundred or so stalwart folks who would maintain it over the winter.

Flying north we saw nothing to say good-bye to. The station was covered with fog, the mountains were ringed with clouds, and the overcast became so dense that when we reached the edge of the continent, everything below us was masked by a dense layer of clouds as thick as cottage cheese. I spent most of the evening flying the plane—a strenuous job because the autopilot had crapped out an hour out of McMurdo, forcing us to hand-fly the beast twenty-two hundred miles. This is akin to driving for eight hours in three dimensions, having to keep your car wheels perfectly aligned on a long stretch of flat road—except you can't see the road.

But we muscled through and, on our arrival in Christchurch, were heralded for our feat by the depot-level maintenance crew, who had been waiting to repair this plane for a number of days. The CO personally came to meet us. He shook my hand, giving me an "Atta boy!" for a job well done. Then he told us he had scheduled us for a twenty-three-hour-long turnaround flight twelve hours from now. I thought that was rough, but then he followed it up by telling me that once the turnaround was done, I would fly our training bird home to our base at Point Mugu, California.

I would be home in four or five days time. Totally exhausted, but home! I was speechless. It was time to find a bed and throw myself into it. Yet as tired as I was, I couldn't sleep. One more flight to the Ice and then home—it was what I had dreamed of for the last few weeks.

The turnaround flight took place on 14 February—it was Valentine's Day, everywhere but on our plane. At least the plane was looking good and was already loaded upon my arrival at the airfield. Wind was a minor concern for the flight south, but we should be able to muscle our way through, as long as the weather at McMurdo didn't get any worse than what the forecasters had said it would be—a thousand and four, poor and poor, if the Shamans were right. *If.*

We launched into what would be a long, dreary, nine-and-a-half-hour flight south. At our PSR, I updated our weather for McMurdo and was happy to learn that it was holding in there, still expected to be a thousand and four for our arrival. At that time I also passed along to Mac Center that we could haul out eighty-five hundred pounds of retrograde cargo—might as well make ourselves useful one last time.

It was clearer than I expected, once we arrived at Willy. I had the field at fifteen hundred feet and five miles, but there was no surface definition. The landing by my turnaround copilot, Patty, was sound. She had to scramble a bit, but she made the right moves when it counted. Paperwork for our return trip was waiting for me in Maintenance Control: it showed a load of ninety-six hundred pounds, not eighty-five hundred. Someone had decided to slip on a few extra passengers for the trip north. I called Term Ops and went over the numbers with them. They wouldn't listen to reason until I simply refused to risk all our lives by taking off in an overweight plane.

I felt terrible for the disappointed folks who, believing today was their day to head home, had eagerly packed up the last of their personal belongings and checked out of their rooms, only to find they had to go get their keys back, get sheets and towels, and so forth, for one more day's stay. But I stuck by my guns: safety first, period.

Back at the plane, Patty said she had left her headset in Maintenance Control. I borrowed a skidoo and gave her a ride for the half a mile back. Zipping over the snow-covered ice surface at fifty miles an hour in minus-35 degrees was brutal, yet it was a thrilling ride. Unfortunately, by the time we returned to the plane some ten minutes later, my ears no longer felt attached to my head; it was to be nearly an hour into the return flight before I could feel them again.

A lowering pall hung over the skiway as we taxied out, departing to the cheers of the thirty-six happy passengers in the rear. The whole of my Antarctic experience came to me in flashes as we passed over McMurdo Station heading north that last time. Never again would I tread those icy and oftentimes muddy streets. No more poor food, no more strange hours, no more communal showers with ever-changing water temperatures, no "Saturday Night Live"—no more McMurdo. I had mixed feelings. It was sad to go, but I was happy to be leaving: going anywhere with my memories was better than staying here and facing another season.

The flight north was smooth for the first four hours, although clouds kept me from any last-minute picture taking. At the two-hour mark Ed informed me we were officially off the continent. Off came my wind pants, never to be put on again. At the four-hour mark, my other copilot made a couple of unfortunate moves while I was in the back fixing a sandwich. He screwed around with our one barely working HF radio and "fixed" it so we were NORDO (no radios); in the process he allowed the plane to drift 70 degrees off course—about fifty miles' worth.

I explained to him the need to pay strict attention to detail, but that didn't seem to be on his agenda. He was going north! I guess it was all he could think about. Using parts from two radios and a lot of fussing and swearing, Bob, our engineer du jour, was able to jury-rig one radio well enough to make it workable. After what seemed the better part of eternity (actually about seven hours) we saw the verdant coastline of New Zealand's Southern Island.

My last landing in Christchurch was uneventful, even dull. With thirty-six passengers, a pilot can't do much out of the ordinary—none of those low-level flybys, breaks, or showboating. On the ground, it took nearly three hours to turn in all my extreme cold weather gear, wind pants, flight jacket, and the like, but each item I handed in was another burden lifted, another step closer to home. After a shower and a taxi ride downtown, I had one last meal at Kanniga's, where I said my good-byes. Then I converted the last of my local money, had a few drinks at a small pub, and went off to bed, after a fifty-two-hour stint.

The next day, well-recovered by a night of good rest, I was winging my way toward the States. Droning along over the Pacific, I felt the excitement of going home beginning to set in—my life would be mine again. No more five-and-a-half-month deployments to nowhere. Working in Antarctica had been a wonderful experience, and nothing would ever change that fact for me. But three years was a long time to be away, and I felt every minute of it on that flight.

[T]he climate was rigorous and our food detestable. In short, we rather vegetated than lived; we withered, and became indifferent to all that animates the soul at other times. We sacrificed our health, our feelings, our enjoyments, to the honour of pursuing a track unattempted before.

—Georg Forster, *A Voyage Round the World, in His Britannic Majesty's Sloop, "Resolution"*

And so it was. I have never considered myself a pioneer, although Antarctica reinforced my independence and my sense of nature in the deepest way. I always enjoyed rock climbing, mountaineering on Rainier, backpacking or cross-country skiing in the knee-high snows of West Virginia. I still had an appetite for these things now. But I could never have spent an Antarctic winter tramping through uncharted wilds and living in a hut with twelve other men, burning seal blubber for heat and light, just to be first at the Pole. I could never have pioneered like Roald Amundsen or Robert Scott.

Scott found no animals to slaughter for food and no wood to build a fire or a hut. His journey was nothing but grief and hardship over a vast ocean of snow and ice—windblown, treacherous snow. He and his party covered over fifteen hundred miles, and everything they needed they had to drag along in a sledge, marking their path along the way by building cairns in the false hope of finding them, and the goods they stored within them, on their way back.

I thought about this on the trip home. How did Scott and his men muster the fortitude to fight every step in freezing cold to reach an obscure objective? It seemed to me that, driven or not, they accepted the hardships as a matter of course—as simply the obstacles they needed to overcome in order to be the first to reach the South Pole. Still, I could not fathom what fearful thoughts they must have had every morning as they crawled from their sleeping bags, exhausted, to face another day of pain and anguish marching through that white, frozen hell.

As pilots we faced the daily flight schedule with the same sense of duty and accepted the hardships as a matter of course, but I was thankful that at least we didn't have to wake each day in pain to face another day of suffering the elements. Antarctica had taught me that each person who traveled there became an explorer of sorts and therefore a part of the rich history of the continent. I went without expectations and came away with a profound sense of how raw and surly the unconquerable Mother Nature can be. She makes it perfectly clear in Antarctica: if you are not prepared, she will kill you.

But my goal, to go there and see what this frozen continent was all about, had been worth the danger. The flying itself was an occasionally exhilarating experience interspersed with life-or-death drama. I'd flown low, gone into places where an airplane had no right flying, and been forced at times to risk not only my life but also the lives of my crew and passengers in the fiercest and most unpredictable weather in the world. But I had lived, and so had they. Maybe I had gained a little insight into Scott and Amundsen. We were all survivors of a different sort.

I had followed orders—orders that sometimes mandated the impossible, orders drawn up by people who had never stared into a white fog of nothingness and been unable to see the ground ten feet below, had never landed a plane filled with explosives on a blue-ice runway bumpier than foot-high rumble strips, had never landed with empty fuel tanks in a whiteout. And I had lived.

Often in Antarctica, around the galley at night, pilots were spoken of as second-raters, as people who are here to serve and nothing else, the means from point A to point B. Sometimes, indeed, it was only a matter of survival for a pilot here—you pitting your best against Mother Nature, proving yourself again and again. Sometimes, that was our only satisfaction; we got little appreciation from anyone else.

In the past, front-office management had protected pilots from the overzealous, from those with the mind-set that it has to be done today, right now. But no more. The front office during my last season on the Ice made it known that they would hang you out to dry if you didn't hang it out to fly. Be safe, yes, but if you can see a few feet ahead, go for the mission. I believe this attitude will kill someone someday. A sad statement, but I believe it.

Pilots who fly Antarctica are some of the gutsiest men and women I have ever known. They put themselves on the line every day, not merely for questionable science but for the gratification and glory of those who plan the missions and whose job is to make numbers look good, to meet predetermined goals and to provide positive data that will ensure continued funding.

I will always remember the flight from SERIS L. The weather had turned bad shortly after our departure. After three approaches (following hours of flying, diverting, guessing the weather) we were on our last legs; we nearly had an unplanned touchdown due to a slight case of vertigo by yours truly. Our lives were saved by my alert copilot, Tim. Carol, the navigator on that flight, gave better heading information than the ground controller (who had better radar); Tim watched for the runway and called my airspeed and rates of descent, all while keeping an eye on me; and Roy, the engineer, let me know how high I was above the ground. We worked in symphony, trusting each other like family to do the job at hand correctly.

Management wasn't concerned. Weather forecasters weren't concerned. They were home tucked away in their beds waiting for the sounds of sirens. But we made it. We did it despite the odds against us. We did it for us. That was all we had left. If I understood Scott and Amundsen at all, it was on this level.

In Antarctica I had some good times, some bad deals, some shitty weather, some anxious moments, and some moments of sheer terror. I had frustrating times when I just wanted to scream. I had moments of unbelievable joy, experiencing sights never before seen by anyone. I forged friendships that will last a lifetime, with people I may never even see again. I made acquaintances who buoyed my sagging spirits when the going got too tough for me to handle alone, and I learned the value of self-control and a good sense of humor.

All in all, I had a good time. What I will remember most vividly is the flying—the bold, terrifying, surprising face of flying on an untamed continent. The frustrations, the bad memories, they'll fade away. But not the fond memories—never them. Carpe diem.

NOTES

2. WELCOME TO CLUB MUD

1. R. Bage, "The Quest of the South Magnetic Pole," chap. 14 in Douglas Mawson, *The Home of the Blizzard, Being the Story of the Australasian Antarctic Expedition, 1911–1914,* 2 vols. (London: Heinemann, 1915), 1:274.
2. Jamesways, which are actually insulated canvas tents that can be erected and disassembled quickly, are used extensively in the open field for extended projects in the summer season.
3. The operations duty officer is usually the PTAC or the Polar navigator of a crew. Each crew rotates through for a week-long stint as the duty crew and stands watch, during which the ODO is responsible for running a smooth daily flight schedule. The ODO uses the rest of the crew as support and is the direct liaison among the flying crews, maintenance, the cargo yard, and the NSFA (Naval Support Force, Antarctica) duty officer, who coordinates with the NSF. The ODO coordinates a myriad of details to ensure that each mission has the proper load, airplane, passengers, fuel load, and so on, prior to the crew's preflight. The ODO also delays, cancels, or reschedules other crews, depending on weather or changes in mission priorities.
4. Derelict Junction is a centrally located spot in town that is marked by a telephone pole (dubbed the "metaphysical pole"); affixed to the pole is a sign stating that you are indeed at Derelict Junction, which is the main stop for the various shuttle busses that ferry the denizens of McMurdo Station around the place.

3. RUNWAYS ARE FOR SISSIES

1. On the skiway during training flights we will, after touchdown, lower the nose and reduce power to ground idle and let the airplane slowly decelerate as we slide to 40 knots, at which point we will add maximum power, and a normal ski takeoff is commenced. This technique is known as "slide and go."

2. When pilots can't make the field for normal landing, they will go around, or "wave it off," and try the landing again. It might be that they are unable to see the field, or they may not yet have completed all required checklists. Or they may suddenly break out of the weather and see that the plane is in a poor position to land. In all such cases, pilots generally elect to go around, or to "take it around," as it is often called.

3. Pressure altitude is the altitude reading on the plane's altimeter when that instrument is adjusted to indicate height above the Standard Datum Plane, a standard barometric pressure of 29.92 inches of mercury. As atmospheric pressure changes, the Standard Datum Plane also changes. In Antarctica the atmospheric pressure is usually very low because of the extremely cold temperatures; therefore, pressure altitude is a key factor in calculating aircraft performance.

4. Sastrugi are rippled patterns resembling ocean waves or sand dunes that are carved in ice-encrusted snow by prevailing winds. Sastrugi can vary from three inches to over four feet in height and thus, depending on their hardness and size, can pose a significant hazard to ski operations.

5. A system of hydraulic pistons, struts, and cylinders controls the nose ski. When the gear is raised, the nose gear itself swings forward and up and, since the nose ski is connected to the nose gear, the ski swings forward and up, too. To prevent the ski from being driven into the body of the plane, the rigger strut (an actuating piston) keeps the nose ski level when the gear is raised or lowered. The nose-gear fairing is a flared panel attached to the plane that makes the nose ski more aerodynamic when up.

6. In order to be valid, every FCF must follow a distinct plan, or profile, which informs the pilot the altitude to climb to and the proper sequential steps to take to test the repaired system.

7. "Nil and nil," meaning "no surface and no horizon visible," is a surface and horizon definition of the type used at the end of every weather observation or forecast to give pilots as accurate a picture as possible of what surface and horizon conditions they will be facing upon landing. Since almost all of Antarctica is white, this information is indispensable. What follows here is a list of surface and horizon definitions and values, drawn from the "Polar Definitions" section of the Operation Deep Freeze's 1992 publication titled *Aircrew Reference & Planning Aid*.

SURFACE DEFINITIONS
Good: snow features such as sastrugi, drifts, and gullies are easily identified by shadow; the sun is unobscured.
Fair: snow surface features can be identified by contrast. No snow definition exists; the sun is partially obscured.
Poor: snow surface features cannot be readily identified except from close up; the sun is totally obscured.
Nil: snow surface features cannot be identified. No shadows or contrast exists; dark-colored objects appear to float in the air; the sun is totally obscured, although the overcast may exhibit considerable glare that appears to be equally bright from surface reflection from all directions.

No Surface: total loss of surface visibility due to blowing snow, fog, ice fog, or any other restriction.

HORIZON DEFINITIONS

Good: the horizon is sharply defined by shadow or contrast.

Fair: the horizon may be identified, although the contrast between sky and snow surface is not sharply defined.

Poor: the horizon is barely discernible.

Nil: total loss of horizon; the snow surface merges with the whiteness of the sky.

No Horizon: total loss of horizon due to blowing snow, fog, ice fog, or any other restriction to visibility.

Whiteout (the word that strikes fear into an Antarctic pilot's heart): no surface and no horizon definition.

8. T. W. Edgeworth David, "Professor David's Narrative," in Ernest Henry Shackleton, *The Heart of the Antarctic, Being the Story of the British Antarctic Expedition 1907–1909,* 2 vols. (London: Heinemann, 1909), 2:173.

9. Aircrews write "gripes"—aircraft discrepancies that are documented on maintenance action forms (MAFs)—when they find a problem with the plane. Gripes for the last ten flights are carried in the aircraft discrepancy book (ADB). A yellow gripe sheet indicates that the required maintenance action has been performed and signed off by Quality Assurance as good. A pink gripe sheet indicates that maintenance actions are pending. Most of our pink sheets were marked "AWP" (awaiting parts to fix the problem). When the pink sheet indicates a major problem, the plane is downed, considered unsafe for flight.

10. As a rule, postflight duties require that the pilot discuss with the maintenance chief any problems the plane may have, that the engineer inspect the plane, and that the loadmaster unload any retrograde cargo remaining aboard.

4. WE BAND OF BROTHERS

1. Like all runways, skiways are numbered from 01 to 36, based on the approach direction; landing to the northeast, we therefore used skiway 02.

2. Everything that is shipped to the South Pole, including the entire fuel supply, is brought by LC-130s. Approximately half of our flights to the Pole are fuel flights, or "tankers." The fuel is carried either in wing tanks or, occasionally, in a large, removable internal tank. Fuel is much easier to off-load than cargo because there isn't any need to open the cargo ramp and door. A defuel port and control panel are located on the right rear section of the plane. For defueling, a hose is connected to the port, and the plane's boost pumps are used to draw the fuel out of our tanks and into the Pole's storage facility.

5. THE WEATHER SHAMANS

1. "Minimums" is a generic term for the minimum altitude to which a pilot may descend on any particular approach. For example, on a precision approach—like the one I was flying that day—the minimum altitude is a hundred feet above the

ground. If a pilot cannot locate the runway environment at that altitude, then he or she is supposed to break off the approach and try again. If a pilot never sees the ground at minimums, the only other choice is to land in the whiteout area.

2. Robert Falcon Scott, *Scott's Last Expedition: From the Personal Journals of Captain R. F. Scott* (New York: Dodd, Mead, 1964).

3. During the warmest part of the summer season in Antarctica, Kiwis stationed near Lake Vanda in the Dry Valleys cut a swimming hole in the ice of the fresh-water lake. Hardy souls strip naked and plunge themselves completely into the ice-cold waters. Once they emerge, nearly frostbitten, they are rewarded with tea and hot scones, a patch commemorating their folly, and the permanent inscription of their names in the official Lake Vanda Swim Club log.

4. So that Mac Center can track the process of each polar flight, mandatory check-points called papa 1, 2, and 3 are spaced about an hour apart from one another. There is no in-route radar for air-traffic control in Antarctica to use to follow a flight, so if a crew fails to check in at one of these three mandatory points, a search effort is begun at the aircraft's last reported location.

6. HAPPY CAMPER SCHOOL

1. In naval aviator slang, a "gouge" is a statement of what's what, practical information related by an experienced person.

7. CHICKEN COOKIES

1. Robert E. Lee, cited in Robert Paul Jordan, *The Civil War* (Washington: National Geographic Society, 1969), 108.

8. A COZY LITTLE ICE SHELF

1. Included in the TAC-PAC portfolio is information about the load the plane will be carrying, the amount of aviation fuel required, the expected weather, the leg loads from previous flights to the same location, and other pertinent details. The put-in sheet, which is completed after every recce, contains pertinent information on a proposed open-field camp site. Usual data include the surface conditions and hazards, the proposed landing area, the prevailing wind, the items to be air-dropped (if any), the snow conditions, and the surrounding terrain. These put-in sheets are prepared with careful attention to the smallest detail so that if for some reason the crew who does the recce is not the one who does the actual put-in, the put-in crew will be completely aware of what they can expect at the site. After each flight the PTAC fills out a leg-load report describing the flight. This is where the pilot would note any problems with Terminal Operations or with the weather office.

2. Scott, *Scott's Last Expedition.*

3. Plunkett Point, also affectionately known as the "Crotch," is the confluence of the Mill and Beardmore Glaciers.

4. "Loose load" is anything that isn't palletized; such items can range from bamboo stakes to Nansen sleds to bags of mail and anything else that might be thrown on the plane at the last minute.

5. The LC-130 is equipped with rollers mounted in the cargo deck so that the crew unlatches a pallet and then basically drives out from underneath it. Usually the pallets just slide down off the ramp and onto the snow, but on a rare occasion they "tombstone"—that is, instead of coming straight out and sliding along the snow, the pallet slides off the ramp and sticks in the snow like a toppled-over tombstone.

9. ICE FOLLIES

1. Herbert Ponting was the photographer for Robert Scott's last expedition in 1911–12. He is still considered by many to have been the finest polar photographer ever. He later wrote of his experiences with Captain Scott and proved himself an able writer as well.

10. OVER A FROZEN EDEN

1. Richard Evelyn Byrd, *Discovery: The Story of the Second Byrd Antarctic Expedition* (New York: G. P. Putnam's Sons, 1935), 4.
2. Scott, *Scott's Last Expedition.*
3. When operating on the LC-130's skis, prior to any taxi evolution the copilot will cycle the skis by raising them (so that the plane rests on its wheels) and then lowering them again. When the plane sits in one spot for very long, the snow has a tendency to bind with the skis, and the resultant friction is almost always impossible to break free of. The skis are cycled to break that surface friction.
4. In an airdrop, pallets of supplies are brought to an area via parachute. The area is selected, the plane's ramp and door are opened, and from an altitude of (normally) three hundred feet, the bundles are pushed out to float to the ground. For field party put-ins, it is usually advantageous to perform these airdrops in conjunction with the recce. During the actual put-in, the plane is limited to 118,000 pounds total weight, including gas to get home on. This leaves the field party enough room for seven to eight thousand pounds of supplies, so if a field party has more than eight thousand pounds, then an airdrop is the best way to get their supplies to them.
5. As part of their emergency equipment, pilots in Antarctica carry a portable HF radio dubbed the "southcom," short for southern communications set. HF radio signals are bounced off the stratosphere, thereby allowing extreme long-distance communication. The radio is battery powered, but it also comes equipped with a solar panel that can recharge the battery or power the radio.
6. James Clark Ross, *A Voyage of Discovery and Research in the Southern and Antarctic Regions during the Years, 1839–43* (London: J. Murray, 1847).
7. We used the ice runway as long as possible at the beginning of the flying season because of the plane's higher gross weight while operating on wheels. On wheels the LC-130 can take off at 155,000 pounds. On skis it is limited to 147,000 pounds, though it can still carry the same amount of fuel as it does using wheels. In other words, we would lose eight thousand pounds of cargo space from a flight when we transitioned to skis.

8. The Naval Academy guys had, on one of their underclassmen cruises, learned the Sea States, which run from 1 to 6 or so and are used to describe the roughness of the ocean. A Sea State of 2, then, would be a choppy and rolling sea.

9. Jean-Louis Etienne, cited in "Theory Is Frozen Out in Antarctica Reality—The Stegar Team Looks Back," St. Paul *Pioneer Press Dispatch*, 18 March 1990.

10. Qin Dahe, cited in "Theory Is Frozen Out in Antarctica Reality—The Stegar Team Looks Back," St. Paul *Pioneer Press Dispatch*, 18 March 1990.

11. THE GOOD, THE BAD, AND THE INEXPERIENCED

1. Roald Amundsen, *The South Pole: An Account of the Norwegian Antarctic Expedition . . . 1910–1912*, trans. A. G. Chater (New York: Barnes & Noble, 1976).

2. A crab is the angular difference between the course of an aircraft and the heading necessary to make that course in the presence of a crosswind. In high crosswinds, in order to keep the nose of the airplane straight, a pilot must land in a crab to compensate for the winds and also to keep the airplane on centerline. We use a wing-down, top-rudder technique, also known as a slip: we put the upwind wing down into the wind (the amount varies with the intensity of the crosswind) and then use the rudder to keep the nose of the plane straight.

3. When the weather is IMC (instrument meteorological conditions, which are any weather conditions below a three-hundred-foot ceiling and one-mile visibility), pilots must follow a separate set of guidelines called Instrument Flight Rules, which dictate what actions and procedures a pilot will use when approaching an airport for a landing.

4. The compressor section is the first of three basic stages in all jet engines. The compressor section compresses the ambient, low-pressure air and converts it to high-speed, high-pressure hot air. This hot air is then channeled into the burner section, where it is combined with fuel. Combustion follows. Now the extremely high-temperature air is forced out of the burner section by incoming compressor air and enters the final section, the turbine. The turbine extracts the energy from the hot gasses and in turn rotates a shaft that spins the compressor section.

13. WE'RE PRETTY SURE THIS WON'T EXPLODE

1. The Transantarctic Mountains are unusual in that they are the only area in the world where there are tectonic boundaries in the earth's crust that are rifting apart rather than moving together. These mountains are a perfect place to study such a phenomenon since they are covered with a layer of snow and ice that has, for the past forty million years, prevented the usual degree of erosion that modifies the surface of a mountain almost as quickly as the mountain forms. The rocks of the Transantarctics therefore preserve far more evidence of their history than is generally available in other mountain chains.

2. The Mill Glacier runs into the Beardmore Glacier at Plunkett Point. Mill has long been considered a possible site for a blue-ice runway.

3. Apsley Cherry-Garrard, *The Worst Journey in the World: Antarctic, 1910–13* (London: Constable, 1922), vol. 1.

14. GOAT ROPES

1. The CSEC building, also known as Crary Laboratory, was hailed as the grand jewel in the tiara of the United States Antarctic Research Program (USARP). The twenty-five-million-dollar state-of-the-art polar research facility contains specialized equipment, laboratory space, a library, and a new aquarium, all under one roof. Replacing structures dating from as early as 1959, Crary Lab was built to extend scientific research beyond the field collections and observations that typified the earlier work conducted in the region. Becoming fully operative in the 1994–95 season, the facility is named for the geophysicist and geologist Albert P. Crary (1911–87), who was the first person to have set foot on both the North and South Poles.
2. "Skidoo"—the name of the most popular snowmobile on the Ice—is also used as a term for snowmobiles in general.

15. FLYING IN THE MILK BOTTLE

1. A pull-out is the opposite of a put-in; that is, when the scientists are finished at the site, we go in and bring them out.
2. On a ground-controlled approach, the glide slope is an imaginary line that extends upwards at normally 3 degrees from the runway to a point eight miles or so out in space. It is the ground controller's job to tell the pilot whether he or she is above, below, or on this line, which is used to bring the plane straight into the runway, passing over the threshold of the runway at fifty feet.
3. A maximum-endurance profile is a fuel-saving maneuver, designed to maximize the amount of time a plane can remain airborne; it is often used when the plane is being kept in a holding pattern.

17. HAPPY LANDINGS

1. The only person who is authorized to grant approval for a plane with a downing discrepancy to be flown is the commanding officer. In granting this approval, the commanding officer issues a one-time waiver for the plane to be flown as is—by which action he or she is acknowledging the fact that the plane is not completely airworthy and is assuming the responsibility for the flight's being undertaken.
2. A fuselage tank is a thirty-six-hundred-gallon fuel tank that can be mounted in the cargo compartment for transporting bulk fuel or, as in this case, for providing supplemental fuel for engine consumption. A major benefit of this tank is that it can be removed quickly to facilitate other missions.

ABOUT THE AUTHOR

Mark Hinebaugh, a 1980 graduate of the University of Maryland, joined the Navy in 1981 and was awarded his wings in 1983. Prior to his service with VXE-6 in Antarctica, he served with VRC-50 in the Philippines, VT-2 at Pensacola, and VQ-4 at Patuxent River, and is still active in the Naval Reserves. He is currently a pilot with a commercial airline in Columbus, Ohio.